W9-BJS-119

BE WHO YOU WANT

Unlocking the Science of
Personality Change

Christian Jarrett

SIMON & SCHUSTER

New York   London   Toronto   Sydney   New Delhi

Simon & Schuster
1230 Avenue of the Americas
New York, NY 10020

First Simon & Schuster hardcover edition May 2021

SIMON & SCHUSTER and colophon are
registered trademarks of Simon & Schuster, Inc.

For information about special discounts for bulk purchases,
please contact Simon & Schuster Special Sales at
1-866-506-1949 or business@simonandschuster.com.

The Simon & Schuster Speakers Bureau can bring authors to your live event.
For more information or to book an event, contact the
Simon & Schuster Speakers Bureau at 1-866-248-3049 or
visit our website at www.simonspeakers.com.

Interior design by Ruth Lee-Mui

Manufactured in the United States of America

1   3   5   7   9   10   8   6   4   2

Library of Congress Cataloging-in-Publication Data
Names: Jarrett, Christian, author.
Title: Be who you want : unlocking the science of personality change /
Christian Jarrett.
Description: New York : Simon & Schuster, 2021. | Includes bibliographical
references and index. | Summary: "From cognitive neuroscientist Dr.
Christian Jarrett, a fascinating book exploring the science of
personality and how we can change ourselves for the better"– Provided
by publisher.
Identifiers: LCCN 2020056797 | ISBN 9781501174698 (hardcover) | ISBN
9781501174711 (paperback) | ISBN 9781501174704 (ebook)
Subjects: LCSH: Personality change. | Change (Psychology) |
Self-realization.
Classification: LCC BF698.2 .J37 2021 | DDC 155.2/5–dc23
LC record available at https://lccn.loc.gov/2020056797

ISBN 978-1-5011-7469-8
ISBN 978-1-5011-7470-4 (ebook)

For Jude, Rose, and Charlie

Contents

Contents

Author's Note

Can people ever truly change? In the more than twenty years I've been writing about psychology and brain science, I've come to realize that for many people, this is the burning question. Put differently: Can bad people turn good? Can the idle become ambitious? Can a leopard ever change its spots?

It's true that a degree of self-acceptance is psychologically healthy (so long as it doesn't slip into resignation and hopelessness). But I wanted to write a book for those of you who are less interested in feeling good about yourself as you are now and more interested in becoming the best version of yourself that you can possibly be.

Through tales of criminals who transformed their personalities, of shy celebrities who found their voice, of drug addicts who reformed and excelled in new endeavors, combined with the latest compelling research evidence from psychological science, you'll learn that people *do* change, and that, yes, if you want to change yourself, *you can*. It won't be quick or easy, but it's possible.

Your personality will continue to evolve through your life, partly as a natural response to your changing situations and also because of gradual changes in your physiology. Most exciting, there are ways you can take control of this malleability to mold yourself more in line with the person you aspire to be.

This book is filled with tests and interactive exercises to help you better understand the various aspects of your personality, your life story, and your passions. The more you engage with the interactive elements in an honest fashion, the greater the likelihood that you will find out more about yourself and benefit from the insights in the book. Building new habits is a key part of successful personality change, and each chapter concludes with suggestions for new activities to adopt and psychological strategies to try out to help shape your different traits.

There are many notes of caution ahead too. I will tell you about good people turned bad and delve into the sometimes devastating effects of injury and illness on a person's character. In short, your personality is a work in progress. Pursuing the best version of yourself is a philosophy to live by rather than a job to complete.

I hope this book will especially appeal to anyone who has ever felt imprisoned or constrained by the way they've been characterized—or caricatured—by others. It is a human weakness that we are prone to drawing premature conclusions about one another, often ignoring the influence of circumstances (known in psychology as the *fundamental attribution error*). If you've ever felt boxed in by other people's judgments on your personality—labeled *introvert, slacker, softie, snowflake*, or whatever else in an overly simplistic way—you will enjoy learning about the profound effects of circumstances on how personality manifests itself at any given time, how we all tend to change throughout life, and how you can smash out of that box by transforming yourself through new habits and pursuing your true passions in life.

People change. I've changed. The other day I was clearing out old papers when I came across my teachers' reports from when I was a teenager at boarding school. "I am not sure how, if at all, Christian can change his naturally placid manner," wrote my personal tutor when I was sixteen years old. "I do agree with his tutor," wrote my housemaster in the same end-of-term report: "Christian's nature and personality do tend to draw comments such as 'too quiet.'" My class teachers were unanimous: "Too reserved and quiet" (geography); "I would encourage him to contribute more to class discussion" (history); "He needs to speak more!" (English). My favorite came from my housemaster a year earlier: "It is not always easy to tell whether Christian's good-natured taciturnity is a sign of diffidence or merely intelligent verbal economy."

But in my freshman year at college, I burst out of my shell, built large groups of friends, and partied all night most nights of the week. I remember my graduation-year dissertation adviser admitting, after I graduated with highest honors, that he had long ago given up on me, having pigeonholed me as a hedonist more interested in sports than learning (based on what he knew of my social life and all my time at the university gym where I worked part-time as a trainer).

Change never ceases. Fast-forward five years or so after graduation, and life was quiet again. With a job working remotely as an editor and writer and living with my then wife-to-be in a rural part of Yorkshire, England, I was back to being an extreme introvert. I had no car, and my wife-to-be was out most days, twenty miles away in the city of Leeds, studying to be a clinical psychologist. It was a textbook example of how circumstances can shape us profoundly. It's tricky to be an extravert when you're working by yourself in a home office in a quiet village. Yet I felt my conscientiousness grow as I became absorbed in the challenge of my first editorial role, and writing about psychology came to feel like my calling. Meeting my deadlines and having the self-discipline to write daily was a pleasure and became part of the rhythm of my life.

In more recent years, I've felt myself changing again. I'm blessed with two beautiful young children—Rose and Charlie—who have boosted my conscientiousness still further (What greater calling in life can there be than parenthood?), but I think they may have also increased my neuroticism a point or two!

In addition, my career has evolved to include more public speaking, such as for live events, radio, and TV. I remember standing onstage at a large bar in London a few years ago, experiencing the euphoric buzz of making a three hundred–strong audience laugh (deliberately, I should add—I was giving a lighthearted talk on the psychology of persuasion). I wonder what my schoolteachers would have thought of me then. Compare the school reports they gave me with the kind of reviews I've received recently for talks I've given in London bars: "Christian is a great speaker," "very relaxed and engaging," "informative and funny," "enriching, engaging, enjoyable." Sure, I was to an extent putting on a performance, but beneath the public mask, I believe there has been a meaningful shift in my disposition and a greater willingness to speak up and take risks in pursuit of my goals.

I also feel changed by the experience of writing this book. I'm now far more receptive to how people and circumstances bring out different features of our characters. I'm less accepting of aspects of my personality that I previously considered immutable. I've learned how the lifestyles we lead, the ambitions we pursue, and the values we live by, all affect our traits.

In fact, I'd go so far as to say that writing this book (and heeding its lessons) gave me the motivation and self-belief to leave my job of sixteen years earlier this year to take up a challenging role at a global digital magazine. I'm out of my comfort zone but confident I can adapt. True to the science of change, it has helped that the ethos of the magazine chimes with my own values: supporting others by sharing practical insights on psychological well-being. I believe it's also in your power to change and adapt in positive ways, to be who you want, especially in pursuit of what matters to you in life, and I've written this book to help show you how.

BE WHO YOU WANT

Chapter 1

THE WE WITHIN YOU

Like many other young men, twenty-one-year-old Femi had fallen in with the wrong crowd. In 2011, when police pulled him over for speeding through Northwest London in his Mercedes, they found 8 oz. of cannabis in his sports bag. He was charged with possession of drugs with the intent to supply.

If you'd encountered Femi back then, you might well have concluded that his was the kind of disagreeable personality you'd rather avoid. After all, the drug arrest wasn't his first brush with the law; it was part of a pattern of behavior that led him to be ordered to wear an electronic tag. He was often in trouble in his younger years. "I got banned from the area I was growing up in because I was getting into too much trouble," he recalls.[1]

However, Femi, or to use his full name, Anthony Oluwafemi Olanseni Joshua OBE, became an Olympic gold medalist and a two-time heavyweight boxing champion of the world, heralded as an impeccable role model of clean living and good manners. "He really is one of the nicest, most down-to-earth young men whose acquaintance you'll ever make," wrote Michael Eboda, chief executive of Powerful Media, publisher of the Powerlist (an annual listing of the most influential Black people in Britain), in 2017.[2] "I could have gone the other way, but I choose to be respectful," Joshua said in 2018 as he laid out his plans to help educate the next generation in "healthy living, discipline, hard work, respect for all races and religions."[3]

People can change, often profoundly. They are one kind of person in one chapter in their lives, but fast-forward to later in their story and they've transformed into a different character altogether. Sadly, it's sometimes a change for the worse. Tiger Woods was once praised for his wholesome and exemplary behavior. In personality, he was the epitome of conscientiousness and self-discipline. But in 2016, after years battling back-related health problems, he was arrested for driving under the influence, his speech slurred. Tests showed he had five drugs in his system, including traces of THC, found in cannabis. His disheveled mug shot stared out of newspapers around the world. It was just the latest scandal to follow the former champion golfer. Years earlier, his world had come crashing down amid tabloid tales of serial infidelity—a dark era of his life that began when he veered his car into a fire hydrant after a nocturnal domestic fight. Happily, negative change is reversible too. In 2019, having previously sunk to 1,199th golfer in the world, Woods won the Masters in Atlanta, Georgia, a feat described as the greatest comeback in sporting history.[4]

Evidence for change doesn't just come from tales of redemption or disgrace. Look around and you'll see examples of less sensational but still surprising change that are everywhere. As a child, Emily Stone was so anxious and prone to such frequent panic attacks that her parents sought the help of a psychotherapist. "My anxiety was constant," she told *Rolling Stone* magazine.[5] "At a certain point, I couldn't go to friends' houses anymore—I could barely get out the door to school." It's hard to believe that this girl would not only overcome her nervous disposition but that as Emma Stone (the name she chose when she joined the Screen Actors Guild), she would become the world's highest-paid actress, decorated with an Oscar, Golden Globes, and a British Academy of Film and Television Arts award.

And consider Dan, an inmate at Ohio's Marion Correctional Institution who was profiled in an episode of NPR's *Invisibilia* podcast. He was serving time for a violent rape, but we hear how Dan, now a published poet, is helping to run a TEDx event at the prison (an offshoot of the famous TED Talks online). The show's guest reporter, who has known and corresponded with him extensively for a year, describes him as "completely charming, playful, fast talking, fast thinking, very poetic, creative." Dan's prison warden says he is "articulate, humorous, kind, passionate." Dan himself says his personality at the time he committed his crime "has truly ceased to exist" and that he now almost feels as though he is in prison for somebody else's crime.[6]

Since researching this book I've been struck by how often people have stories like Dan's and Emma Stone's to tell and how their transformations are consistent with, and explained by, the findings coming out of the exciting new psychology of personality change. Radio phone-ins, online chat forums, and glossy magazine pages are filled regularly with stories of change, often for the better: lazy people finding purpose, shy people discovering their voice, criminal offenders turning good.

Learning these lessons from the science of personality change is arguably more important today than ever before. The pandemic has shaken all our lives, testing our adaptability. Sources of distraction, from social media to smartphone games and apps, are more ubiquitous, draining our focus and self-discipline. Outrage and political polarization are everywhere as people get sucked into Twitter pile-ons and political discourse plumbs new lows, draining civility. Sedentary lifestyles are also on the increase (the World Health Organization describes physical inactivity as a "global public health problem"), which research shows has damaging effects on personality traits, weakening determination and fermenting negative emotions.[7] Yet the inspiring tales of positive personality change show you don't have to submit to these harmful influences passively; it's possible to take the initiative and shape your own character for the better.

PLENTY TO HOLD ON TO AND PLENTY WE CAN CHANGE

The fact that we are capable of change does not mean we should entirely dismiss the concept of personality. Far from it. According to decades of careful psychological research, there *is* such a thing as "personality"—a relatively stable inclination to act, think, and relate to others in a characteristic way. This includes whether we seek out social company and how much we like to spend time deep in thought. It reflects our motivations, such as how much we care about helping others or being successful; and it's also related to our emotions, including whether we tend to be calm or prone to angst. In turn, our typical patterns of thought and emotion influence how we behave. Combined, this constellation of thoughts, emotion, and behavior forms your "me-ness"—essentially, the kind of person you are.

When it comes to defining and measuring personality, a problem for psychologists has been the vast number of possible character labels available, some more flattering than others: *vain, chatty, boring, charming, narcissistic, shy, impulsive, nerdy, fussy, arty,* to name just a handful. (In 1936, the grandfather of personality psychology, Gordon Allport, and his colleague Henry Odbert estimated there are no fewer than 4,504 English words pertaining to personality traits.)[8] Thankfully, modern psychology has weeded out all the redundancy in these descriptions, distilling the variation in human character into five main traits.

For an example of this distillation process, consider that adventurous, thrill-seeking people also tend to be happier and more chatty, so much so that these characteristics seem to stem from the same underlying trait, known as extraversion. Following this logic, psychologists have identified five main traits:

- *Extraversion* refers to how receptive you are at a fundamental level to experiencing positive emotions, as well as how sociable, energetic, and active you are. In turn, this affects how much you enjoy seeking out excitement and company. If you like parties, extreme sports, and travel, you most likely score high on this trait.

- *Neuroticism* describes your sensitivity to negative emotion and your levels of emotional instability. If you worry a lot, if social slights hurt you, if you ruminate about past failures and fret about upcoming challenges, you probably score high on this trait.

- *Conscientiousness* is about your willpower—how organized and self-disciplined you are, as well as your industriousness. If you like your house to be tidy, you hate being late, and you're ambitious, you're probably a high scorer here.

- *Agreeability* refers to how warm and friendly you are. If you're patient and forgiving and your first reflex is to like and trust new people you meet, you're probably highly agreeable.

- *Openness* is about how receptive you are to new ideas, activities, cultures, and places. If you dislike opera, films with subtitles, and breaking your routine, you're probably a low scorer.

The Main Personality Traits and Their Subtraits

Big Five Trait	Its Facets (or Subtraits)
Extraversion	Warm, gregarious, assertive, active, fun-seeking, happy, cheerful
Neuroticism	Anxious, prone to anger, prone to sadness and shame, self-conscious, impulsive, vulnerable
Conscientiousness	Competent, orderly, dutiful, ambitious, self-disciplined, cautious
Agreeability	Trusting, honest, altruistic, accommodating, compliant, modest, empathic
Openness	Imaginative, aesthetically sensitive, in touch with emotions, curious, open to other perspectives and values

Most psychologists believe these five traits don't fully capture the darker sides of human nature. To measure these, they propose three more—narcissism, Machiavellianism, and psychopathy (known collectively as the dark triad).[9] We'll deal with these in detail in chapter 6, including looking at whether it's possible to learn lessons from the jerks, schemers, and braggers of this world, without ourselves going over to the dark side.

Personality can seem a bit woolly and purely descriptive, but it's reflected in your biological makeup, even down to the ways your brain is structured and functions. For instance, introverts don't just prefer peace and quiet; their brains respond more sensitively to loud noises. Neurotic (less emotionally stable) folk don't just experience more mood swings; they also have less surface area and folding in the parts of their cerebral cortex that are responsible for regulating emotions.[10] In the front of their brains, people with more advantageous personality traits—such as greater resilience and conscientiousness—have more myelination, the insulation around brain cells that helps them communicate efficiently.[11] Personality traits are even related to the microbiome in your stomach, with neurotic people having more harmful gut bacteria.[12]

Personality traits are manifested in the structure and function of the brain in various ways (see main text).

Higher conscientiousness is associated with lower levels of the stress hormone cortisol, as measured in the hair.

Lower neuroticism and higher conscientiousness are associated with lower blood pressure. Low heart rate, meanwhile, can be a mark of trait psychopathy.

Higher openness and conscientiousness are associated with fewer markers of chronic inflammation in the body.

Higher neuroticism is associated with more unhealthy gut microbacteria.

Personality trait scores are not merely abstract; they also get under the skin and are associated with many aspects of your physiology, from the microbacteria in your gut to your patterns of brain activity. It's a two-way relationship, so maintaining good physical health, such as through a healthy diet, adequate sleep, and regular exercise, is also associated with benefits to personality, such as lower neuroticism and higher conscientiousness, agreeability, and openness.

So personality is a genuine concept with biological underpinnings. Yet as the stories of Anthony Joshua, Tiger Woods, and others imply, personality is not set in stone—or plaster, for that matter. That was the metaphor preferred by the great American psychologist William James in the nineteenth century, who observed in his *Principles of Psychology* that by age thirty, our personalities are set in plaster and our capacity for change is over.

In fact, there's a sense in which your capacity for change is more apparent beyond age thirty. It's notable that whereas the genetic influences on cognition—things like your intelligence and memory abilities—increase through life, the genetic influences on personality decline, arguably reflecting the increasing scope for life events and other experiences to leave their mark, like new jobs, relationships, or moving abroad.[13]

Humans have evolved to be adaptable. You can think of your current personality traits as the behavioral and emotional strategy that you've settled on to best survive and thrive in the circumstances you find yourself in. Your genetic disposition makes it more likely that you might settle on some strategies more than others, but it doesn't confine you to one approach to life and relationships, and you are not stuck with your current way of being.

It's true that personality tends to become more stable with increasing age, but this isn't because of a lost capacity for change. It's because most people's circumstances become progressively less varied as they settle into the grooves of adult life.

Zoom out, and it's clear that most of us change throughout life. If you follow the typical pattern, you'll become friendlier, more self-disciplined, and have less angst as you get older. Occasionally the big choices you make in life—the career paths you take, the relationships you form—will bring about more profound changes. The effect of major events like graduation, parenthood, divorce, bereavement, illness, and unemployment also accumulate. The longest-ever personality study, published in 2016, involved a comparison of participants' personalities at age fourteen and then again at age seventy-seven, and it failed to find much correlation between the two times.[14] Another compared nearly two thousand people's personalities across fifty years, again finding evidence of significant change, showing that personality is malleable and that people's traits typically mature as they age.[15]

Of course you also show trait-like changes in your behavior over the short term (psychologists call these "state changes"), in response to things like your mood, the people you're with (think how you act around your boss or grandmother compared with your best friend, for instance), or what you've had to drink. Consider how tennis star Rafael Nadal's persona on and off court are said to be so different that it's like Superman and Clark Kent. His mother "never ceases to be amazed by how brave he is on the tennis court and how fear-ridden off it."[16]

The mixed message that personality is both stable and changing is perplexing for the many of us who prefer things to be black or white. Simine Vazire, a personality psychologist at the University of California, Davis, captured the paradox neatly. She wrote an open letter to NPR in response to the episode of the *Invisibilia* podcast I mentioned earlier—the one featuring Dan, the convicted rapist with the now charming, kind personality. The episode was called "The Personality Myth," implying that because personality is malleable, it is a meaningless concept. But that's going *way* too far, Vazire explained. "With personality," she said, "there is plenty to hold on to, and plenty we can change."[17]

WHY PERSONALITY MATTERS

Your personality has a powerful influence on your life, from your chances of success at school and work, to your mental and physical health and relationships, and even your longevity. Consider how a teenager's grit and self-discipline are even more important to her academic results than her IQ.[18] In fact, according to a controversial study from 2017, a child's level of self-control—a key component to having a conscientious personality—continues to reverberate for decades.[19]

To show this, researchers charted the lives of 940 people born in Dunedin, New Zealand, in 1972 or 1973 to the present day, finding roughly 20 percent went on to account for a huge slice of the entire cohort's burden on society in terms of things like obesity, crime, smoking, and broken homes. Crucially, those with low self-control as children were much more likely to be members of this high-burden minority.

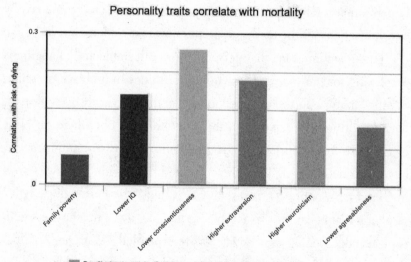

Predictive power of traits vs. IQ and family socioeconomic status

The significance of personality traits is evidenced by how strongly trait scores correlate with future risk of dying (mortality), as shown in this graph based on data from dozens of studies featuring thousands of volunteers. Source: Data from Brent W. Roberts, Nathan R. Kuncel, Rebecca Shiner, Avshalom Caspi, and Lewis R. Goldberg, "The Power of Personality: The Comparative Validity of Personality Traits, Socioeconomic Status, and Cognitive Ability for Predicting Important Life Outcomes," Perspectives on Psychological Science 2, no. 4 (2007): 313–345.

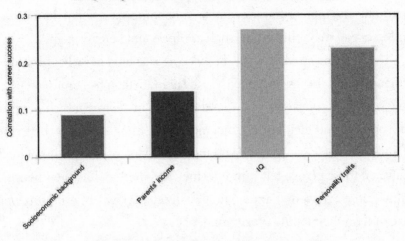

Personality traits correlate with future career success

▓ Predictive power of traits vs. IQ and family background

Personality traits also correlate with future career success more than factors related to family and parental background, and nearly as much as intelligence. *Source: Data from dozens of studies, collated by Roberts et al., "The Power of Personality: The Comparative Validity of Personality Traits, Socioeconomic Status, and Cognitive Ability for Predicting Important Life Outcomes,"* Perspectives on Psychological Science *2, no. 4 (2007): 313–345.*

Another study, this one of over twenty-six thousand people in the United States, found that, independent of their family's social status, individuals' personality traits at high school were related to their longevity, even in their seventh decade, with more impulsive people likely to die earlier and people with more self-control likely to live longer.[20] Similar research shows having a conscientious personality is as important a factor as socioeconomic status or education level if you hope to lead a long life.[21]

In terms of happiness, a recent estimate placed the monetary value of a small reduction in trait neuroticism (a propensity for negative moods, stress, and worry) as equivalent to an extra $314,000 income per annum.[22] Another way to put this in perspective is to consider the results of an Australian study that followed over ten thousand people for three years: the influence of their personality traits, especially being less neurotic and more extraverted, on their happiness was about double the influence of major life events such as illness and bereavement.[23]

More extraverted, less neurotic people also tend to be happier with their material success. A Swedish study of more than five thousand people, age thirty to seventy-five, found that the link between their personality profile and their current income was as strong as the link between family economic background and income.[24] Moreover, in terms of how satisfied these people felt with how they had done in life, their personality (more extraverted, more emotionally stable) was an even stronger factor than their family background.

Another important aspect of personality is open-mindedness. A worker's ability to innovate and learn new skills, as so many modern employers demand, is based on having high levels of this trait. Your personality could even make it less likely that your job will be taken over by a robot![25] When researchers tracked the careers of three hundred and fifty thousand people for over fifty years, they found that those who displayed higher levels of extraversion and conscientiousness when they were teenagers were less likely to enter careers that are easily computerized.

So personality matters massively. But remember that although your traits show some stability through life, especially if you make no conscious attempt to change them, they are not fixed and they are not destiny. In fact, the ways in which your personality changes are incredibly important for your future happiness, possibly even more so than other obvious factors you might think of, such as your wealth and marital status.

THE CASE FOR CHANGE

Your personality traits make you who you are and shape the life you will lead, so this idea that they are to some extent constantly evolving and readily molded by life may seem unsettling. But it's also an empowering revelation. By familiarizing ourselves with the ways that our personalities shift and bend at different life stages and in response to different circumstances, we can anticipate and exploit our capacity for change. More than that, we don't have to be passive observers, waiting for events to shape us. Inspiring new research shows that with the right attitude, enough dedication, and suitable techniques, we can literally choose to change our personalities at will, to be who we want. This book will help you understand how to do this, including through outside-in approaches—placing yourself in the right situations, choosing carefully whom you spend your time with, and taking up new hobbies and meaningful projects—and inside out, through mental and physical exercises and altering your habits of thought and emotion. After all, your personality arises from your style of thought, motivations, emotions, and habits. Address these, and you will change yourself and your life.

Before setting out to shape your personality, it's worth reflecting deeply on what your current priorities in life are. Deliberate personality change is also a goal that should be undertaken with care, bearing in mind the importance of your sense of identity and authenticity. That said, feeling authentic is arguably about acting as much as possible as the kind of person you want to be rather than how you actually are.

GETTING TO KNOW YOURSELF

What kind of personality do you have today? You will have a rough idea based on the things you enjoy or the reputation you have among friends and family. If you like parties and meeting new people, for instance, you probably see yourself as being an extravert.

In fact, many of our everyday habits and routines can be surprisingly revealing. A recent study involved profiling the personalities of nearly eight hundred volunteers in Oregon and then four years later asking them to rate how often they had engaged in four hundred different mundane activities over the preceding year.[26]

Some of the findings were obvious: extraverts went to more parties and open-minded people to more operas, for example. But other results were more surprising. Do you enjoy wallowing in hot tubs, decorating, and getting a tan? This might suggest you're an extravert (in the study, extraverts were especially likely to say they'd engaged in these activities).

If you spend lots of time ironing, playing with kids, washing up, or even singing in the shower or car, then you're likely to be a high scorer in agreeability (presumably you're trying to keep everyone happy, including yourself). If you avoid swearing, wear a watch,[27] keep your hair combed and shoes polished[28] (or a more modern equivalent—your phone apps are all up to date), then you're probably highly conscientious—so too if you're more of a morning person, as opposed to a "night owl," or evening person.[29] And if you lounge around the house in the nude a lot, this apparently is a sign of your open-mindedness!

THE LEMON JUICE PERSONALITY TEST

If you want to get more scientific, there are also some messier, more hands-on ways to discover your personality. The lemon juice test of extraversion and introversion was introduced decades ago by Hans Eysenck, one of the pioneers of personality psychology. To try it, you'll need some concentrated lemon juice, a Q-tip, and a piece of thread (alternatively, skip the next two paragraphs if you'd rather not get sticky—probably a sign that you're super-conscientious!).

First, tie the thread to the center of the Q-tip. Now place one end of the Q-tip on your tongue and hold it there for twenty seconds. Next, place a few drops of lemon juice on the other end of the Q-tip before placing that juicy end on your tongue for twenty seconds. Finally, hold the Q-tip by the thread and see if the juicy end hangs lower. If it does, this suggests that you are an introvert, at least at a physiological level. Introverts are known to respond more strongly to stimulation and pain than extraverts, which explains why they tend to shy away from loud noise and high excitement. This sensitivity also applies to lemon juice, which causes the introvert's tongue to salivate, making the Q-tip extra heavy on the juicy end. Extraverts, by contrast, aren't so physically sensitive, and so they don't salivate so much in response to the juice and the Q-tip stays evenly balanced.

The lemon juice test is fun and thinking about our daily habits is somewhat informative, but to get a really accurate and more complete read of your entire personality—of the kind that's used in psychology research—what you need is to take a detailed questionnaire that taps into each of the so-called Big Five personality traits.

TAKE A BIG FIVE PERSONALITY QUIZ

The thirty descriptive statements that follow are adapted from the shortened version of the Big Five Inventory-2, developed by psychologists Christopher Soto and Oliver John at Colby College in 2017.[30] By completing the quiz now and then again after you've finished reading this book, you'll get a good sense of your current personality and then how much and in what ways you've changed while reading it.

For each of the following thirty items, mark from 1 to 5 how much the description matches you (1 = Disagree Strongly; 2 = Disagree a Little; 3 = Neutral/No Opinion; 4 = Agree a Little Bit; 5 = Agree Strongly). Be as honest as you can. If you try to manipulate the scores, you'll just end up with a skewed picture:

Measure Your Personality Traits

1.	Tends to be chatty.	1	2	3	4	5
2.	Is compassionate, has a soft heart.	1	2	3	4	5
3.	Tends to be organized.	1	2	3	4	5
4.	Worries a lot.	1	2	3	4	5
5.	Is fascinated by art, music, or literature.	1	2	3	4	5
6.	Is dominant, acts as a leader.	1	2	3	4	5
7.	Is rarely rude to others.	1	2	3	4	5
8.	Good at getting started on tasks.	1	2	3	4	5
9.	Tends to feel depressed, blue.	1	2	3	4	5
10.	Has lots of interest in abstract ideas.	1	2	3	4	5
11.	Is full of energy.	1	2	3	4	5
12.	Assumes the best about people.	1	2	3	4	5
13.	Is reliable, can always be counted on.	1	2	3	4	5
14.	Is emotionally unstable, easily upset.	1	2	3	4	5
15.	Is original, comes up with new ideas.	1	2	3	4	5
16.	Is outgoing, sociable.	1	2	3	4	5
17.	Is never cold and uncaring.	1	2	3	4	5
18.	Keeps things neat and tidy.	1	2	3	4	5
19.	Is highly strung, handles stress badly.	1	2	3	4	5
20.	Has many artistic interests.	1	2	3	4	5
21.	Prefers to be in charge.	1	2	3	4	5
22.	Is respectful, treats others with respect.	1	2	3	4	5
23.	Is persistent, works until the task is finished.	1	2	3	4	5

24.	Feels insecure, uncomfortable with self.	1	2	3	4	5
25.	Is complex, a deep thinker.	1	2	3	4	5
26.	Is more active than other people.	1	2	3	4	5
27.	Rarely finds fault in others.	1	2	3	4	5
28.	Tends to take care over things.	1	2	3	4	5
29.	Is temperamental, gets emotional easily.	1	2	3	4	5
30.	Has lots of creativity.	1	2	3	4	5

So what do your answers say about you? Let's take each trait in turn, beginning with extraversion.

Extraversion: The Rock Star Trait[31]

To find your extraversion score, add the ratings you gave yourself for items 1, 6, 11, 16, 21, and 26. Your total will sit somewhere between 6 (a leave-me-alone, highly sensitive introvert) to 30 (a fully pumped, adrenaline junkie of an extravert). Most of us tend to score somewhere in between these extremes.

If you're a strong extravert, not only are you very sociable with lots of friends, you are probably drawn to professions that involve risk and reward, such as sales or trading stocks, as well as leadership and the chance for status. You're optimistic and happier more of the time than most introverts are. The chances are that you also like a drink or two. In fact, when researchers have studied groups of strangers mingling together over a drink, they've found extraverts are especially likely to say that the alcohol boosted their mood and that drinking helped them feel closer to their new acquaintances.[32] Summed up, strong extraversion is about living fast and dying young—and indeed, strong extraverts take more drugs and have more sex than introverts, and on average they also die younger. This is why personality psychologist Dan McAdams calls extraversion the "all-time rock star" of personality.[33]

If you're an introvert (you scored very low on extraversion), the picture is basically the opposite: you're a chill seeker, not a thrill seeker. It's not that you're unsociable necessarily, but the intense buzz of a party is not very appealing. In fact, you likely find parties overwhelming. Brain imaging studies show that introverts like you respond more sensitively at a neural level to stimulation, which probably explains why, in contrast to extraverts, you are careful about seeking out too much excitement.

Neuroticism: How Stable Are You?

To find your overall neuroticism score (also known as "negative emotionality" or "emotional instability"), add your ratings for items 4, 9, 14, 19, 24, and 29. Again you will end up with a number between 6 (it's like you have ice running through your veins) and 30 (like a Woody Allen character, you are probably too nervous to even venture outside).

If extraversion is about sensitivity to the good things in life, then neuroticism is sensitivity to all that can go wrong. If you have a high score, it's probable that you are moody, shy, prone to stress, volatile, and spend a lot of time feeling unpleasant emotions such as dread and shame and guilt. High scorers on neuroticism are more vulnerable than average to mental health conditions, such as depression and anxiety, and to physical ailments. This shows up at a neural level; for example, neurotic people's brains are especially sensitive to unpleasant images and words.[34] Indeed, while there may be poetic and philosophical reasons for finding virtue in emotional distress, from a practical perspective it is hard to deny that it is better to be a low scorer on this trait.[35]

If you are lucky enough to have scored low on neuroticism, it probably takes quite a lot to make you upset, and even when you are feeling down or nervous, you get over it quickly.

Agreeableness: How Friendly Are You?

For your agreeableness, add your ratings for items 2, 7, 12, 17, 22, and 27, placing you somewhere between 6 (there's no easy way to say it: if this was your score, you're not a very nice person, though the honesty of your self-appraisal is remarkable!) and a maximum of 30 (you, sweetie, are an angel!).

High scorers are warm and kind, and they see the best in other people (and bring out the best in them). They are gentle, welcoming of strangers and outsiders, empathic, and good at taking others' perspectives. These characteristics show up in their brains; for example, they have structural differences in neural areas linked with looking at things from other people's point of view,[36] and they show more activation in regions involved in dampening down negative feelings.[37] In short, these are the sort of people you want to have as your friend. No wonder they tend to be popular and well liked.

A recent study provides a graphic illustration of the difference between high and low scorers on agreeableness.[38] Researchers gave participants alcohol to drink and paired each of them with a partner with whom they could give and receive electric shocks (this was partly a ruse; the participant's partner was fictitious, and the shocks were preprogrammed). Participants who scored lower in agreeableness showed more aggression: if their partner provoked them with a mild shock when they were intoxicated, they were especially prone to lashing out in retaliation, answering with an extreme electric shock of their own. But the more agreeable participants were far less fiery; even when disinhibited with alcohol, they were more inclined to respond to provocation by turning the other cheek.

Openness to Experience: How Thoughtful and Creative Are You?

The relevant items for this trait are 5, 10, 15, 20, 25, and 30. Again, you will have a total score lying somewhere between 6 at the low end (I'm guessing you don't have a passport and you eat the same cereal every single morning) and 30 at the high end, which would make you the kind of person who eats spices for breakfast while listening to opera, of course. To "closed-minded" people who score low on this trait, high scorers can seem dreamy, high-minded, and pretentious, overly keen to advertise their individuality.[39] To open people, low scorers can seem bigoted, boring, and boorish (or uncultured at least).

Fundamentally this trait is about how motivated you are to have new, unfamiliar experiences and how sensitive you are to beauty and aesthetics. This manifests at a basic physiological level; for example, higher scorers on this trait are more likely to experience shivers down the spine in response to what they consider to be beautiful music or art.[40] And it can even protect you from the ravages of dementia. It's as if a life of greater intellectual variety builds up a kind of cognitive reserve or spare capacity that provides a buffer against decline.[41]

Openness correlates with but is not the same as intelligence. It also manifests in our attitudes—for example, toward politics and religion. High scorers tend to be more liberal and drawn to spirituality rather than organized religion; in contrast, low scorers are more traditional and conservative, and they see things in more black-and-white terms. Individuals with an open-minded personality are not morally superior as such (except perhaps in terms of showing less prejudice toward outsiders), but they are usually more questioning of moral values and more prepared to change their mind or even accept that many questions don't have straightforward answers.

Conscientiousness: Do You Have Grit and Determination? [19]

Here's how to calculate your score for the fifth and final of the Big Five personality traits: you need to find and add your ratings for items 3, 8, 13, 18, 23, and 28. The very lowest you can score is 6 (kudos if this is you, because given your usual tendencies, it's pretty impressive that you managed to stay focused long enough to even get this far in the quiz), and the highest is 30 (in which case I'm guessing it's probably very early in the morning, the rest of your household is asleep, and you're getting in some extra study time).

Extreme scorers at the high and low ends of conscientiousness are a little like the Ant and the Grasshopper, respectively, from Aesop's eponymous fable. The conscientious Ant has the long-term goal to ensure he doesn't go hungry next winter. Crucially, he also has the motivation and self-control to work through the summer accumulating food so that he can fulfill this goal. The Grasshopper, by contrast, succumbs to the hedonistic temptations of summer, lacking the self-discipline or motivation to plan ahead for the winter.

At a fairly trivial level, if you're very conscientious, you're probably punctual, neat, and tidy. More significant, conscientiousness, more than any other trait, is associated with important life outcomes, such as academic success, career success, and satisfaction,[42] lasting personal relationships, avoiding getting into trouble with the law, and a longer, healthier life. This is little surprise because those who are highly conscientious have the self-control and persistence to focus on their studies and work, follow rules, stay loyal, and resist the lure of often harmful temptations such as smoking, overeating, fast driving, unprotected sex, and extramarital affairs.

Armed with your scores from the quiz, you now have a detailed breakdown of the kind of person you are *today*. If you're like most other people, there will be some aspects that you're happy with and others that you'd like to change. Now that you know your official personality profile, some obvious questions spring to mind that I'll help you answer in the next chapter: What were some of the first factors to influence your character? How might your parents, siblings, and friends have cultivated the kind of personality that you started out with in life? Of course, your personality today might feel quite different from the one you had as a bright-eyed eighteen-year-old with the world at your feet. How have life's ups and downs left their mark on you, and what changes can you expect in the future?

Ten Actionable Steps to Change Your Personality

To reduce neuroticism	Whenever you are upset or angry, write down how you are feeling and label your emotions. Research suggests that doing so has a calming effect and reduces their intensity.	Keep a gratitude diary. Each day, make a note of three things that happened that you are grateful for. Gratitude increases positive mood and reduces stress.
To increase extraversion	Commit to inviting a friend over for a drink this week. Loneliness and social isolation increase introversion, and part of the way to combat this is to plan social activities. If you don't know where to start, try a friendship app like Frim to find like-minded people in your area.	Set yourself the challenge of saying hello to a stranger this week, and if you feel confident enough, try engaging in a little small talk. Research suggests we find talking to strangers far more enjoyable than we think we will and that we also tend to make a better impression than we realize.
To increase conscientiousness	Before you go to sleep at night, make a note of the things that you have to do the next day. Not only will this help you be more organized, but a recent study also found that it helped reduce insomnia through providing some closure on as-yet-incomplete tasks.	Reflect honestly on a chore or task that you've been putting off and commit to doing it this week. If you don't know where to start, ask yourself: What is the very next action I need to take to get this done?
To increase agreeability	Send a thank-you note to a friend, relative, or colleague. One recent study found that the recipients of thank-you notes benefit from them much more than we expect.	Give someone at work (or in your neighborhood) a compliment. Civil acts like this tend to propagate as people pay forward the kindness they received.
To increase openness	Start watching subtitled dramas on TV; exposing yourself to other cultures will broaden your mind.	Join a book group. Reading literary fiction in particular has been linked with an increased ability to consider other people's perspectives.

Chapter 2

SLINGS AND ARROWS

The Verrio, a painting by Antonio Verrio, depicts the foundation of the Royal Mathematical School in England in 1673. It has hung in the cavernous dining hall at Christ's Hospital boarding school for hundreds of years. At around eighty-six feet long, divided into three panels, it is one of the largest paintings in the world. Many generations of staff and pupils have marveled at it.

Some pupils are more awestruck by this enormous painting than others. When I attended the school in the 1990s, one of my more boisterous peers named George (not his real name) stabbed a slab of butter with his knife and then flung it straight at *The Verrio*, seemingly just for the hell of it. The congealed blob lingered on the canvas for a moment, before leaving a greasy smear as it fell with a quiet slap onto the dining hall floor.

The butter chucker was punished heavily at the time, but less than twelve months later, he was appointed to be our new house captain (the pupil chosen by the housemaster to help keep order in the board-inghouse). My friends and I were not angels, but we were certainly more discreet in our antics than our new house captain. To say we were surprised by his appointment is an understatement. I'm telling you this tale not out of lingering bitterness, but because whether they knew it or not, the teachers at my school had acted with shrewd insight into the psychology of personality change.

One of the main theories for how personalities change through life is known as social investment theory: the roles you take on, whether getting married, starting a new job, or becoming boardinghouse cap-tain, can shape your personality—especially if the roles lead you to be rewarded consistently for certain patterns of new behavior.

Giving my housemate George, who was a bit of a rascal, the respon-sibility of being house captain was a clever move. The extra responsi-bility, the public gesture of belief in his capacity to be good, and the requirement for him to be disciplined to fulfill his duties all combined to increase his trait conscientiousness (in fact, today George works as a teacher himself!).

In this chapter, I give you an outline of the many ways personality tends to change through life—not only in the social roles you take on, such as getting married and having kids, but also in response to the slings and arrows thrown your way, including getting divorced or los-ing your job. I'll show you how we tend to change on average through the different life stages as we typically mature and mellow into old age. Being aware of these changes will allow you to anticipate them, capital-ize on the positive, and do what's possible to avert the negative.

You're not a blank slate. The kind of person you are is not en-tirely the product of the things that you've done or have happened to you. Your personality comes from a mix of your experiences and your genes: in fact, between 30 and 50 percent of the variation in personality between people stems from the genes they inherited from their parents and the rest to differences in their experiences.

Things aren't entirely separate when it comes to these two sculpting forces. The traits you're born with, by virtue of your genes, are a little like your factory-setting approach to life, and so they also shape the kinds of situations you find yourself in. For instance, it stands to reason that if you're genetically inclined to be extraverted, you're likely to spend more of your time in social situations (which will likely make you even more extraverted). If you're genetically inclined to be open-minded, you're more likely to read and discover new ideas and viewpoints, making you yet more open-minded. Highly agreeable people tend to place themselves in pleasant situations, and they're skilled at diffusing arguments, which makes it a lot easier to be friendly and easygoing. In this way, even modest genetic influences on personality can snowball by affecting the kind of experiences you have.

Before looking in detail at the ways that personality develops through adult life, let's rewind and consider the kind of personality you had as an infant and child. Specifically, what factors influenced you back then, and is there any connection between the way you were as a child and the kind of person you are as an adult?

YOUR ORIGIN STORY

Armed with your scores from the personality quiz in the previous chapter, you have a detailed breakdown of your personality profile today. That said, there is always a thread of continuity running through people's lives. Even the way you behaved as a baby might have given clues to the kind of person you've become.

Infants don't have fully formed personalities. Instead, psychologists talk about infant "temperament," which is defined according to three traits. "Effortful control" is how well an infant can focus and resist distraction—for example, persisting with one play challenge rather than flitting impetuously from one toy or object to another (like an early form of adult conscientiousness). There's also "negative affectivity," which is essentially how much a baby cries and gets scared and frustrated (it's clearly the forerunner to adult trait neuroticism). And finally, there's "surgency," which has to do with striving, sociability, and energy levels and is the baby version of extraversion.

Your infant temperament certainly isn't destiny, but some of what makes you *you* may have been starting to show. A recent Russian study looked for links between the same individuals' temperaments when they were just a few months old and their personalities as eight-year-old children, rated in both cases by their parents.[1] They found some striking consistencies. For instance, infants with more energy and who smiled more grew into more emotionally stable eight-year-olds. Similarly, infants with more focus and concentration went on to be the kind of children who keep their bedrooms tidy and get to school on time. But not everything matched up; for example, smiley, more outgoing babies didn't score higher on extraversion as children.

The later you measure a child's personality, the stronger the relation it is likely to have to her adult character. When researchers compared the adult personality profiles of just over a thousand twenty-six-year-olds (all of whom had been born in Dunedin, New Zealand, in 1972 or 1973) with the behavioral scores these same individuals had been given as three-year-olds, they found many striking consistencies. To take just one example, the "confident" children became the most extraverted adults, and the inhibited children became the least extraverted.[2]

While they're certainly not fixed, your early habits of behavior, thought, and relating to the world also have far-reaching consequences. You may have heard of psychologist Walter Mischel's iconic marshmallow test experiments. He challenged young children to resist eating a delicious-looking marshmallow that he placed in front of them for fifteen minutes while he left the room. If the sweet was left uneaten by the time he came back, they would be rewarded with the chance to gobble up two marshmallows. Later in life, the children who'd shown strong powers of self-control in Mischel's tests (suggesting they scored highly in the temperamental trait of effortful control) tended to be healthier and to have done better in their schooling, careers, and relationships. Similarly, researchers in Luxembourg recently compared the conscientiousness ratings that hundreds of people received from their teachers when they were eleven years old and found that the higher they scored, the better their careers were going forty years later in terms of their status, pay, and job satisfaction.[3]

Now let's look at how your own childhood experiences—your parents, siblings, and friends—might have shaped the kind of personality that you started out with in life.

Your Parents

"They fuck you up, your mum and dad," wrote the poet Philip Larkin.[4] This is a harsh assessment. In fact (excluding cases of maltreatment), modern psychology views the influence of parents over their children as surprisingly modest. I say "surprisingly" because of the huge advice industry built around telling parents how they should and shouldn't raise their kids. However, to borrow a metaphor from developmental psychologist Alison Gopnik, we should think of parenting less like the intensive training of an animal (although it may sometimes feel like that) and more akin to a gardener gently tending to her plants, "providing a rich, stable, safe environment that allows many different kinds of flowers to bloom."[5]

Think about your own parents. Did they try to control everything you did, and to what extent? How much did they invade your privacy? Did they seem emotionally cold? Did they never praise you? If you answered yes to all four questions, this would suggest that your parents were controlling and cold.[6] Think back again: Did your parents shower you with affection? Did they talk to you? Did they encourage you but set boundaries and sometimes prevent you from doing what you wanted? If so, this sounds more like an authoritative style, which is generally considered to be more beneficial to the child.

Studies suggest that the children of more authoritative parents tend to be better able to regulate their own emotions (they would probably ace Mischel's marshmallow test), are more likely to excel in their school studies, and are usually better behaved in general—for example, they are less likely to get into trouble at school.[7] In terms of personality, we can think of this as lower neuroticism and higher conscientiousness and openness. It's a similar story if you look at research that has asked adults about their memories of how their parents raised them: those less fortunate individuals who say their parents were cold and controlling tend to score higher as adults in neuroticism and lower in conscientiousness.[8]

Parenting style is also relevant to the development of grit, a concept that has gained traction in the past few years because of claims that it is the secret to dramatic success in life. Grit is really a subcomponent of conscientiousness. It is associated with having passion *and* perseverance—in other words, having a single-minded focus on one or more specific goals and having the willpower and dedication to work toward them. In her definitive book on the subject, *Grit* (2016), University of Pennsylvania psychologist Angela Duckworth argues that it is parents who are highly supportive of their children but also demanding, pushing them to achieve (she calls this "wise parenting"), who are more likely to have children who grow up to have grit.[9]

Another fascinating concept to bear in mind when thinking about how your parents may have shaped your personality is that some of us may be much more sensitive to these influences, good and bad, than others. In their landmark paper published in 2005, pediatrician W. Thomas Boyce and psychologist Bruce Ellis coined the beautiful term "orchid children" to describe kids who are particularly vulnerable to wilting when they are treated harshly but who bloom magnificently when they are treated with care and attention.[10] They refer to less sensitive children, whose development is much more immune to their upbringing, good or bad, as "dandelion children."

Check out these statements based on the Highly Sensitive Child Scale; the more you agree with, the more likely that you're an orchid:[11]

> I find it unpleasant to have a lot going on at once.
> I love nice tastes.
> I notice it when small things have changed in my environment.
> I don't like loud noises.
> When someone observes me, I get nervous. This makes me perform worse than normal.

If you think you might have an orchid disposition and your parents had leanings toward the authoritarian style or worse, I feel for you, but I hope it's also motivating to think that in the right environment, you could yet thrive and blossom. As an adult, you may have more control over the situations and cultures you place yourself in, giving you the chance to reach your potential.

Your Siblings

Another popular idea is that your personality is influenced by your family birth order. Kevin Leman, a psychologist and author on the subject, wrote, "The one thing you can bet your paycheck on is the firstborn and second-born in any given family are going to be different."[12] The usual argument is that firstborns get all their parents' undivided, and somewhat nervous, attention (because this is their first child), which shapes them to be conscientious; later-borns, by contrast, are caricatured as being more carefree and attention seeking.

These suggestions are intuitively compelling and backed up by anecdotal evidence. Consider that firstborns are overrepresented among former American presidents, making up twenty-four out of the first forty-six presidents, including George W. Bush, Jimmy Carter, Lyndon Johnson, and Harry Truman. More recently, Bill Clinton was a firstborn, and Barack Obama was raised as such (he had older half-siblings he didn't live with). Elsewhere, the European leaders Angela Merkel and Emmanuel Macron are both firstborns. Among astronauts, twenty-one of the first twenty-three astronauts who were sent into space were firstborns.[13] It's a similar story in business, with Sheryl Sandberg, Marissa Mayer, Jeff Bezos, Elon Musk, and Richard Branson, to name just a few famous CEOs, all being firstborns.

Nevertheless, the idea of a firstborn personality was undermined convincingly by two definitive studies published in 2015. These investigations were more carefully devised than any previous ones. Most prior research had relied on siblings rating each other's personalities, not the most trustworthy of measures. The new studies were also huge in scope. One involved data on personality traits and birth order from over twenty thousand people.[14] The other had nearly four hundred thousand participants.[15] Together, the new studies found that the anecdotal evidence is misleading and that birth order actually has few or negligible associations with personality. "The conclusion is inescapable," wrote US personality experts Rodica Damian and Brent Roberts in a commentary: "Birth order is not an important factor for personality development."[16]

Although birth order is not meaningfully relevant to personality development, birth spacing might be. This is the size of the gap in age between one sibling and another. A recent British study involved repeated personality tests over forty-two years of more than four thousand people born in 1970, all of whom had one older sibling.[17] This study showed that the bigger the age gap between the siblings, the more likely that the younger brother or sister had an introverted, emotionally unstable personality.

Speculating as to why birth spacing has this effect, the researchers at Maastricht University suggested that having siblings closer in age is beneficial because they get to play and compete together and they're more likely to receive joint attention and teaching from their parents (consistent with this, other research has found that preschoolers with more siblings tend to perform better at theory of mind tests, which measure the ability to think of things from other people's perspectives, a key part of having an agreeable personality). The Maastricht researchers even went so far as to suggest governments might want to encourage shorter age gaps between siblings—for example, through incentives related to parental leave as a way to foster more adaptive personalities in children. However, given that the previously popular idea that birth order affects personality has been debunked recently by rigorous research, it is wise to treat the new birth spacing findings with caution until more evidence is gathered.

What if you don't have siblings? There's a widespread negative stereotype about only children: because they get all their parents' attention and don't have to share, they become spoiled and selfish. Of course this is a sweeping generalization, but—and I say this reluctantly, as an only child myself—there may be a kernel of truth to it, at least according to research in China, a country that for years had a one-child policy enforced by the government as a way to control overpopulation. One study that compared the personality traits and behavioral tendencies of people born just before or after the introduction of China's one-child policy found that those in the latter group, predominantly only children, tended to be "less trusting, less trustworthy, more risk-averse, less competitive, more pessimistic and less conscientious."[18]

In another study, Chinese researchers scanned the brains of adult volunteers, some of whom were only children and some of whom had siblings, and then these volunteers completed personality tests and a creativity challenge. The only children scored significantly lower on the trait agreeableness than the participants with siblings (they described themselves as less friendly, sympathetic, and altruistic), and this seemed to correlate with their having less gray matter in a frontal part of their brain that's involved in thinking about the self in relation to other people.

On the plus side, the only children outperformed the others on the creativity task, which, among other things, involved coming up with unusual uses for a cardboard box. So perhaps all the time playing alone as a child is not great for developing a warm and sociable persona, but helps instead to foster a more creative mind. (This does jibe with my own personal experience. I used to spend hours devising elaborate game plots with my toys.)

Your Friends

Pop psychology makes such a big deal about the powerful effects of parenting and birth order, but it's your early friendships that probably had the largest influence on your personality. Indeed, looking again at the twin and adoption studies that have revealed the modest influences of parenting on personality, they have also shown that in terms of environmental influences (i.e., nongenetic influences), what's most important is the unique experiences that we each have rather than those that we share with our siblings.

To test the influence of very early friendships, researchers at Michigan State University recently had crews of observers go into classrooms several times between October to May.[19] The observers rated two classes of preschoolers—one of three-year-olds, the other of four-year-olds—in terms of their temperament and the kids they played with. The fascinating finding was that the children acquired the traits of the friends they played with most often, especially in terms of how much positive emotion they tended to display and how much planning and impulse control they showed (or failed to show) in the way they played and related to others. For instance, a child who spent a lot of time playing with a happy, well-behaved friend was more likely to show more happiness and good behavior when observed again a few months later. Consistent with the idea that personality is more plastic than plaster, it was also noticeable that most of the children showed a moderate level of change in their traits over the course of the study. "The dynamic nature of personality development is evident as early as three to five years of age," the researchers said.

The important influence of our peers on our personalities continues into adolescence. One of the largest–ever studies to look into interventions to help at-risk teenagers showing early signs of difficult, antisocial behavior found that, more important than parents' behavior or teachers' efforts to help, was the kind of friends they hung out with: mixing with agreeable, conscientious buddies was key to ensuring the effectiveness of any organized initiatives.[20] In early adulthood too, there's research showing that people in their twenties tend to acquire the traits of their friends; for instance, having a strongly extraverted friend will tend to increase your own extraversion.[21]

Think back to your own friendships. Was your best friend a rebel or a hard worker? Did you fall into a crowd that admired risk taking, experimentation, and pushing against the rules, or was it a group of ambitious and self-disciplined friends? Of course, to an extent, your own personality will have influenced the kind of peers you ended up mixing with. However, there is also a large element of luck and convenience involved in friendship (classic psychology research from the 1950s showed that proximity plays a key role: you were more likely to have ended up friends with the kids living next door than those who lived two blocks away). Reminiscing about these early relationships may help make sense of your personality today: it's highly likely that some of your friends' characteristics rubbed off on you.

TRIALS AND TRIBULATIONS

One major reason that your childhood nature doesn't map perfectly onto your adult personality is the small matter of adolescence to get through—the tumultuous time of life when we're finding ourselves and when personality typically shows the greatest change.

There's evidence that personality actually regresses for a short while in early adolescence (many parents will surely attest to this) in the sense that most teens tend to show temporary reductions in their self-discipline, sociability, and open-mindedness—suggesting there's some truth to the cliché of the moody young teen who prefers to listen to music alone in a messy room than venture out with friends. Also, for girls, but not boys, there's usually an initial, temporary increase in emotional instability. Psychologists haven't yet pinned down the reason for this gender difference, though it suggests that early adolescence may be an emotionally trickier time for girls or that they find it more difficult than boys to get the support they need from their parents or other relationships.

Then, whatever your gender, as you approached late adolescence and early adulthood, your personality probably started to mature again: on average, people at this age typically begin to mellow emotionally and show greater self-discipline and self-control. And even once you reached adulthood, you will likely have found that your personality continued to mature. To investigate these lifelong changes, psychologists have compared the average personality profiles of people at different stages of life. One impressive piece of recent research compared the personality of more than one million volunteers age ten to sixty-five.[22] They've also conducted many studies in which they've measured the same people's personalities repeatedly over many years or even decades.

Whatever approach they take, researchers generally find the same thing: as people get older, they tend to become less anxious and less moody, friendlier and more empathic but, on the downside, also less outgoing and sociable and open-minded. Meanwhile, self-discipline and organizational skills tend to increase through the first half of adult life, peak in midlife, and then decline again, possibly in part due to what's been dubbed the dolce vita effect—the easing of responsibilities and concerns in later life.

In the jargon of personality science, as you age, you can expect increases in emotional stability and agreeableness but drops in extraversion and open-mindedness (your conscientiousness will typically first rise and then fall). These typical patterns are worth bearing in mind in relation to your own personality development. Take a look back at your personality scores from chapter 1 and think again about the traits you'd like to change.

If you're a young woman who'd like to be more emotionally stable and more conscientious, for example, the good news is that you'll probably find that this is how you will change naturally as you mature into middle age (that is, without taking conscious steps to alter your traits). If you do make deliberate efforts to change yourself—for example, using the advice later in this book—then you will be working with the grain, so to speak. Conversely, if you're a senior and you pride yourself on your open-mindedness, it could be useful to know that the typical trend is for this trait to decline at your stage of life.

These are the broad, lifelong trait changes you can expect across a lifetime. But what about the impact on personality of more specific experiences, such as divorce, marriage, unemployment, and bereavement?

Few other life events are as turbulent as divorce. After years spent thinking as a "we," divorce forces an abrupt change in self-identity. As Elizabeth Barrett Browning is reported to have said to her husband, Robert Browning, "I love you not only for what you are, but for what I am when I am with you." It's little surprise that psychologists have found that divorce is one of the major life events that can leave a mark on personality. Take as case in point what happened to the former Bond girl and supermodel Monica Bellucci and her actor husband, Frenchman Vincent Cassel. They were a true supercouple, Europe's answer to Brad Pitt and Angelina Jolie. But after eighteen years together, including fourteen as wife and husband, two children, and joint appearances in at least eight films, they announced their split in 2013.

The fallout hit Bellucci and Cassel just as it would any less famous couple. Bellucci says that the split forced her to become "more structured, more grounded"; in personality terms, more conscientious, and less neurotic. 'I was just emotion before," she said in a 2017 interview.[23] "This is a new part of me I am discovering now in my 50s." Meanwhile,

Cassel moved from Paris, where he'd lived with Bellucci, to Rio de Janeiro. "Later in life, a man has the possibility to reinvent himself again and again," he said.[24]

Research into the effects of divorce on personality has uncovered mixed results. One US study tested the personalities of over two thousand US men and women twice across a period between six and nine years.[25] Among the women, those who'd gone through a divorce in that time tended to show signs of increased extraversion and openness to experience, perhaps because they found it a liberating experience (while this doesn't quite match Bellucci's description of her postdivorce personality change, she is also on record as saying that she "felt very alive" and "very energized" after the split).[26] By contrast, the men in this study who went through a divorce showed changes in personality suggesting they'd become more emotionally unstable and less conscientious, as if the relationship had given them a support and structure that they were now badly missing.

Other research has uncovered different patterns. For example, a German study of five hundred men and women found that for both genders, divorce tended to lead to reduced extraversion, perhaps because when marriages break up, some people tend to lose the friends they had made as a couple. Yet another study, this one involving over fourteen thousand Germans, found that divorce increased men's openness to experience, which would seem to parallel Vincent Cassel's move to Brazil and his belief in the chance for reinvention.[27]

The research on divorce shows how we can use the science of personality change to anticipate the impact of major life events. The German study that found that men and women tended to become more introverted postdivorce is a case in point. If you ever experience the misfortune of going through a divorce (or another significant relationship breakup), or even if you're going through the ordeal now, you could benefit from recognizing that one possible outcome is that you will become more introverted at just the time in your life when you could well benefit from becoming more outgoing.

Indeed, other research shows how feeling lonely, whether due to divorce or any other reason, can have this counterproductive effect on personality. Yet another study from Germany, this time involving more than twelve thousand women and men, found that those who described themselves as lonely at the start tended to show reduced extraversion and agreeableness at the end of the study compared with the start.[28]

This isn't too surprising, since other research on the psychological effects of loneliness shows it tends to make us highly sensitive to social slights and rejection. This is probably an evolutionary hangover; a degree of paranoia would have given some advantage to our ancestors who found themselves alone in a dangerous world. But the unfortunate side effect is that lonely people are quicker to spot signs of rejection, such as turned backs or angry faces, and their brains are highly tuned to negative social words like *alone* and *solitary*.[29]

A completely different major life experience that the research suggests can have an even larger impact on your personality is losing your job. If you're like many other people, your work role provides an important part of your identity and lends important structure to your life. If you ever have the misfortune of losing your job (as you will know already if this has happened to you), you'll find that time will suddenly all be your own, and you now have no answer to the inevitable, "So, what do you do?" question from new acquaintances at parties. All of this could lead to big changes in how you think, feel, and behave—the foundations of your personality traits.

The precise effects on your personality are likely to vary over time depending on how long your joblessness lasts. A team of psychologists led by Christopher Boyce demonstrated this by studying thousands of

German people who completed personality tests four years apart.[30] During this time, 210 of the volunteers lost their jobs and stayed unemployed, while another 251 lost their jobs but found new employment within a year.

The results were different for men and women: newly unemployed men showed an initial gain in their levels of agreeableness, perhaps as they strove to adjust and make a good impression on their friends and family. Remaining unemployed for years, however, took a toll, and they ended up less agreeable than men who worked. Unemployed men also became gradually less conscientious over the years. We can imagine this manifesting in various ways, such as being less ambitious, less focused, lazier and less motivated, less punctual, and taking less pride in their appearance. In contrast, fired women showed early drops in their agreeableness and their conscientiousness took a dive, but they later rebounded if they stayed unemployed over many years. The researchers think this might be because women can find new ways to structure their days and find reward for hard work that are related to traditionally feminine gender roles.

On a positive note, the study participants who had returned to employment before the study concluded didn't show any personality differences compared with those who'd stayed in work all the way through, suggesting that those who found new jobs had recovered from any adverse effects of unemployment.

What's worrying is the way that chronic unemployment led men's personalities to change in counterproductive ways, similar to what happens with loneliness reducing trait extraversion. Higher agreeableness and conscientiousness will increase your odds of finding a new job, yet the research showed that the longer that men were unemployed, the lower their scores dropped on these traits—a worryingly negative spiral.

Thankfully, experiences and opportunities in life can most definitely change us in positive ways too (think back to my rebellious classmate who thrived after being made boardinghouse captain). The Oscar-nominated actor Tom Hardy knows this better than most others. A rebel through and through, his addiction to drink and drugs, which began in his teens, reached its nadir in 2003 when, at age twenty-six, he woke from a heavy night of bingeing in a gutter in London's Soho, covered in his own vomit and blood. He has since turned over a new leaf and is one of the hardest-working and most respected actors in Hollywood. For this, he credits the opportunities that came his way courtesy of his job: "Acting was something I could do—and because I found that I was good at it, I wanted to make the effort to invest time and effort into doing it. These days, I'm lucky enough to do it for a living; and I love it and I learn from it every day."[31]

Hardy's experience jibes with the research on the positive effects of work and jobs on personality, which are the opposite of the harmful effects of job loss. When young people start their first jobs, their conscientiousness increases considerably compared with before they started.[32] The psychological explanation is that jobs make demands on us that shape the way we think, feel, and behave, such that over time, we change to meet these demands. For most jobs, this means greater orderliness, self-discipline, and impulse control—the characteristics that make up the trait of conscientiousness, and which help us get projects in on time, and foster smooth relations with colleagues and clients. Research also shows that promotions can have a similar effect as first jobs: presumably as the demands of a role increase, they again stretch us to adapt, leading to further gains in conscientiousness and openness to experience.[33]

Another major, usually happy, event that occurs in many of our lives is moving in with a partner and then, for some, getting married. As for moving in together, a consistent finding among heterosexual couples is that men tend to become more conscientious afterward, perhaps in an attempt to match their partners' expectations for tidiness and cleanliness (women on average score higher on conscientiousness).[34]

What about the effects of marriage? Anyone single who has ever been surrounded by a dinner party of married couples might wonder if tying the knot somehow warps people's personalities to make them self-satisfied (as captured in that scene in the movie *Bridget Jones's Diary* in which Bridget is surrounded by condescending couples feigning concern for her singleton status). Psychologists haven't fully answered that question, but another German study in which researchers looked at personality changes among nearly fifteen thousand people over a period of four years found that volunteers who got married during the course of the research showed reductions in extraversion and openness to experience—concrete evidence, perhaps, that marriage makes people at least a little more boring than they were before.[35]

There's also evidence that marriage can act as a sort of training ground for certain personality skills, particularly self-control and ability to forgive, presumably brought about by all those times you have to bite your tongue rather than risk an argument, or turn a forgiving eye when your spouse leaves you the dishes to wash or flirts with the neighbor. Dutch psychologists showed this by asking nearly two hundred newlywed couples to fill out questionnaires soon after getting married and then again each year for the next four years.[36] These married volunteers showed significant improvements in both traits; in fact, the increases they showed in self-control were similar to those seen in people who take part in training programs specifically designed to increase self-discipline.

Of course, the effects of personality on marriage will depend somewhat on the character and behavior of your spouse and the trajectory of your relationship. Another study of nearly five hundred fortysomething Dutch mothers that measured their personality repeatedly over six years found that those who reported more daily experiences of love and support from their partners (and/or their children) also tended to show increases in their own agreeableness and openness and reductions in neuroticism over time.[37] It's another example of how your personality evolves and adapts depending on the circumstances you find yourself in.

Unfortunately, there are also some happy events in life that won't necessarily have positive consequences for your personality. The most joyful moment I've ever experienced occurred on a sunny day in April 2014: my twins were born. The two little monsters (a girl and a boy) have brought me untold pride and happiness, and trying to care for them the best I can has redefined the meaning of my life. It's given me a clear purpose and direction that I didn't have before. But ever since that April day, it's also fair to say that life has been something of a whirlwind. It's funny now to look back on life before kids and wonder what on earth my wife and I did with all our free time. The constant demands on our freedom, the anxieties, and burden of responsibility are all a challenge.

Perhaps it is these challenges, and especially the stress of trying to live up to the ideals of being a good mother or father, that partly explain why research has shown that parenthood can have adverse effects on personality, particularly in relation to self-esteem (an aspect of trait neuroticism). For example, in a recent study, over eighty-five thousand mothers in Norway completed questionnaires while pregnant and then several times for three years after they gave birth.[38] As you might expect, most of the women were buzzing for the first six months after giving birth and their self-esteem increased over this time. But for the next two and a half years, their self-esteem dropped lower and lower. The good news is that this didn't seem to be a permanent state of affairs. Some of the mothers participated more than once in the survey, and when they returned to the study years after one birth, their self-esteem levels were usually back to normal.

However, other research involving many thousands of people has similarly found that becoming a parent seems to be associated with adverse effects on personality, including decreases in conscientiousness and extraversion.[39] The effect on extraversion makes obvious sense: it's difficult to be fun-loving and sociable when you're sleep deprived and have a baby constantly in tow. But the adverse effect on conscientiousness is something of a puzzle. You'd think the huge responsibility of having a child would boost conscientiousness, just as has been found for jobs and work promotions. One plausible explanation is that the demands are simply too overwhelming and confusing with children.

Finally, what about the inevitable, often devastating, impact of bereavement? In one particularly moving firsthand account published by the *Guardian*, Emma Dawson describes the grief she experienced after the loss of her younger sister, only thirty-two years old, as less like waves and more akin to "gargantuan freight trains that ram into your very soul."[40] She documents how "it feels as if someone has sucked out everything you have—your guts, your heart, your oxygen, your whole being," and she details the isolation (from avoiding speaking to friends), anxiety (including thoughts of her mortality), guilt (that she hadn't been able to protect her sister), and anger (triggered, for instance, by frustration at her three-year-old for throwing things that belonged to her late sister).

In personality trait terms there is surprisingly little systematic research on the effects of bereavement. Of the few studies that have been done, some have found no standard patterns of change in the bereaved compared with control participants, perhaps because the effects of bereavement are simply so varied and complex that consistent effects on personality have not been uncovered. One study found evidence for increased neuroticism following a loss, which would reflect the increased anxiety and anger that Emma Dawson described.[41] Most recently, researchers in Germany followed the same group of people for decades and uncovered a series of personality changes related to losing one's spouse.[42] For instance, prior to their loss, people showed increases in extraversion—presumably due to all the social effort involved in caring for their spouse and liaising with medical professionals—followed by reductions in extraversion after the loss. And unsurprisingly, people showed increased neuroticism leading up to the time of the loss, but gradually they regained their emotional stability in the years that followed. The findings provide another clear example of the dynamic interaction between personality and experience.

Life Isn't Completely Random

The dynamic between life events and personality isn't entirely one way: while your experiences shape your traits, your traits also influence the kind of life you are likely to lead. Swiss researchers recently assessed the personality of hundreds of participants and then interviewed them six times over three decades.[43] They found that people with certain personality profiles (especially those who were more emotionally unstable and less conscientious) were not only more likely to develop depression and anxiety over the course of the study; they were also more likely to go through more relationship breakups and job losses—upsetting experiences that we've seen are likely to feed back and shape personalities.

Of all the personality types, highly agreeable people seem to be the most skilled at shaping their own experiences. This helps explain why they always seem to be in a good mood. Researchers confirmed this in the psychology lab recently by measuring how much time participants chose to spend looking at a range of positive or negative pictures (such as of a cute baby or a photograph of skulls) and asking them to choose between a range of pleasant versus less pleasant activities, like listening to a lecture on baking or body dissection, or watching a horror movie

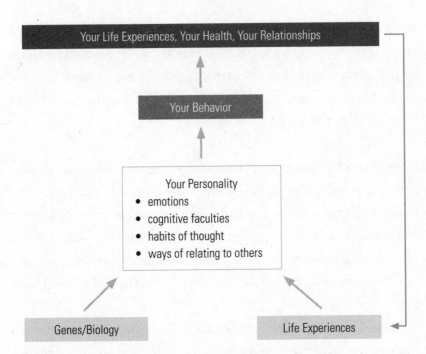

Personality both shapes and is shaped by life. By choosing to alter your behavior, habits, and routines, it's possible to change your traits and so influence the kind of life you will lead.

or a comedy.[44] Compared with others, higher scorers on agreeableness showed a consistent pattern to prefer exposing themselves to positive situations and experiences.

So, your personality traits clearly influence the kind of experiences you have. They also affect how you react to those experiences. Consider marriage. Decades of research have found that while tying the knot usually comes with a temporary spike in happiness, this soon fades back to the baseline as the newlyweds adjust to their new lifestyle. However, a recent study found that this isn't true for everyone. We often talk about some people being good husband or wife "material" (while others seem more suited to a life of singlehood). Consistent with this view, a study published in 2016 found that for some people, marriage did appear to lead to a lasting happiness boost: specifically, more conscientious, intro-verted women and more extraverted men showed prolonged increases in life satisfaction following marriage, presumably because the new married lifestyle suited these personality types, although this remains to be tested by future research.[45]

I hope I've given you a vivid sense in this chapter of how your person-ality is constantly shaping and being shaped by your experiences. In the next chapter, I focus on an all-too-common experience in life that is particularly powerful in this regard: brain injuries and mental and physical illness. Injury and illness can cause particularly dramatic and permanent personality change, and so it is important to consider their effects in detail.

Before we move on, though, take a few minutes to reflect once more on the bigger picture: the story of your life and how it has shaped you so far.

EXERCISE: WHAT'S YOUR LIFE STORY?

The difficulty with extracting lessons from research into how life events can change us is that no single study can possibly capture the messy complexity of real life. Alongside major life experiences are the many subtle accumulating influences to consider. And the big impacts don't affect us in isolation, but within the context of all that's gone before. The past is a prologue. Profound events might mark out the chapters of your life, yet to truly understand the forces that have shaped who you are today, you need to contemplate your entire story. "If each life event is a star," writes psychologist Tasha Eurich in *Insight* (2017), her best-selling book on self-awareness, "our life story is the constellation."[46]

Here's a writing exercise you can perform to reflect on your life story.[47] The way you go about this reveals fascinating things about your personality and how it has been molded by what you've been through. Whereas the personality quiz toward the end of chapter 1 revealed your personality in a series of trait scores, reflecting on your life and describing your own story gives you a sense of what Dan P. McAdams, a psychology professor at Northwestern University, calls your "narrative identity."[48]

First, think back through your life and come up with two notable, self-defining high points or "peak experiences"; two low points (or nadir experiences); two turning points (these can be decisions, emotional experiences such as meeting someone, or events that were like a fork in the path of your life); two key early memories; and finally two more significant memories. The idea is for you to take your time and write one to two paragraphs about each of these ten scenes from your life. Write about who, what, where, and when the event took place; what you were feeling; and why you chose this episode or scene.

When you have finished, read back through your accounts and see if there are any overarching themes—a desire to fit in, for instance; a constant striving to improve; a yearning to forge new relationships; a sense of good things turning bad (called "contamination sequences") or perhaps the opposite: challenges turned into opportunities (also known as "redemption sequences").

Complexity and contradictions in your narrative are a good sign because they reveal a sophisticated and honest account of your life—in short, greater self-awareness. The contradictions can also make sense of things you do that appear, superficially at least, at odds with your personality traits. For instance, if a key theme in your life is helping others, this might explain why you spend a lot of time engaging with other people even if you're an introvert. "Embracing the complexity, the nuances, and the contradictions [of your life story] will help you appreciate your inner reality in all its beautiful messiness," says Eurich in *Insight*.

Not surprisingly, research generally shows that people whose accounts are filled with more redemption sequences are happier, whereas those with more contamination sequences are more likely to be depressed (and to score higher in neuroticism). Note that the same kinds of events can be recalled in opposing ways. Being bullied at school could, for instance, be recalled purely as a time of misery and trauma (a contamination sequence), but it could also be remembered as leading to increased personal resilience and, ultimately, the discovery of genuine, more meaningful friendships (as a redemption sequence).

The complexity of your account, in terms of lots of twists and turns and how many different perspectives you present, is an indicator of your openness, and frequent mentions of forging relationships are a sign of high agreeableness. The way you tell your story is your narrative identity, and it's almost like another aspect of your personality, superordinate to your traits. An important thing to remember is that your narrative identity, like your personality traits, tends to be stable over time, but it *is not set in stone.*

If you repeat this exercise again in a year's time, you might find that your mind wanders to different key events from your past. And if you do return to any of these events, you might write about them in a different light. Indeed, if your accounts on this occasion were filled with dark tales and sad endings, next time you could deliberately aim to reframe at least some of what you've experienced, seeing setbacks as learning opportunities and past tribulations as a source of strength. This is precisely the aim of what's known as narrative therapy because how we think about our past stories can influence our character today and the course of the episodes to come. When people tell more positive personal narratives, this has been shown to lead to subsequent increases in their well-being.[49] "The most important story that we ever tell," says McAdams, is "the story of our lives."[50]

Ten Actionable Steps to Change Your Personality

To reduce neuroticism	Spend a few minutes writing about how a challenging experience in life changed you for the better. Focusing on such redemptive sequences in your life story has been shown to increase resilience.	Take the time to hug your partner, friend, or a colleague (with consent and taking suitable precautions in a pandemic, of course). Affectionate touch is emotionally powerful. In fact, recent research suggests that a major reason that people who have more sex are happier is that they cuddle each other more.
To increase extraversion	Consider joining your local chapter of Toastmasters, a club founded in 1924 that promotes public speaking skills. The speech consultant John Bowe likens it to Alcoholics Anonymous for shy people.	Plan this week to ask one of your colleagues if he or she wants to go out for coffee or have an informal phone chat or Zoom call. Research suggests that when introverts act more outgoing and sociable, they enjoy the experience more than they think they will.
To increase conscientiousness	Commit to regular gym visits with a friend. You are less likely to flake on your plans if doing so means letting someone else down. Also you will probably enjoy the gym experience more if you go with someone you like spending time with. Incidentally, any commitment you make to changing your behavior is more likely to stick if you ask a close friend or relative to cosign a written pledge. There's something about feeling accountable to someone we care about that increases our determination.	Put temptations like wine or cookies out of sight in the kitchen, and make healthier options readily available. Research into willpower suggests that people who appear more self-disciplined are actually better at avoiding temptation in the first place.

Ten Actionable Steps to Change Your Personality *(continued)*

To increase agreeability	The next time that someone irritates you, take a moment to consider how circumstances might have affected that person's behavior for the worse. We're very good at taking the situation into account in this way when judging ourselves, but we tend to be far less lenient with others.	Spend a few minutes writing down the characteristics you admire in the people you live and work with.
To increase openness	Watch a nature documentary— something like the BBC's *Planet Earth* should do the trick. The awe that you experience will increase your humility and open-mindedness.	The next time you plan to go out to a restaurant, try somewhere new.

Chapter 3

PATHOLOGICAL CHANGE

When Alice Warrender regained consciousness on the night of February 19, 2011, in Fulham, London, she had no idea what had knocked her off her bike or if she'd just fallen. According to newspaper reports, she was lucky there were paramedics nearby attending to another incident.[1] They spotted Alice and persuaded her to let them take her to the hospital where a CT scan showed that the twenty-eight-year-old, a digital business owner and college friend of the Duchess of Cambridge, had a blood clot on her brain. The next day, she was in surgery for over five hours to remove it.

Alice's story isn't that unusual. Every year in the United Kingdom, hundreds of thousands of people are admitted to the hospital with damage to their brains, and in the United States, the annual figure is in the millions. In the worst cases, brain injuries can lead to death or coma, paralysis, loss of speech and comprehension, and other disabilities. Alice's arduous rehabilitation over the ensuing months was largely successful, although she endured many of the complications often associated with even mild brain injuries, including headaches, memory difficulties, and extreme lethargy.

Yet another profound effect that Alice experienced after her accident, and the reason I'm sharing her story, was that her personality had changed dramatically, another common occurrence for brain injury survivors.[2] The idea that brain injury should lead to personality change is not too surprising when you consider that at a physical level, our traits are partly rooted in the functioning of the neural networks in our brains. If an injury or illness alters the workings of these networks or the delicate balance between them, then changes to our habits of thought, our behavior, and our ways of relating to others are almost inevitable.

The chances that you, or someone you know, will experience some kind of injury or illness that leads to personality change are extremely high, meaning that alongside the slings and arrows of life discussed in the previous chapter, pathological change is another key part of the story of what shapes us.

In this chapter, I share the stories of people who have experienced profound personality changes after brain injury, dementia, or mental illness, and I'll look into the latest research on how and why this happens. The tales provide another striking lesson in the malleability of personality and the fragility of the self.

GAGE "WAS NO LONGER GAGE"

In terms of the effects of brain injury or insult on personality, the emphasis over much of the medical and psychological history understandably has been on the negative side. Indeed, probably the most famous neurological case study, that of Phineas Gage, has often been held up as providing the classic example of these dramatic, disruptive effects.

Gage was a conscientious railway worker who, in 1848, survived an accidental explosion on the Rutland and Burlington Railroad in central Vermont that caused a three-and-a-half-foot-long iron rod to shoot into the front of his brain and clear out the other side. The front of the brain is critical for many functions that are especially related to personality, such as decision-making and impulse control. Little surprise, then, that one of the first doctors to attend to Gage, John Harlow, famously wrote that his "mind was radically changed, so decidedly that his friends and acquaintances said he was 'no longer Gage.'" Specifically, Harlow wrote that the once "well-balanced . . . shrewd, smart" Gage was now "fitful . . . irreverent," "impatient of restraint or advice," and "pertinaciously obstinate, capricious and vacillating."[3]

Historians have recently revised the story of Gage's recovery: they now believe that he went on to make a far more complete recovery than previously realized. Nonetheless, the picture of initial personality change that Harlow presented matches frontal lobe syndrome, which is often seen in individuals who suffer any kind of damage to the front of the brain. Although personality is not affected in a uniform way, four distinct patterns of change can emerge (depending on the precise neural circuits that have been compromised):[4]

- Poor judgment and problems planning ahead
- Lack of control of emotions (including becoming irritable and impatient) and disturbances in social behavior, like being aggressive, insensitive, or otherwise inappropriate
- A flattening of emotion, apathy, and withdrawn behavior
- Excessive proneness to worry and feelings of an inability to cope

These are overlapping clusters rather than completely discrete categories. Most people with frontal lobe syndrome share problems to varying degrees with things like planning, social inappropriateness, angst, and apathy. In terms of the main personality traits, this would translate as increases in neuroticism and reductions in conscientiousness and agreeableness.

In everyday life, these changes can manifest in some dramatic, yet paradoxically mundane, ways. Take, for instance, the middle-age man described by neuropsychologist Paul Broks, who one day decided his life was going nowhere and began taking spontaneous trips to the seaside, indulged in petty theft, bought himself a Fender Stratocaster electric guitar, and eventually left his wife and job and relocated to a beach resort to become a bar worker.[5] The case had all the hallmarks of a midlife crisis until the man started having seizures and a brain scan revealed a huge tumor in his frontal lobes, a growth that, as Broks puts it, had been "insidiously recalibrating his personality."

Research suggests it is changes like these, in which a person begins to act as if they have a completely different moral compass, that can be most distressing for relatives and friends. More than other aspects of personality, the moral faculty is seen as core to a person's true self.[6]

Surprisingly there has been a growing recognition that brain injury can sometimes also lead to beneficial personality changes. This is what Alice Warrender, the woman I introduced at the start of the chapter, experienced. She told the *Daily Mail,* "I think I've become a nicer person. . . . I'm more patient, and more openly emotional, I've got a calmness that I've never had before."[7] In trait terms, Alice had increased in agreeableness and enjoyed a reduction in neuroticism.[8]

Some elements of welcome personality change following neurological damage are also apparent in the remarkable story of Lotje Sodderland, the star and codirector of the 2014 Netflix documentary *My Beautiful Brain.* In 2011, at the age of thirty-four, Sodderland, a documentary producer, suffered a stroke related to a congenital malformation in her brain that she was unaware of. Living alone, she awoke to great confusion, was unable to speak, and lapsed in and out of consciousness. She received emergency medical care only after she had collapsed in the public restroom of a nearby hotel.

Following brain surgery and many years of grueling rehabilitation, Sodderland has regained many of her basic cognitive functions and is able to live a happy life. Though she says her "essence" is unchanged from before her stroke, her personality has clearly been altered in other ways, and she's had to adapt to being far more emotionally sensitive. Yet in other ways, she has been aesthetically awakened (together suggesting marked increases in neuroticism and openness to experience).

"Every aspect of your experience is intensified," Sodderland told the *Times*. "Sounds are much louder, images are much brighter and emotions are much, much stronger, so when you're happy you are ecstatic and when you are sad it's devastating and you can't handle it. You have these ups and downs like a wild storm."[9]

This sounds unpleasant, but Sodderland has found ways to adjust and now lives what she describes as a simple "monastic life."[10] "I prefer my new life with my new brain," she told the *Times*. "I am grateful to have been forced to reassess the value of my life, but also to simplify my life, to figure out what I can focus my energy on because I can't do everything."

That a blow to the head or bleed in the brain could lead to any kind of beneficial personality changes seems far-fetched, like something out of a Hollywood movie (as in *Overboard*, the 1980s cult classic romantic comedy, in which Goldie Hawn's spoiled socialite character becomes caring and compassionate after hitting her head in a yachting accident). Yet psychologists at the University of Iowa recently conducted the first systematic investigation of positive personality effects following brain injury.[11] They found that of ninety-seven previously healthy patients who had suffered a neural insult, twenty-two went on to enjoy positive personality changes.[12] For instance, a seventy-year-old woman referred to as patient 3534, who sustained frontal brain damage during the excision of a tumor, was described by her husband of fifty-eight years as having previously been "stern," irritable, and grumpy, but after her injuries as having a "happier, more outgoing, and more talkative" personality. Another patient, a thirty-year-old man, suffered brain injuries from surgery to correct an aneurysm and went from being short-tempered and "mopey" to jokey, "passive and easy-going."

Why is it that most people experience adverse personality changes after brain injury but a significant minority appear to enjoy some positive effects? There is no simple answer, but it is likely related to the precise pattern of damage and how that interacts with a person's pre-injury personality traits. Those typical features of frontal lobe syndrome caused by brain injury that I described above, such as apathy and disinhibition, might have a beneficial calming and socializing effect for some people with a previously highly strung, withdrawn personality.

The findings also suggest that positive change is more likely when damage affects the front-most part of the brain that is involved in making decisions and taking the perspectives of others. The implication is that the brain damage can lead to a rewiring in this region with beneficial effects on psychological function. (Incidentally, this is the same part of the brain that is sometimes targeted deliberately in neurosurgery to treat extremely severe depression or obsessive-compulsive disorder.)

The stories of these patients remind us of a deeper lesson: that personality has a physiological basis; it is not merely an abstract concept but arises in large part from the wiring of our brains. Moreover, that physical foundation is much more like plastic than fired clay. Usually such changes are subtle, but even small changes can accumulate over time, and it's empowering to think that when you develop new, constructive habits, you can purposely begin to shape the neural networks that underlie the kind of person you are. In contrast, in the case of brain injury survivors, the change can be random, sudden, and dramatic. The dice are rolled, and while the effects on personality are usually harmful, the changes are welcome for a lucky few.

"HE STOPPED BEING THE GUY WE KNOW"

The beloved actor and comedian Robin Williams had one of the biggest, most contradictory personalities in show business. Onstage, in public, he was the ultimate supercharged, freewheeling extravert. Yet he admitted in an interview with James Lipton in 2001, in his downtime, he was introverted, quiet, and "absorbent."[13] But even allowing for this extraordinary variation in his character, those closest to him began to notice from 2012 onward (a year after the star's third marriage, to Susan Schneider, and two years prior to his death by suicide in 2014) that his personality was beginning to undergo changes.

Williams had battled depression and drinking problems in the past, but in 2012, after five years sober and free from psychiatric medication, he began to show signs of chronic anxiety. "He would spend less time in the green room talking to other performers. He was having more difficulty letting go of his fears," his widow, Susan Schneider Williams, recalls.[14]

From there, his anxiety only intensified. During a fall weekend the following year, Susan describes how "his fear and anxiety skyrocketed to a point that was alarming." She adds that "having been by my husband's side for many years already, I knew his normal reactions when it came to fear and anxiety. What would follow was markedly out of character for him."[15]

Around the same time, Williams's friend, the comedian Rick Overton, was starting to have concerns that something was amiss. They were still performing improv shows together in Los Angeles that year, and Overton recalls how Williams came to life onstage, but in the evenings afterward, he would see his friend's "eyes dimming." "I can't imagine the weight of it," Overton says. "I can't even dream of it."[16]

The changes to Williams's character worsened still further in 2014, the year of his death. In April, on the set of what would be his last movie appearance, *Night at the Museum: Secret of the Tomb*, he suffered a full-blown panic attack. His makeup artist, Cheri Minns, recalls that afterward, he told her, "I don't know how anymore. I don't know how to be funny." He told his wife that he wanted "a reboot for his brain."[17]

The following month Williams was diagnosed with Parkinson's disease, a progressive neurological illness that mainly manifests in difficulties moving. But according to his wife, he was skeptical that this could fully account for all the changes he was experiencing or explain why "his brain was out of control."[18]

In August, Williams visited his son Zak and his daughter-in-law. According to his biographer, Dave Itzkoff, he "showed up like a meek teenager who realizes he's stayed out past his curfew"—in other words, entirely out of character. The once bombastic showman had become a shadow of his former self. Then, on August 11, 2014, he took his own life, "cloaking the planet in a shadow of sadness," to quote Itzkoff. "He wasn't Robin at that point," recalls Overton. "He stopped being the guy we know. That part shut down."

It was only during a postmortem exam that the reasons for Williams's profound personality change became clear: he had been suffering from diffuse Lewy body dementia ("diffuse" meaning it had spread through his brain), a relatively rare form of dementia that can only be conclusively diagnosed at autopsy based on identification of clumps of protein that interfere with the function of brain cells. There is some evidence that Parkinson's disease is associated with trait changes too, especially high neuroticism and reduced extraversion.[19] With Lewy body dementia, the changes are much more dramatic and more in keeping with the tragic descriptions of those close to Williams in the years preceding his death.

Just as neurological damage from head injuries, internal bleeds, or brain tumors can cause personality change, Robin Williams's story provides a tragic demonstration of how neurodegenerative illness can do so as well. "My husband was trapped in the twisted architecture of his neurons and no matter what I did I could not pull him out," Susan Schneider Williams wrote in an article for the journal *Neurology* with the apt title, "The Terrorist Inside My Husband's Brain."[20]

Around 1.5 million people in the United States are suffering with Lewy body dementia, so it is relatively rare. However, another form of dementia that can also cause personality change and is far more common is Alzheimer's disease, which affects nearly 6 million Americans. Although most obviously associated with memory problems, relatives and caretakers of those with the illness report that its arrival precipitates marked increases in neuroticism and reduced conscientiousness.[21] (Such changes are obviously very distressing, although some relatives and the people with dementia themselves do find comfort in islands of continuity, such as taste in art and music, that are usually unaffected by the illness.)

Other research has compared people with Alzheimer's disease with healthy volunteers of similar age and background.[22] Researchers have found that people with Alzheimer's typically have much higher levels of neuroticism and lower levels of openness, agreeableness, conscientiousness, and extraversion. (With this kind of comparison, it's possible that at least some of these group differences were present prior to the illness. Certainly both lower openness and lower conscientiousness are associated with a higher risk of developing dementia.)

Any personality changes that do occur are likely due at least in part to the way Alzheimer's causes the loss of cells in regions of the brain that are linked with these personality traits. For instance, lower brain volume in the hippocampus, near the ears, and the dorsolateral prefrontal cortex, near the temple, has previously been shown to correlate with higher trait neuroticism.[23] Alzheimer's causes cell death in these very regions.[24]

The question of when exactly Alzheimer's begins to alter personality has become highly contentious among experts because some believe these changes could be used to detect the disease early on, thus increasing the opportunity for coping measures and support to be put in place. Those with a skeptical take point to research showing that the personality changes do not start until the disease has set in, but advocates for personality testing point to other research showing that personality changes *do* occur prior to a dementia diagnosis, especially marked increases in neuroticism.[25]

Undeterred by the skeptics, in 2016, Zahinoor Ismail at the University of Calgary and his colleagues proposed a thirty-four-item checklist tapping different signs of personality change that Ismail told the *New York Times* are a "stealth symptom" of the illness.[26] Some example items from that list follow. The questionnaire is completed by a physician or a close relative of the patient, and the more signs of change lasting six months or more, the greater the likelihood that the patient has what the checklist's creators call "mild behavioral impairment," essentially a form of pathological personality change. I've put in parentheses how the domains of the checklist relate to the main personality traits:

Changes in interest, motivation, and drive (reduced openness to experience and extraversion, in personality trait terms)

Has the person lost interest in friends, family, or home activities?

Does the person lack curiosity in topics that would usually have attracted her/his interest?

Has the person become less spontaneous and active—for example, is she/he less likely to initiate or maintain conversation?

Changes in mood or anxiety symptoms (increased trait neuroticism)

Has the person developed sadness or appear to be in low spirits? Does she/he have episodes of tearfulness?

Has the person become less able to experience pleasure?

Has the person become more anxious or worried about things that are routine (e.g., events, visits, etc.)?

Changes in the ability to delay gratification and control behavior, impulses, oral intake, and/or changes in reward-seeking behavior (reduced conscientiousness)

Has the person become more impulsive, seeming to act without considering things?

Does the person display a new recklessness or lack of judgment when driving (e.g., speeding, erratic swerving, abrupt lane changes, etc.)?

Has the person recently developed trouble regulating smoking, alcohol, drug intake, gambling, or started shoplifting?

New problems following societal norms and having social graces, tact, and empathy (reduced conscientiousness and agreeableness)

Has the person become less concerned about how her/his words or actions affect others?

Has she/he become insensitive to others' feelings?

Does the person seem to lack the social judgment she/he previously had about what to say or how to behave in public or private?

Other forms of dementia are associated with their own distinct personality changes. For instance, frontotemporal dementia, which is caused by brain cell loss at the front of the brain and in the temporal lobes, tends to lead to impulsive, socially inappropriate behavior, to an extent mirroring the effects of frontal brain damage. In contrast, dementia with Lewy bodies (the disease that afflicted Robin Williams) is associated with "increased passivity":[27]

Loss of emotional responsiveness

Losing interest in hobbies

Increased apathy

Purposeless hyperactivity (being highly active, but not in a way directed toward any goals)

If you read through the checklists above and on page 63 and worry that you have experienced a few such changes yourself or that someone close to you has, it may be wise to consult a physician, but do not panic. As I mentioned, the personality change approach to detecting forms of dementia remains controversial—not only because of the debate about whether personality changes really do precede, rather than follow, dementia, but also because some experts fear such lists could lead to erroneous overdiagnosis and undue anxiety.

After all, as I described in the previous chapter, at least somewhat similar changes can be caused by a number of other more mundane reasons, from losing your job to going through a divorce. So while looking for personality change as a way to spot Alzheimer's or Lewy body dementia early might sound like a good idea in theory, in practice it is problematic.

"IT CLEARLY WASN'T HER"

Initially famous for her colorful, eye-catching handbags, the American entrepreneur and designer Kate Spade went on to lend her name and creative genius to an entire lifestyle brand. The vibe of her products, from stationery to fashion, was said to reflect her own personality— vibrant, fun, and sweet. Millions of women, including Michelle Obama and Nicole Kidman, were drawn to their happy, retro appeal. Yet unbeknownst to all but those closest to her, Spade had spent much of her life battling inner demons. On June 5, 2018, at age fifty-five, it became too much and she hanged herself in her Manhattan apartment.

In the ensuing days, her husband and business partner, Andy Spade, issued a public statement. "It clearly wasn't her," he told the world, explaining that she had been suffering from depression and anxiety.[28] The gifted designer who'd once explained that fashion accessories should "assume the personality of the wearer, not the reverse" had succumbed to the tragedy of her own colorful character being overshadowed by depression.

Stories like Kate Spade's are tragically common. In 2016, over ten million Americans experienced at least one bout of major depression[29] and nearly fifty thousand people took their own lives.[30] When people write about their experiences of depression and anxiety, the distorting effect of these afflictions on personality is a common theme.

Your personality arises from your habits of thought and ways of relating to others—the very aspects of the self struck by clinical depression and anxiety as they suck your energy and hijack your mind—breeding negative, fearful thoughts and an aversion to socializing. It is almost inevitable, then, that one of the major consequences of mental illness is how it reduces trait extraversion and increases neuroticism. Writing for *Vice* magazine about his depression, the Australian comedian Patrick

Marlborough put it succinctly: "When your mind feels groggy and your day is a looping cycle of inaction and despairing thoughts, it can be hard to work up the strength to go to a friend's gig, grab a coffee, or reply to a text."[31]

These firsthand accounts are backed up by long-running studies that have measured people's traits before they became depressed and then again after they developed depression. These have confirmed that people high in neuroticism are more vulnerable to anxiety and depression, but also that experiencing these mental health problems increases neuroticism. For instance, one Dutch study involving thousands of volunteers looked at clinical depression and anxiety and found that both had the effect of increasing neuroticism, while depression in particular also led to decreases in extraversion and conscientiousness.[32]

There is also a psychiatric diagnosis known as "bipolar disorder" that can involve not only the lows of depression, but also manic phases of great energy, excitement, distraction, or irritability. For those with bipolar disorder who switch between phases of depression and mania, it is as if they have undergone a radical personality change. In the case of mania, this can appear like they have suddenly become an extravert on hyperdrive—a self-declared prophet with sky-high levels of trait openness, say—or they might transform into having a ridiculously short fuse, like a person with meager agreeability.[33] "Mania brings with it the thought that you're this amazing person, who can do anything, someone who deserves to be with people," a young woman called Cat told the *Guardian* in 2017. "The bad side of mania is that loss of control."[34]

A highly neurotic personality puts you at greater risk of bipolar disorder, just as it does more common, so-called unipolar depression, and anxiety. Specific to bipolar disorder, though, some experts have argued, controversially, that there is such a thing as a more particular "hypomanic personality" type that predisposes people to developing bipolar disorder at some (or multiple) points in their life. Here are some of the items on the scale, developed by Mark Eckblad and Loren Chapman in the 1980s, that's used for measuring this kind of personality:[35]

- I have often felt happy and irritable at the same time.
- There are often times when I am so restless that it is impossible for me to sit still.
- I often get so happy and energetic that I am almost giddy.
- At social gatherings, I am usually the "life of the party."
- I would really enjoy being a politician and hitting the campaign trail.
- I do most of my best work during brief episodes of intense inspiration.
- I sometimes have felt that nothing can happen to me until I do what I am meant to do in life.

People with a hypomanic personality tend to agree with these kinds of statements. The first three items are meant to tap into having tendencies toward a hypomanic mood—being highly excitable and having boundless energy. The fourth and fifth items relate to grandiosity and thinking of oneself as the life and soul of any gathering. And the final two relate to feeling highly creative.

This questionnaire and the idea that it can predict the risk of developing bipolar disorder are controversial because some psychologists believe it is not only measuring a lifelong personality style but might also be detecting symptoms of mania. They say it's not a surprise that the questionnaire predicts the risk of developing bipolar disorder if it's actually sensitive to current symptoms of the condition.[36] Another controversy, related to both unipolar and bipolar depression, concerns whether the effects of these mental illnesses on personality disappear once symptoms have lifted or whether they are more lasting—an idea known as the scar hypothesis.

The results to date are mixed. While most studies have found that the personality changes that occur during unipolar depressive illness — including increased neuroticism and introversion — return to pre-illness levels once volunteers have recovered, a few others have uncovered signs of more lasting harmful change.[37] For example, a five-year study of hundreds of psychiatric patients in Finland found that accumulated episodes of depression led to prolonged increases in neuroticism, especially what the researchers called "harm avoidance" (they explained that a "harm-avoidant" person would be "pessimistic, inhibited, and fatigable").[38] Other research with people who have had bipolar disorder has found that they tend to score higher on impulsivity, aggression, and hostility than people who have had unipolar depression and that they tend to score higher than folks without mental illness on neuroticism and openness but lower on agreeableness, conscientiousness, and extraversion — again, perhaps indicative of a scarring effect (although it's possible these personality differences were also present before their illness).[39]

The idea of depression leaving personality scars sounds unpleasant, but the Finnish researchers said that these effects could be advantageous in this evolutionary sense: if adverse circumstances brought on the depression in the first place, it arguably increases one's chances of survival to develop a more vigilant, guarded personality style. The problem, of course, is that while switching to a more defensive, vigilant personality style may have been advantageous for our ancestors in times of threat, it is not necessarily so useful in modern life, especially in a world that tends to reward bold, sociable behavior. Sadly, if the scarring effect of depression is a reality — and remember the jury is still out — it would imply that one effect of the illness is to trap people in a negative spiral, increasing their risk of relapse (by increasing their trait neuroticism, which further increases vulnerability to the illness).

On a more optimistic note, treatment with antidepressants, anti-anxiety drugs, and various forms of psychotherapy can reverse at least some of the harmful personality effects of mental illness. In particular, antidepressant drugs that target the functioning of the brain chemical serotonin (so-called SSRIs, or selective serotonin re-uptake inhibitors) have been shown to increase extraversion and reduce neuroticism. In one study that tracked depressed patients over a year, those who took the drug paroxetine showed increases in extraversion that were 3.5 times greater and reductions in neuroticism that were 6.8 times greater compared with those patients on a placebo.[40] Deeper analysis suggested that at least some of these trait changes are due to the drugs directly altering the biological basis of personality rather than being merely a consequence of the reduction in depression symptoms.

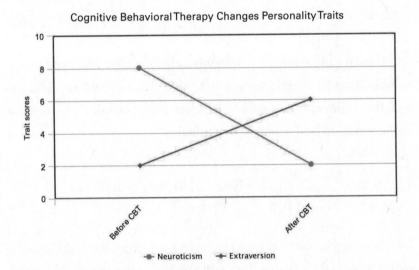

Research with mental health clients undergoing cognitive behavioral therapy has shown that the experience changes their personality traits, especially neuroticism and extraversion.
Source: Data from Sabine Tjon Pian Gi, Jos Egger, Maarten Kaarsemaker, and Reinier Kreutzkamp, "Does Symptom Reduction After Cognitive Behavioural Therapy of Anxiety Disordered Patients Predict Personality Change?" Personality and Mental Health 4, no. 4 (2010): 237–245.

It's a similar story with anxiety. For instance, a study of patients with anxiety who underwent cognitive behavioral therapy (CBT)—a form of psychotherapy that focuses on biases in the way people think about themselves and the world around them—found that they showed reductions in neuroticism and increased extraversion (see figure on page 69).[41] This wasn't entirely due to an alleviation of anxiety symptoms, but seemed to be a direct effect of the therapy on personality, likely due to changing the patients' habits of thought and behavior.

The British journalist and author Oliver Kamm described these effects of CBT based on his experience working with a clinical psychologist to overcome his own depression and anxiety: "The treatment was not Freud but Socrates," he writes, "a process of dialogue to test and change destructive ways of thinking. The psychologist explained that my depression was a severe illness but not at root a mystery: it was born of cognitive error. Recovery, and then guarding against a relapse, could come by interrogating the beliefs that had caused my mental collapse and replacing them with better ones."[42]

Mental illness can steal a person's character, transforming a bold extravert into an anxious hermit, but these changes are reversible, and with the appropriate support and treatment, it is possible—at least some of the time—to heal a damaged personality.

TRAUMA CAN SPLIT PERSONALITIES BUT ALSO LEAD TO POSITIVE CHANGE

Like many other mothers who are confronted with their children's loss of innocence, the day that Tara discovered that her teenage daughter, Kate, was taking birth control pills, she felt shocked and emotional. But unlike most other mothers, the effect of this intense emotion was to trigger Tara into a radical personality change, such that she suddenly slipped into the identity and rebellious traits and interests of a teenage girl nicknamed "T."

When Kate returned home, she found T in her bedroom, rifling through her wardrobe looking for trendy clothes to put on. With a teenage swagger, T invited Kate to go shopping with her, using credit cards she'd taken from her main identity of Tara. Kate was not as freaked out as you might expect: she recognized T as one of her mother's "alters"—alternative identities that she shifted into during times of stress. In fact, Kate even gave T a big hug; she was the favorite of her mother's alternative personalities, after all.

This scene appears in the Showtime comedy drama *The United States of Tara*, which has been praised for the accuracy of its portrayal of a psychiatric condition known as dissociative identity disorder (DID), previously referred to as multiple personality disorder, one of the most controversial psychiatric diagnoses in history. People with DID switch between different, often dramatically varied, personalities and identities—or at least they appear to—sometimes claiming to have little memory of their experiences in the different roles.

The fictional character of Tara Gregson, played by Toni Collette, and her three alters (besides T, her other alters are Alice, the archetype of a clean-living, pious mother, and Buck, a macho male war veteran who smokes and wears glasses; more alters develop through the series) might sound far-fetched to some. Yet there are many real-life cases that are just as dramatic.

DID evokes memories of Robert Louis Stevenson's *The Strange Case of Dr Jekyll and Mr Hyde*. Indeed, "Meet Dr Jekyll . . ." is the title of a recent case study in medical literature featuring a retired psychiatrist also diagnosed with DID: one of his alters was "Lewis," a promiscuous nineteen-year-old, and another was "Bob," a depressed four-year-old in a wheelchair.[43] When the psychiatrist, referred to in the paper as Dr. S, had extramarital affairs, he claimed to have no memory of them and blamed Lewis, and when he attempted suicide in his sixties, he blamed Bob.

Clearly DID is an extraordinary condition that challenges our very conception of the self. Confronted with such a mysterious, dramatic phenomenon, it's little wonder that experts disagree about how to interpret what is going on. The dominant view is that it is a kind of defense mechanism against intense trauma, usually suffered in childhood, and especially when the child does not have a secure attachment figure— an adult who loves and cares for him. The theory is that the child develops one or more alternative personalities as a way to escape from his trauma and better cope with the hostile world they find themselves in—a coping strategy that then persists into adulthood. As Melanie Goodwin (who has DID and is the director of the DID charity First Person Plural) told *Mosaic* magazine, "If you're in a totally impossible situation, you dissociate to stay alive. Trauma can freeze you in time. And because the trauma is ongoing over the years, there are lots of little freezings happening all over the place."[44]

Consistent with this account, most cases of DID typically feature a traumatic history. For instance, the psychiatrist with DID, Dr. S, was confined to bed for many months as a young child, his infant sibling died, and his mother was reportedly cold and distant. Melanie Goodwin says that she was abused as a child, beginning at age three. And one of the most famous cases of DID, Chris Costner Sizemore (whose alters included Eve White and Eve Black, among others, and whose story was turned into the 1957 film *The Three Faces of Eve*), says that before the age of three, she witnessed her mother being badly injured, saw a drowned man pulled from a ditch, and saw another man sawn in half in an accident at a lumber mill. To follow these typical patterns, a history of abuse and rape was also written into the fictional character of Tara Gregson in the television series.

Nevertheless, some clinical psychologists, such as the late Scott Lilienfeld and Steve Lynn, are skeptical that people with DID really do develop separate personalities. They point out, for instance, that careful tests show that people with DID don't *really* have amnesia for the experiences of their different personas; they just *think* that they do. These skeptics don't believe that patients with DID are faking (at least not consciously) but rather that the condition is better explained by the patients' problems with insight into their own emotions and consciousness. In turn, this contributes, along with their sleep problems and emotional difficulties, to their struggling to form a coherent sense of self. According to this sociocognitive account, some people—especially those who are highly suggestible, prone to fantasy, odd perceptual experiences, and rapid shifts in their emotions—make sense of their confusing mental world by resorting to a narrative of having multiple separate personalities, one that is (at least in some cases) shaped by the notion of split personalities they've encountered through fiction or the ideas that their therapists put forward to them.

Complicating matters still further is that a traumatic early life can also give rise to a closely related personality diagnosis known as borderline personality disorder, or emotionally unstable personality disorder. As with DID, people with this kind of personality also experience frequent mood swings, relationship difficulties, and problems forming a coherent sense of self, but they don't usually believe they have separate personalities as such. (People with borderline personality disorder are at much higher risk than normal of also developing DID.)

The hopeful news, consistent with this book's central thesis about the promise and potential of positive personality change, is that there has been great progress in how to help people with these kinds of disorders. In the case of DID, therapists aim to create a trusting relationship with their client, help them process their past traumas, teach them techniques to better regulate their emotions, and finally support them to reconcile and integrate their different personalities—efforts that initial research suggests are helpful.[45] When it comes to borderline personality disorder, there was a pessimistic belief for many years that it couldn't be treated because the problems were believed to infuse the person's personality, and because personality was considered to be written in stone, the condition was seen as permanent too.

Thankfully, today, by using dialectical behavior therapy (DBT) and similar approaches, it's widely recognized that it *is* possible for people with a borderline personality to alter their mental and emotional habits (e.g., by learning to better tolerate and manage negative emotions), acquire new social skills, and gradually shift their traits in a healthier, happier direction.

DBT borrows Buddhist principles to teach people with borderline personality a balanced perspective, to accept those aspects of themselves that they can't change while working to adjust the parts they can. It's accomplished with one-on-one sessions with a therapist and group work to develop social and emotional skills. Another approach is mentalization therapy to help improve the person's insights into the reasons behind their own and other people's behavior, with the aim of enabling them to form more meaningful, healthy relationships. For instance, a therapist might help her client better understand how his own behavior could affect the people around him, and how he might appropriately respond to the emotions shown and felt by others.

So, while trauma can harm your personality, with enough dedication and support, and through learning new social skills and emotional habits and techniques, it is also possible to take back control and achieve lasting, beneficial personality change.

It's also uplifting to learn that just as brain damage can sometimes cause beneficial personality changes, traumatic life experiences for some people can actually trigger welcome changes in personality—a process that psychologists call posttraumatic growth. The idea is that trauma can trigger a reevaluation of one's life, a changing of priorities, and a fresh outlook. Researchers have now documented this kind of posttraumatic positive change in many groups, from patients with cancer to the survivors of a natural disaster.

To measure posttraumatic growth, psychologists typically use a scale, first developed by the American psychologists Richard Tedeschi and Lawrence Calhoun, that taps change in five areas:[46]

- Relating to others (Do you have a greater sense of closeness with others? Or do you realize now that there are wonderful people who you can rely on?)
- New possibilities (Have you developed new interests? Or recognized new opportunities that weren't there before?)
- Personal strength (Do you feel stronger? Are you better able to deal with difficulties that life throws up?)
- Spiritual change factor (Has your religious faith increased?)
- Appreciation of life (Do you value each day more than you used to?)

In terms of the main personality traits, posttraumatic growth can be seen to manifest as increased openness, agreeability, and conscientiousness and lower neuroticism, although little research to date has focused on trait changes per se in this context. (One important exception was a study that measured personality change among the bereaved spouses of patients who had died of lung cancer. The surviving spouses became more extraverted, agreeable, and conscientious as they adapted to their loss.)[47]

I believe I too may have experienced my own minor equivalent of posttraumatic growth in 2014 when, with the expected birth of my twins just two weeks away, I was told by my new employer, a fast-growing tech start-up based in New York, that they were letting me go. This wasn't a natural disaster or a car crash, but imagine you lose your job two weeks before your twins are due to arrive in the world!

I'd joined the team a month earlier to lead the start-up's new blog, tempted by the opportunity for change, a huge pay raise, and amazing employee perks of the kind I'd never encountered before (my favorite was the Starbucks card chargeable to the firm). I didn't make the move lightly, but my close family agreed with me that it was an exciting opportunity.

I was hired by the newly appointed director of marketing to write psychology-based articles offering advice and inspiration to designers, which sounded right up my alley. Unfortunately, not long after I started, it became clear that the founder and CEO had other ideas (no doubt this confusion is quite common in a fast-changing company, one that I'd add is now hugely successful). The company kindly softened the blow with a parting payment, but when they gave me the news, I had an awful sense of rising panic in my stomach. Telling the news to my wife was a trauma in itself.

In the days and weeks that followed, however, I felt my priorities change. I came to see the advantages in my previous, less exciting, but much more stable role—one that I ultimately managed to get back in a couple of months (that's another story). True, I missed the Starbucks card, but I saw the value in my old, secure job and experienced a new sense of balance between my career ambitions and my burgeoning family responsibilities (in fact, the layoff meant I had an extra-long period of paternity leave). I felt humbled by all that happened, but also somehow wiser and happier.

The concept of posttraumatic growth lends scientific reality to the old adage about every cloud having a silver lining. If you are going through a particularly tough time or you ever do in the future, you may find comfort in this idea that the experience may end up changing you for the better. As the psychologist Scott Barry Kaufman wrote on Twitter recently, "Adversity sucks, but overcoming adversity is awesome. The more we can overcome, the more resilient we become."[48]

Some psychologists have expressed skepticism that posttraumatic growth is a real phenomenon. They suggest, for example, that it might simply be a case of trauma survivors looking on the bright side rather than actually changing for the better. However, I believe there is more than a grain of truth to the concept, especially if we have already managed to build up our resilience or emotional stability. For instance, a recent meta-analysis (a study that takes a big-picture view by combining the results from existing research) concluded that posttraumatic growth *is* a real phenomenon for some children and young people with cancer.[49] Other recent research also found that on average, people who have experienced adversity tend to be more compassionate (a form of increased agreeability),[50] and people who have lived through more trauma have more mental control than average over their thoughts and memories (an important component of trait conscientiousness).

I've shared with you frightening and inspiring examples of the personality changes that can arise from injury and illness, mental and physical. These stories and research findings further demonstrate the fragility and plasticity of personality—how the kind of person you are rests on biological processes that are susceptible to accident, stress, and pathology. On the bright side, sometimes these changes can be for the better or, if unwanted, they can be reversed with the right treatment, help, and support. (If you, or someone you know, is affected by the conditions raised in this chapter, I would strongly urge you to seek professional help if you haven't already.) Ultimately, though, cases of pathological change are another example of how your personality is a work in progress—an ongoing process, not an end result.

Ten Actionable Steps to Change Your Personality

To reduce neuroticism	Write down the emotions you're struggling with on one side of a card. On the other side, write down what you value most in life. Now reflect on how the two are linked, and that if you tear the card up (to banish the emotional difficulties), you will also lose all that most matters to you. The lesson, from acceptance and commitment therapy, is that a rich, meaningful life is not necessarily the easiest or happiest path.	Many apps teach you mindfulness meditation and similar techniques; Headspace is one of them. Commit to meditating two to three times per week, and this will help you feel more relaxed and lower your neuroticism.
To increase extraversion	Join a group that will bring you into contact with other people, such as an improv acting class, a choir, or your local soccer team. If the activity is challenging or there is a team element to it, this will help you form bonds with the others. Even strong introverts usually find that they enjoy the social contact more than they anticipated.	Volunteer for a charity that you care about. This will bring you into contact with others in pursuit of the values that matter to you. A side effect is that you will become habituated to greater social contact.

Ten Actionable Steps to Change Your Personality *(continued)*

To increase conscientiousness	The next time that you require focus, try going to a place where other people are exhibiting the concentration that you require. This could be going to work in a library or co-working space, or deliberately sitting next to your most diligent colleague. Research suggests that being next to someone who is highly focused can rub off on your own behavior.	Take practical steps to make it as easy as possible to fulfill your commitments. For instance, if your aim is to attend an early-morning exercise class once a week, ensure that you pack your gym bag the night before so that in the morning, you need only walk out the door. Generally the less arduous you make your goals, the easier it will be to fulfill them.
To increase agreeability	Send a friend or relative a supportive text at least once each week. Research shows that receiving a message of this kind can help people cope with challenging tasks and reduce their stress levels.	Commit to making a kind gesture to a stranger at least once every week. Not only will this benefit others, but there's evidence that practicing kindness regularly will increase your own physical and mental well-being.
To increase openness	Try keeping a weekly "beauty log" for a few months. At the end of each week, write down a few lines about something in nature that you felt was beautiful; do the same for something human-made that you found beautiful; and, finally, write a few lines about human behavior (good deeds) that you found beautiful.	When you face a tricky decision, try describing your predicament from a third-person perspective (e.g., "He was comfortable and happy in his current job, but the new opportunity was exciting and more of a challenge"). Using this ancient rhetorical technique, known as illeism, can increase your open-mindedness and the ability to see things from other people's perspectives.

Chapter 4

DIETS, HIGHS, AND HANGOVERS

Three and a half minutes into the speech, tears began to trickle down his cheeks. The man, nicknamed "Mr. Spock" by some for his cool detachment, was crying. As he paused to compose himself, the room fell silent. Then an eruption of applause.

That was in Chicago, when President Barack Obama was thanking his campaign staff the day after winning reelection in 2012.[1] "Whatever good we do over the next four years," he told them, "will pale in comparison to what you guys end up accomplishing for years and years to come, and that's been my source of hope."

The video went viral as commentators worldwide remarked on this surprisingly open demonstration of feeling from "no drama Obama." Yet there are many other examples of Obama's emotions getting the better of him. In 2015, for example, he fought back tears when he delivered a eulogy for Beau Biden, the son of Vice President Joseph Biden Jr.[2] And in 2016, the Internet was again abuzz when Obama's tears flowed freely during his speech about gun control. In fact, many times over the preceding years, Obama had fought to contain his emotions when discussing this issue.

There are so many instances of Obama getting emotional, in fact, that it can seem odd in retrospect to read the headlines that his emotional displays tended to provoke, such as the *New York Times* in 2015, "Obama Lowers His Guard in Unusual Displays of Emotion,"[3] and a *Washington Post* story from 2016 that began with this stark one-line introduction, "President Obama cried in public on Tuesday," as if this emotional event on its own were newsworthy.[4]

In another sense, however, the public and media reactions to Obama's emotions are not a surprise because forming strong and somewhat simplistic impressions (or caricatures) of each other's personalities is something we do all the time. Whether we're thinking about a president or a friend, we're nearly always shocked when people we think we know behave in a way that we feel is out of character for them.

There's no question that Obama's personality has—most of the time, at least—been characterized by coolness and emotional control. As Kenneth Walsh, former president of the White House Correspondents' Association, put it in 2009: "Obama is a cool customer. He doesn't seem to get really angry, depressed or frustrated or to lose control of his emotions."[5] And in an in-depth analysis for the *Atlantic*, James Fallows observed how "whether things are going very well or very badly . . . [Obama] always presents the same dispassionate face."[6]

In terms of the Big Five personality traits, Obama would surely score as a strong introvert and even more strongly on emotional stability (low neuroticism). So what to make of his free-flowing tears on multiple occasions? Which is the real Obama? Well, both. Obama is human, and sometimes the strength of the situation overpowers our personalities.

WHAT EXPLAINS THE WAY YOU BEHAVE: THE SITUATION OR YOUR PERSONALITY?

The apparent contradiction in Obama's behavior neatly encapsulates a debate that consumed personality psychology for decades through the latter twentieth century. At the extreme were those who said that personality is meaningless because the situation is all-powerful. Probably the most infamous example these situationists pointed to was Philip Zimbardo's Stanford prison experiment, conducted in 1971, which had to be abandoned after volunteers recruited to play the part of guards started mistreating the others who were acting as prisoners—as if their usual personalities had been taken over by the power of the situation.

Later, the situationist argument became more nuanced. Psychologist Walter Mischel and his colleagues proposed an account of behavior that emphasized the idiosyncratic ways people are affected by social context. In a study of children at a six-week summer camp, they showed how the children's behavior varied strongly depending on who they were with but, crucially, how this played out was different for different campers.[7] For instance, one boy might flare up much more angrily than his peers whenever he was told off by an adult, and yet the same boy was supercool when his friends teased him. His buddy, by contrast, might show the opposite pattern. The implication was that it would be misleading to label either child as aggressive or laid-back, as if these were core traits fundamental to their characters.

On the backs of these kinds of studies, some commentators went so far as to declare the notion of personality a myth. However, as I argued at the start of this book, there is no question that personality—the constellation of our habitual tendencies in thought, feelings, and behavior—is real and clearly very important, predicting all sorts of outcomes in life, from wage earnings to longevity. Today few experts endorse the idea of personality as a myth. The scholarly debate has moved on, approaching something of a consensus that sees both personality and situation as about equally important for explaining behavior.[8]

You will see the dual influence of situation and personality play out among your friends and family. Over the long term, your extraverted friend will be more outgoing and pleasure seeking than your more introverted cousin, but that doesn't mean your garrulous friend will be outgoing and game for a laugh every moment of every day.

Psychologists recently demonstrated this mixture of consistency and adaptability in behavior when they videoed hundreds of undergraduates taking part in three different kinds of social situations in a group with two strangers, spaced a week apart.[9] The first was an unstructured meet-up (the students were told they could "talk about anything you like"), whereas the second and third weeks involved structured tasks with a financial incentive: one cooperative, the other competitive. Each week, the researchers counted how much the students displayed sixty-eight different behaviors, including laughing, relaxing, smiling, loquaciousness, and irritation.

In some ways, the students' behavior varied a lot across the situations, just as you'd expect. For example, on average they volunteered more information about themselves at the informal meet-up. Yet there were also clear consistencies in behavior: students who acted more reserved than others in one situation also acted relatively reserved in the other situations. Behaviors that are more automatic, like smiling, showed the most trait-like consistency across contexts, which makes sense, because personality is more likely to shine through in the behaviors over which we have the least control.

These recent findings make sense of President Obama's personality. Yes, he sometimes gets emotional, but he probably gets emotional less often than a lot of us, especially averaged over time and many different situations. That's because he is low in neuroticism and extraversion. But situations are important too. Even if you are emotionally composed and resilient like President Obama, there will be certain contexts that cause you to behave out of character, especially strong situations that override your usual disposition (such as when giving a speech to your closest supporters after a tumultuous and exhausting period of campaigning).

To take a more extreme example, if someone points a gun at your head, it doesn't really matter whether you are high or low in neuroticism, you will still feel scared—although if you're highly neurotic, you will probably feel more intense fear and be more vulnerable to developing posttraumatic stress afterward. Thankfully, for many of us, the kind of personality-defying strong situations that we are likely to encounter in everyday life are not a gun to the head, but a clearly defined and demanding social or occupational role—say, giving a speech at a wedding, visiting the doctor for test results, or participating in a job interview.

People who work in the sports or entertainment worlds provide dramatic examples. I've already mentioned how tennis ace Rafael Nadal is almost like two different people: Superman on court and Clark Kent off it. Many boxers are similar, especially because they are cocooned away for months in training camp prior to a fight. For example, former World Heavyweight Champion Joseph Parker from New Zealand has stated that he is an entirely different person in camp, where he lives a rigid lifestyle and strict diet (indicative of extreme conscientiousness), than he is outside, where he enjoys eating pie and playing guitar (a switch to lower conscientiousness, greater extraversion, and openness).

Some athletes speak of more sudden personality changes triggered the moment they walk onto the field. Consider the Australian cricket legend Dennis Lillee, renowned for his aggressive fast bowling. An agreeable extravert off the pitch, he was hostile and intimidating on it. "Soon as I stepped over that line on the field my personality changed," he told the *Telegraph*. "To me, it was battle. Australia v England was a war. You wanna try to smash them into the ground."[10] Another former heavyweight boxing champ, American Deontay Wilder, has described his own sudden personality change: "When I'm in a real fight there's a transformation. I'm no longer Deontay. Sometimes I frighten myself when I'm like that. It's scary."[11]

Sometimes there is a personality leak between roles—the actor Benedict Cumberbatch has described how playing Sherlock Holmes led to him being more curt and impatient in his personal relationships long after filming (a shift to lower agreeability).[12]

It's not just sports stars, singers, and actors who show personality differences. For example, Brian Little, a professor of personality, has described how he transforms into a temporary extravert when he's delivering lectures. Or to take a completely different example, this time from the world of business and activism, look at Florence Ozor, one of the leaders of the Bring Back Our Girls movement (a social movement established to raise the profile of the plight of schoolgirls kidnapped by Boko Haram in 2014) and founder of her own Florence Ozor Foundation that aims to empower women in Nigeria. As Tasha Eurich describes in her book *Insight*, Ozor is a strong introvert, but she learned early in her work as an activist that to achieve the change she wanted, she needed to act like an extravert, at least when in that role. "Never again will I run away from something just because I'm scared of the spotlight," she vowed to herself.[13]

The bottom line in understanding the dynamic between situations and traits is that both matter for how we behave in any given moment. Personality, however, will always express itself over the longer term (although remember that your personality can itself evolve more permanently over time).

The rest of this chapter is about the situation-personality interaction—how different situations, moods, substances, and other people affect the way that we behave in the moment and how this interacts with our longer-term traits.

UNSTABLE VERSUS ADAPTABLE

When considering the power of the situation, something to bear in mind is that some of us will show more short-term variability than others depending on our scores on the Big Five personality traits. Especially if you are highly neurotic, you might find that your behavior is more unpredictable and changeable, whereas if you are an extravert, you are probably more consistent. A key distinction in this regard is between instability and adaptability.

The behavior of highly neurotic folk from one occasion to another is often unstable and hard to predict. This is because it arises in large part from their erratic inner emotions and moods. The behavior of resilient extraverts, in contrast, is more stable and easier to predict because they tend to behave more similarly across different situations. When their behavior does change, it is more often as they adapt appropriately to the demands of the social situation.

Psychologists showed this recently when they asked undergraduates to use a smartphone to record their behavior and feelings during all their social interactions for five weeks.[14] They found that highly neurotic people were much more unpredictable in their friendliness from one encounter to the next, even if it was in exactly the same social context (this probably helps explain why highly neurotic people can be hard to live with and tend to go through more relationship breakups). At the same time, the highly neurotic types showed the least adaptability across different situations; that is, they didn't seem to have the flexibility to tailor their social behavior to match different contexts in a consistent, advantageous way.

In contrast, extraverts and highly agreeable people were more consistent: they were generally happier and friendlier on average over time, yet they also showed greater adaptability to situations, tailoring their behavior appropriately to fit the social context. (Picture the agreeable extravert who is consistently chatty and funny when with friends but also has the skill to display compassion and concern in a more solemn situation.)

PRESENT COMPANY

One of the most important aspects of any situation is who we are with. You can probably think of at least one person who seems to bring out a particularly strong or usually well-hidden side to your character when you're with him or her.

When I was growing up, it was my grandmother. Sure, I was usually fairly well behaved, but around Nanna, I was an absolute angel. I'm surprised I didn't sprout wings and a halo. In her company, I acted several years older than my true age—never silly or disobedient, always helpful and polite. I was nauseatingly precocious: I'd nod along sagely whenever she spoke about the decline in manners these days or expressed disapproval about the bad language on TV, as if I was nine going on ninety. It felt like a self-fulfilling dynamic: I knew she thought butter wouldn't melt in my mouth, and it became a role I felt a pressure to live up to.

That's an extreme example, but most of us tend to adapt our behavior depending on the social role we're in. Maybe you start acting more like a bro around your boss who's heavily into sports, or you become uncharacteristically introverted when you're with your boyfriend's judgmental mother. The word *personality* comes from *persona*, which is Latin for "mask." Psychologists have been studying these short-term personality changes for a while, and some of the patterns seem to be fairly universal.

One study that's typical involved hundreds of people rating their personality traits as they are when with their parents, with friends, and with work colleagues.[15] Predictably they rated themselves as most extraverted when with friends, most conscientious when with work colleagues, and most neurotic (emotionally unstable and needy) when with their parents. Extraversion showed the most amount of variation across social contexts (which isn't really surprising when you consider it is largely a social trait), while conscientiousness showed the least amount of variation.

In another study, this one involving in-depth interviews with eight people about their experience of wearing a social mask with parents, friends, or colleagues, the interviewees described how draining it can be to put on a masquerade.[16] For instance, Mary, a thirty-five-year-old hedge fund manager, talked about the tiring effort of adopting a conscientious persona at work: "It's not something I want to do but it's like, you've already, it's like you're on a treadmill and you can't stop otherwise you'll fall off." Trudy said her personality almost regresses when she's with her family: "My whole character changes back to how I was and I'm sort of really insecure, really shy, just waiting to be told off all the time. . . . Parts of being an extravert will, sort of, come out but it will be so squashed by them, yeah, that I just become more withdrawn." The gist from the interviews was that it's easier to be your "real self" with friends than with colleagues or parents, although sometimes it can be tiring with friends too, especially if you're not in the mood for being sociable or lighthearted.

Something I think is much harder for research to pin down is how specific individuals can have specific effects on our own characters, the way my Nanna used to do with me. Sometimes this can be advantageous. My social life got a kick-start at college because in my freshman year, I formed an early friendship with a party animal who drew out my own inner extravert. In fact, I'd say that generally I've always enjoyed being around people who make me feel more extraverted, whereas I can find it uncomfortable being around people who exacerbate my self-consciousness.

Arguably one of the defining features of what makes for good friends is that they help you be (or at least feel like) the kind of person you'd like to be.

ARE YOU A SOCIAL CHAMELEON?

The temporary effects of present company on our personality may be greater for some of us than others. In the late 1970s, psychologist Mark Snyder proposed that it's possible to divide people into two categories: some of us behave like a chameleon, being highly motivated to make a good impression and skillful at adapting our behavior to suit the current situation (he called them "high self-monitors"), whereas others are more concerned with being genuine and showing their same true self, regardless of who they are with or what is going on ("low self-monitors").

Snyder says that high self-monitors ask themselves, *What does this situation require of me?* and they're adept at picking up social cues to find out. Low self-monitors, by contrast, ask themselves, *How can I be me in this situation?* and they turn their attention inward for answers. It is little surprise, then, that high self-monitors tend to be considered friendlier and easier to get along with by work colleagues and that this can help them get ahead. Snyder told the *Cut*, "It's the difference between living a life that's built on projecting images that are designed to further particular ends, or whether it's a matter of you living a life that's about being true to your own sense of self."[17]

The difference between these personality types plays out in attitudes too. A high self-monitor will bend her preferences and opinions on controversial topics to match the group mentality of whatever crowd she's in, whereas the low self-monitor will pride herself on sticking to her guns and being authentic. High self-monitors also tend to have more friends, but of a more superficial quality, preferring to be with the kind of person who most matches whatever the situation demands (they'd rather go to the football game with their new friend who's a big football fan than with their longtime buddy who's not that into it). Low self-monitors are the opposite: they have fewer but deeper friendships, preferring to be with the person they like best, whether that person matches the occasion or not.

The self-monitoring concept even applies to dating: when they look through personal ads, high self-monitors are more concerned by the physical appearance of potential partners (they think they'll simply adapt to their date's personality); low self-monitors, in contrast, care more about the personality descriptions because for them, rapport is so important and impossible to fake.

You probably have an idea what category you fall into, but to get a more accurate sense, here's a short test that I've adapted from one that Snyder devised with his colleague Steven Gangestad:[18]

1. At parties I say things that I think other people will like. Yes or no?
2. If I'm going to argue for something, I have to believe what I'm saying. Yes or no?
3. I was good at drama at school and would make a good actor. Yes or no?
4. I'm like a different person, depending on whose company I'm in. Yes or no?
5. I'm not very good at ingratiating myself with others. Yes or no?
6. I'm happy to switch opinions if it can help me get ahead or please someone I like. Yes or no?
7. I have trouble putting on a show to suit different social situations. Yes or no?

8. I get socially anxious and I'm not very good at making
    new friends.   Yes or no?

9. I could really dislike someone, but they'd have no idea
    because I'm good at hiding my feelings.   Yes or no?

10. I'd find it really hard to look someone in the eye and tell
    an outright lie.   Yes or no?

How much of a social chameleon are you? Count the number of times you answered yes to items 1, 3, 4, 6, 9. Now count the times you answered yes to items 2, 5, 7, 8, 10. If the first number is higher than the second, you tend to wear a social mask (you're a high self-monitor); if the second number was higher, you are more inclined to just be you, regardless of who you are with (you are a low self-monitor).

You might find that it's helpful to see people in this binary way; perhaps it even makes sense of conflicts among your friends and relatives. Low and high self-monitors tend not to think too highly of each other: the lows see the highs as fakers, and the highs see the lows as rigid and awkward.

To me, it's definitely a fun and interesting way of thinking about how people relate to the world. But I should point out that from a scientific perspective, there are problems with the self-monitoring concept. Some experts say that self-monitoring is really an expression of extraversion; that is, high self-monitors are strong extraverts, better able to play to the crowd and wear a mask of happiness for their friends (which matches what I explained earlier about the difference between stability and adaptability in behavior, with extraverts being highly adaptable).

Also, if you're prone to social anxiety, as I am, you might find the two categories inadequate, feeling that you fall squarely between the two. I certainly feel a pressure to make a good impression (I even get performance anxiety when I'm talking to Siri). But I wish I didn't, and

I'm always chiding myself for trying too hard to be nice rather than being more open and honest. Does that make me a reluctant high self-monitor? Probably not, because they're supposed to be skillful at playing different social roles and supposedly don't get stressed by social challenges. Given these issues with the concept, I'd recommend seeing your self-monitoring score as fun and thought-provoking rather than taking it too seriously.

FEELING MOODY?

I was at a small house party with some fellow twentysomethings I barely knew, nursing a terrible hangover and trying to keep a low profile. "Ah, you're one of *those kinds* of people," the guy opposite me said, jolting me out of my trance. "You don't say very much, do you?" he added, obviously unimpressed.

This rude dude seemed to have made some rapid assumptions about my personality, and from his tone, he didn't much like what he saw. I hate admitting that his words stung. Okay, maybe I am an introvert—at least I was back then—but no one should have to apologize for that. Mainly, though, I resented how he'd assumed my behavior revealed an inherent truth about me rather than merely reflecting my mood, which at that moment was under a cloud thanks to the alcohol-fueled pounding in my head. Yes, I was acting quiet and introverted now, but he should have seen me on the dance floor the night before!

We often assume of other people that their current behavior reflects their underlying personality—the deeply rooted "kind of person" they are—and discount the contribution of the particular circumstances, including their mood. In contrast, and rather conveniently, when it comes to our own behavior, we are often much more aware of the effects of mood and emotion—like the Polish model Natalia Sikorska who was spared jail in 2017 after attempting to shoplift from Harrods in London. She had acted like a completely different person than she normally does, she told the London court, because of the stress and cultural shock of returning from a vacation in the United States.[19] Poor Natalia. What an ordeal!

To be fair to the hungover me and Natalia the model, it really is true that mood has strong effects on how our personality manifests at any given moment. In a recent study, psychologists gave hundreds of students brief email surveys to complete several times a day for up to two weeks.[20] Each email included a short personality test, and space for the students to report their levels of positive and negative mood and to say what they were doing, including whether they were studying or doing something more fun.

The students' personality scores varied to a degree from one time to another; crucially, this was largely explained by differences in their mood. When the students felt happier, they tended to score higher in extraversion and open-mindedness. Conversely, when they felt less happy and more sad or down, they scored higher on neuroticism and lower on

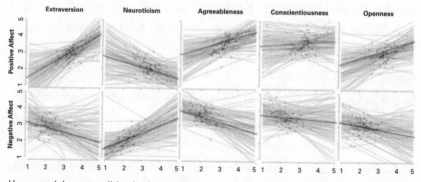

How people's personalities in the moment (rated 1–5, from low to high) vary according to their mood (top row: positive moods; bottom row: negative moods; each line represents a different volunteer). Source: Reproduced from Robert E. Wilson, Renee J. Thompson, and Simine Vazire, "Are Fluctuations in Personality States More Than Fluctuations in Affect?" Journal of Research in Personality 69 (2017): 110–123.

agreeableness. Curiously, conscientiousness came out as largely unrelated to mood, but that may be because the association was opposite for different people (so the effects would have canceled out across all the students).

Speaking for myself, I know that my conscientiousness dips momentarily when I'm feeling down—I'm more likely to start browsing YouTube videos rather than knuckling down to write. I can imagine, though, that other people might become more focused when they're fed up, perhaps using work or chores as a distraction.

The students' personalities also changed when they were studying, becoming less extraverted, less agreeable, less open, and more neurotic (can you blame them?) but also more conscientious. Importantly, though, these in-the-moment trait-like shifts were almost entirely explained by the effects of studying on the students' moods.

The influence of mood on our personality makes me wonder if some of the effects of present company on personality might be largely explained by how different people make us feel. In fact, psychologists recently proposed that there is such a thing as "affective presence," the consistent tendency each of us has to influence the moods of those around us, akin to leaving an emotional footprint on them. A study of hundreds of well-acquainted business students found that some popular individuals consistently lifted the mood of those around them, while others (especially those low in agreeability and, surprisingly, also high in extraversion) consistently made other people feel more fed up.[21]

Moody effects on your momentary personality are also likely to arise as a result of the movie you just watched or the song you just listened to (and probably the book you've just been reading too). In another study, researchers had volunteers complete a personality questionnaire before and after watching either a sad clip from the film *Philadelphia*, accompanied by a somber, stirring piece of classical music, Barber's "Adagio for Strings," or before and after watching a happy video clip of families reuniting after the fall of the Berlin Wall, accompanied by Mozart's uplifting "Eine Kleine Nachtmusik."[22] The volunteers' personalities came out as less extraverted and more neurotic after watching the sad video, and there was a slight increase in their extraversion after watching the happy video.

Lots of things in life we cannot control, but we can choose what we listen to and watch on TV (although you might have to wrestle the remote off your partner), and we usually have at least some influence over whom we spend our time with. Being more mindful of how these decisions influence our mood, and therefore our momentary personality, is part of a simple yet powerful psychological strategy that I'm going to tell you about next.

THE SITUATION-SELECTION STRATEGY

Where you are, what you're doing, and who you are with all affect your personality in the moment. Over time, these influences can accumulate, shaping the kind of person you become. But you don't have to accept this state of affairs passively. The poet Maya Angelou said, "Stand up straight and realize who you are, that you tower over your circumstances."[23] She was certainly right in the sense that we can be canny about how we choose to spend our time: we can shape our circumstances so that they work for, not against, us. For instance, if you would like to develop a more open-minded, sociable, warm personality, an important way to achieve this is to strive to place yourself into situations that lift your mood. This may sound obvious, but if you think honestly for a moment, how often are you strategic when planning your time?

Take next weekend—what are your plans? Did you really consider how what you are planning to do will make you feel? It's quite likely your schedule will be based much more on habit or convenience. Of course, you may have unavoidable responsibilities. Yet for many of us living in free societies and with even a modest income, it is possible to think more deliberately than usual about what we plan to do, taking into consideration how we are likely to feel, and therefore—over the long term—allowing us to exert more deliberate influence over the kind of people we will become. Rather than gritting your teeth as you endure yet another spell of boredom or even a storm of emotional angst, try making a greater effort to plan ahead and seek out the sunlit places that promise more joy. Psychologists at the University of Sheffield in England tested this approach recently.[24] They gave half of their volunteers the following situation-selection instruction before the weekend and asked them to repeat it three times and to commit to doing it: *"If I am deciding what to do this weekend, then I will select activities that will make me feel good and avoid doing things that will make me feel bad!"* On Monday, all the volunteers provided a breakdown of what they'd spent the weekend doing and the emotions they'd experienced. The key finding was that those who followed the instruction experienced more positive emotion over the weekend. This was particularly the case for the volunteers with more neurotic personalities, who said they usually struggled to regulate their emotions. If you would like to be less neurotic, this could be a particularly useful approach for you.

The situation-selection strategy is not all easy sailing, though. An unfortunate and important obstacle to taking this more strategic approach to life and our own personality development is that a lot of the time, we are not very good at anticipating how different situations will make us feel. Psychologists call this skill "affective forecasting," and they've found that we tend to overestimate the impact of rare, dramatic events on our positive and negative emotions. We think that winning the lottery will leave us in a permanent state of euphoria, or that failing

97

next week's exam will leave us devastated, but in reality, we are quick to adapt to these isolated events and return to our usual emotional baseline.

At the same time, we tend to underestimate the cumulative effect of repeated, minor, mundane experiences. I'm referring to simple, everyday things like the route you take to work. Consider how, if you walk through the park, it might take longer to get to work, but it would lift your mood a little every day. Studies suggest that as little as ten minutes of exercise a day can increase our happiness.[25]

Or what about that colleague you always hang out with at lunch? Sure, it's easy to chat with the person you've known for years, but if she is grumpy by nature—or has poor "affective presence"—she is bound to leave you feeling demotivated every day.

And then there's all the time you spend watching TV in the evening. As a veteran of countless box sets, I certainly know how tempting it is to reach for the remote. But watching the latest drama about drug dealers or serial killers probably won't do much for your mood or help you find meaning in life, for that matter.[26]

You could even see your decisions around when to go to bed as part of the situation-selection strategy. Getting enough sleep is one of the surest ways to lift your mood. A recent study of over twenty thousand people found that falling just one hour short of the optimum amount of sleep—seven to nine hours—was associated with a 60 to 80 percent increased risk of experiencing negative moods like hopelessness and nervousness.[27] Despite this, many of us time and again put off going to bed at an appropriate time, preferring to stay up bingeing on *Game of Thrones* or chatting on social media, a modern malaise that psychologists have dubbed bedtime procrastination.[28] Setting yourself some simple ground rules, like no digital devices in the bedroom, can help you get over this bad habit.

Taking a more strategic approach to life will come more easily to some people than others. In particular, those who are very agreeable tend to have shrewd instincts for how they choose to spend their time, frequently placing themselves in pleasant situations, which helps them be more warm, upbeat, and avoid conflict. Those of us not blessed with this instinct can still learn a lot from it by making a greater effort to choose situations beneficial to our mood and personality development.

A simple rule of thumb may be to try to pursue any activities and company that help you to behave as outgoing and friendly as possible. A fascinating study that involved over one hundred undergraduates recording their behavior and mood in a nightly diary for two weeks found that they felt happier on days when they had been relatively more sociable, friendlier, and more conscientious.[29] Critically, this was true regardless of their usual personality profile, including whether introverted or extraverted. This is probably because behaving in these ways helps fulfill our basic human needs to feel connected to others, to feel competent and in control of our lives.

TUMMY RUMBLES AND DUTCH COURAGE

There's an elephant in this chapter that I've yet to address. Much of the time, our behavior and mood are influenced not only by who we are with and what we're doing, but also what we put in our mouths to eat, drink, or smoke. It almost goes without saying that substances that affect our brain functioning will also induce short-term changes in personality. After all, they're altering our thinking and behavior. But what are these effects, and do they vary depending on our usual personality type?

The most mundane example is hunger (or low blood sugar). Hunger affects our brain function in a similar way to the fight-or-flight response, increasing our inclination for risk taking (temporarily higher extraversion and lower conscientiousness) and making us impatient and intolerant (lower agreeability)—an effect that some call "hanger."

My favorite demonstration of this is a study that involved heterosexual couples inserting pins in a voodoo doll of their partner each night before bed: the angrier they felt toward their partner, the more pins they were told to put in the doll.[30] The researchers also monitored the participants' blood sugar levels. They found that on nights that these levels were lower, the participants tended to stick more pins in the doll. These effects of hunger on mood and in-the-moment personality are certainly worth bearing in mind if you plan on going on a diet or tend to skip breakfast.

Alcohol provides an even more dramatic example of how substances can affect personality. At a basic level, as you may well have experienced firsthand, alcohol's neurological effects mean that we become disinhibited and more impulsive; in personality terms, we are more extraverted and less conscientious. This is a pattern that's been confirmed scientifically by asking people to rate their own personality when sober and when drunk[31] and to have a buddy rate them as well.[32] Other studies have videoed people getting mildly drunk, and then unacquainted observers have rated the drunk people's personalities.[33]

Overall this research has confirmed what we already knew: being drunk usually makes us more extraverted, but lower on everything else—less agreeable, less open, less conscientious, and less neurotic (i.e., more emotionally stable). The one nuance from the research is that the observers detected in the drinkers only increases in extraversion (especially increased gregariousness, assertiveness, and activity levels) and, to a lesser extent, lower neuroticism. They didn't spot the other (self-reported) personality changes, like less openness, perhaps because these depend more on changes to our private thoughts and feelings.

Most studies of alcohol's effects have averaged the personality changes brought on by moderate amounts of liquor, but of course we don't all respond in exactly the same way. When psychologists recently looked at variations among people in how their personalities changed in response to alcohol, they found four main types of drunk personality and gave them some funny names.[34] See if you can recognize yourself:

Ernest Hemingway: You don't change as much as others when you're drunk, and you especially retain your openness to experience and intellect.

Mary Poppins: You're charming when drunk, manifested as your usual sober agreeableness being especially unaffected (this was the rarest category in the research).

The Nutty Professor: You're an introvert when sober and show a drastic increase in extraversion and lower conscientiousness when you're drunk. (I hate to admit, but this is me.)

Mr. Hyde: You're unpleasant to be around when drunk, showing especially large decreases in agreeability and conscientiousness—so more likely to take risks and cause offense to others (in the research, more women than men apparently fit this category).

Before you proudly pin the Hemingway or Mary Poppins label on yourself, it might be worth checking how your friends categorize you. I bet many of us have somewhat dubious insight into our own drunk personalities. In fact, an amusing survey of hundreds of British undergraduates recently suggested as much. The researchers found that the students tended to describe themselves, more than others did, as acting when drunk the way they do when sober, and they also saw themselves, but not others, as being "good drunks." "When I drink I become very happy and fun to be around, I am not like others that become overdrunk and are no longer in control of themselves," was a typical comment.[35]

A natural question at this point, especially if you're the Nutty

Professor type and looking to make yourself temporarily more extra-verted, is whether it is sensible to use alcohol to alter your character de-liberately. Of course, any momentary benefits must be weighed against the harmful medical and social effects of alcohol abuse, including in-creased risk of cancer and marriage breakdown. Note too that in terms of personality change, research that has looked at the effects of chronic risky alcohol use has also found that, yes, it leads to increased extra-version, but also lower agreeableness, conscientiousness, and increased neuroticism—not the most appealing combination.[36]

But even putting aside the serious issue of unhealthy alcohol de-pendence, something else to consider if you're contemplating using alcohol to induce short-term personality changes (not just to be more extraverted, but perhaps also less neurotic and anxious) is that its ef-fects can be context specific. Take mood. Although we usually think of moderate alcohol consumption as lifting our mood, more nuanced studies have shown that its effects are rather more specific: it makes us feel more connected to the present moment, more narrowly focused, and less affected by emotional inertia or recent experiences.

This is good news if you're in a happy situation, doing something you enjoy, and with people you like, because then drinking is likely to enhance your pleasure. In social situations, it apparently also makes positive moods more catching from one person to another. But if you're currently down or distressed or you're just sitting on your own with your own worries, then be warned that drinking is likely to make you feel worse.

There's a similar nuance to consider in relation to alcohol's calm-ing effects. What alcohol seems especially good at is helping reduce our general fear of uncertainty—hence, why it can sometimes be an effective tonic for social anxiety. However, it's not so effective at alleviat-ing fear about a specific threat that you know is coming, such as a work presentation or best man's speech that you've got to deliver. It's also worth noting that even if a drink or two calms your nerves before a talk, the alcohol is likely to harm your performance because of its detrimental effects on your mental skills,[37] although it can apparently boost your fluency when learning to speak a foreign language, presumably because it alleviates self-consciousness.[38]

The short-term personality effects of alcohol may also depend on your usual personality type. Research that has filmed strangers getting to know each other with the benefit of an alcoholic drink has found that it's extraverts who are especially likely to say that they found the booze mood enhancing and that it helped them feel socially closer to the other people, perhaps because extraverts are already enjoying themselves and alcohol tends to accentuate your current mood. This difference in alcohol's effects on introverts and extraverts could also help explain why extraverts are more prone to alcohol abuse: they find it more pleasurable, so there's a greater temptation to drink more of it.

WIRED ON CAFFEINE

It won't surprise you to hear that caffeine is the most widely taken psychostimulant in the world. Psychostimulants are a category of drug, also including illegal substances like cocaine and amphetamine, that increase the activity of the brain and nervous system. In the United States, around 80 to 90 percent of adults get a regular caffeine hit, most often from coffee but also in tea and from energy drinks and chocolate. Regular coffee drinkers—I'm looking at you, writers and students—will be very familiar with its effects on their mind, especially increased alertness and concentration, and therefore, momentarily at least, on their personality.

Caffeine exerts its stimulating effect by rapidly blocking the action of the brain chemical adenosine that usually acts to make us more chilled by slowing our breathing and lowering our blood pressure. By blocking this chemical, caffeine speeds us up. A huge literature shows that in moderate doses—say, one to two cups at a time—coffee really does sharpen the mind, especially for so-called low-level mental functions, like our reaction times and our ability to sustain attention over a long period of time.[39] And this is all the more so for people who are feeling fatigued, like the student or security guard pulling an all-nighter.

What does this mean for short-term personality change? It's clear that these mental and physical effects of caffeine are likely to lift our conscientiousness in the immediate moment. If you're falling asleep in front of the spreadsheet on your computer screen or struggling to motivate yourself to get to the gym, then coffee or a caffeine-based energy drink ought to help you out, effectively leading you to behave temporarily like someone with more inbuilt conscientiousness and extraversion (given that extraverts typically have higher energy and activity levels).

However, it's not all good news. Caffeine's effects are dose dependent, and as you may have found out for yourself, if you drink too much, it can make you jittery and anxious. There were some early studies that suggested thrill-seeking extraverts were more likely to enjoy the benefits of drinking coffee than introverts,[40] based on the idea that they have lower levels of baseline nervous energy, so they're less at risk that coffee will make them overly anxious. (If this is true, it would explain why novelty seekers drink more coffee than chill-seeking introverts do.)[41] Some later studies failed to replicate this interaction between caffeine's effects and personality, although it still seems likely that at least in terms of people's subjective experiences (rather than objective effects on performance), personality makes a difference.[42] For instance, another study found that extraverts said coffee made them feel more energetic, while high scorers in neuroticism said it made them feel more anxious.[43]

Indeed, if you're highly neurotic and prone to excess anxiety, you might want to be extra careful about drinking too much caffeine. There's even an official psychiatric condition, caffeine-induced anxiety disorder. Drinking too much coffee is unlikely to turn you into a nervous wreck if you are generally a relaxed person, but if you're susceptible to anxiety, then there's evidence that you may be more sensitive to the physical and psychological effects of caffeine and that it can trigger in you bouts of extreme nervousness or even a panic attack.[44]

These potential anxiety-inducing effects apply as much to popular energy drinks like Red Bull and Monster as they do to old-fashioned espresso. Energy drinks contain more caffeine than a double espresso, as well as high amounts of sugar, and there have been calls in the United States and United Kingdom to ban their sale to children and teens.[45]

Concerns about energy drinks peaked in Britain early in 2018 after the parents of a young man blamed his excessive consumption—fifteen cans a day—for his suicide.[46] This wasn't such an outlandish claim to make. Research has linked energy drinks with relapse for people with mental health problems—who are most likely high scorers in neuroticism—partly through the anxiety-inducing effects of caffeine, but also because they can interfere chemically with the effects of psychiatric medication.[47] Another worry is the popular trend to consume energy drinks alongside alcohol, which can lead people to underestimate how intoxicated they are and, by keeping them awake for longer, make it easier to binge-drink.

Yet another issue to bear in mind is that like most mind-altering drugs, there is a withdrawal effect as your brain gradually decaffeinates, which can include headaches and feeling moody.[48] This is yet another way that coffee drinking could, after its benefits wear off, lead you to experience temporarily increased neuroticism.

SPACE CAKES AND PSYCHEDELIC TRIPS

In some cafés, caffeine isn't the only drug on the menu. I'm reminded of the time my then wife-to-be and I were in Amsterdam as part of a research trip for her undergraduate thesis, and (you guessed it) we couldn't wait to visit the cafés to try out the local delicacy of "space cake" and "space tea," baked and brewed with cannabis.

We felt like such rebels—cannabis was, and still is, illegal back home in the United Kingdom.[49] I remember how we stared with excitement into each other's eyes waiting for the adventure to begin. Truth be told, it was a bit of a downer at first: not much happened. Unbeknownst to us at the time, the mind-altering effects of cannabis take a lot longer to hit when consumed this way instead of smoking. However, it was still fun. Instead of enjoying a mind-blowing trip, we ended up with the giggles as we both tried to spot any hint of an effect in each other's words and behavior.

Though hundreds of millions of people around the world use cannabis, it is a very different prospect from caffeine or alcohol. Its composition and effects are much more complicated and somewhat mysterious. The main psychoactive compounds are delta-9-tetrahydrocannabinol (THC) and cannabidiol (CBD), which act with contrasting effects on cannabinoid receptors in the brain and throughout the rest of the body. However, a typical marijuana leaf will contain over one hundred other related chemicals, each with its own mental and bodily effects that medical science is still uncovering. This chemical complexity and variety could explain why the subjective effects of cannabis vary so much. People report that cannabis affects them in many different ways, including making them feel calm and euphoric, time slowing down or speeding up, and that it allows them to experience revelations or rare insights.

In terms of basic mental functioning as measured in a psych lab, the effects of cannabis contrast starkly with caffeine. It impairs memory and the ability to sustain and switch attention.[50] Over the longer term, some experts also believe there is such a thing as cannabis amotivational syndrome, consistent with the stereotype of the stoner who is too chilled out to bother doing very much at all. One recent study of hundreds of undergraduates found that those who smoked weed showed less initiative and persistence, even after controlling for any initial underlying personality differences from nonusers.[51] In personality terms, you could read these research findings as meaning that cannabis is likely to hit your conscientiousness both in the moment and also longer term if you use it repeatedly.

Combine taking cannabis with other drugs, and of course the risks are multiplied. The world of rock and roll, where such a lifestyle is so common, unsurprisingly provides endless anecdotal evidence for how drug taking can have adverse effects on personality. For instance, Charlie Watts of the Rolling Stones who for years drank heavily, smoked cannabis, and took heroin, among other indulgences, told the *New York Times* how his drug taking was a "nightmare" for his loved ones and how his "personality changed completely."[52]

To be fair, when it comes to cannabis specifically, there are also many positive anecdotal accounts of its effects from the music world, including how it can boost creativity. For instance, the Beach Boys' cofounder, Brian Wilson, credits marijuana with helping him finish his landmark 1966 album *Pet Sounds*: "I listened to 'Rubber Soul' and smoked some marijuana and was so blown away that I went right over to my piano and wrote 'God Only Knows' with a friend of mine," he told the Denver-based music website the *Know* in 2015.[53]

Some studies back up the idea of cannabis having this acute mind-expanding effect, which would imply a temporary boost to trait openness to experience, especially for people who are normally more closed-minded.[54] Other research has found that even when sober, cannabis users perform better on tests of creativity than nonusers do, possibly indicative of a more lasting impact of cannabis on their openness to experience. Alternatively, perhaps people who are already more open-minded are simply more likely to use cannabis, as a recent study claims.[55] The same research also found that cannabis users are more extraverted than nonusers but less conscientious.

In terms of the effects of weed on anxiety, some nervous people swear that it helps them, yet there is also evidence that cannabis can cause anxiety problems.[56] Part of the reason for the mixed effects is that weed simply varies so much chemically depending on where you get it, in terms of its content and strength (worth noting is that the strength of recreational cannabis has increased dramatically over recent decades, according to the US Drug Enforcement Administration).[57] Its effect will also vary depending on your own personality (though exactly how has not been thoroughly researched), your expectations, and how often and for how long you use cannabis.

Psychologist Susan Stoner, the author of a recent report on the mental health effects of cannabis for the University of Washington, recently summed things up well, telling *Vice* magazine that "it is practically pure speculation what any given strain or product might do to any particular person with regard to anxiety."[58] Some advice suggests you should try to source weed with more CBD and less THC if you want it to have a calming effect, but given the state of the science, you're surely taking a gamble if you try to use cannabis to reduce your trait neuroticism, whether in the moment or longer term.

Another class of drug with some powerful effects on personality is psychedelics, including LSD (also known as acid), psilocybin (found in "magic mushrooms"), ketamine, and MDMA/ecstasy.

Psychedelics are consciousness altering and hallucination provoking.

At a neural level, they boost levels of entropy in the brain, meaning there is less synchrony and more unpredictability in the activity seen across diverse cerebral regions. Such changes are thought to facilitate new learning and the breaking of old habits of thought. They also reduce activity in the brain's so-called default mode network, which is involved in self-reflection and self-consciousness. This is thought to lead to ego dissolution, facilitating a sense of oneness with the world. "I felt like a grain of sand on a beach—both insignificant and essential in my own small way" is how one user described the first trip.[59]

Almost by definition, the way these drugs provoke users into seeing the world differently suggests a temporary increase in the personality trait openness to experience. Indeed, research involving magic mushrooms has reported personality changes of at least six months' duration, including increases in "interpersonal closeness, gratitude,

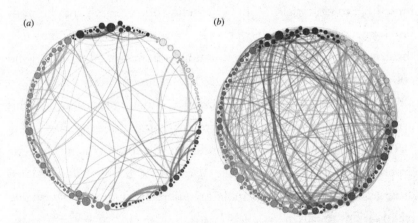

A simplified image from a 2014 study showing neural connectivity in a normal brain (a) and in a brain under the influence of psilocybin (b), in which there is greater communication among diverse brain areas that are usually not connected. Such brain changes are thought to underlie the profound alterations to personality caused by psychedelic trips, including greater open-mindedness and ego dissolution. *Source: Reproduced from Giovanni Petri, Paul Expert, Federico Turkheimer, Robin Carhart-Harris, David Nutt, Peter J. Hellyer, and Francesco Vaccarino, "Homological Scaffolds of Brain Functional Networks,"* Journal of the Royal Society Interface *11, no. 101 (2014): ID 20140873.*

life meaning or purpose, death transcendence, daily spiritual experiences, and religious faith and coping" — in personality trait terms, increased openness, reduced neuroticism, and increased agreeability.[60] More than half the volunteers described their session on the drug as the "single most spiritually significant experience of their life."[61] Other recent research has suggested that MDMA can help increase the effectiveness of psychotherapy and that it does this by increasing people's openness, helping them to see previous traumatic experiences in a new light.[62]

Remember that psychedelic drugs are illegal in most places, and whereas research studies use carefully controlled amounts of drug, it is much more difficult to control dosage in a recreational situation. Used without sufficient care, LSD, MDMA, and mushrooms all come with various dangers, from flashbacks to dehydration to anxiety.[63] There is also a risk of "bad trips," especially in the absence of a "guide," and for those high in neuroticism.[64] In both therapeutic research and the study into longer-lasting personality change, the volunteers didn't simply take the drug; they also received intense support from trained therapists and counselors acting as guides. In fact, the mushroom study I mentioned also incorporated meditation and spiritual training. Practitioners in this area have long referred to the importance of establishing the correct "set," as in mind-set, and setting, for shaping the tone of the psychedelic experience. It would be a mistake, then, to see taking acid or related drugs as an easy or fast-track route to a more open-minded personality based on this research.

A safer approach to developing a more open-minded personality could be to try to re-create the mind-blowing effects of a psychedelic trip but without the drugs. Practitioners of meditation often report moments of bliss or transcendence that change their relationship with reality forever. For others, such peak experiences can come from nature — a view from a mountaintop, especially if the challenge to get there taught you something new about yourself,[65] say, or witnessing the fluorescent brilliance of a tropical fish while scuba diving, might be enough to change you forever, no drugs required.

NO MAN (OR WOMAN) IS AN ISLAND

The lesson from this chapter is twofold: our personalities do not exist in a vacuum (rather, they are shaped by the people we are with and the roles we play), and while our personality traits manifest themselves over the longer term in our behavioral and emotional tendencies, our characters also fluctuate in the moment, especially in strong situations and whenever we ingest mind-altering substances.

These dynamics between situation and personality make sense of research that has shown how aspects of personality and emotion can spread through social networks like a contagion. One study found that you are more likely to be happy (a mark of low neuroticism and high extraversion) if your friends are happy; even the emotional state of the friends of your friends makes a difference.[66] Similarly, a company culture that is rude and disagreeable can effectively shift your own personality in a congruent fashion, making it more likely that you too will be cranky and impatient.[67]

Thankfully the same rules apply for positive aspects of emotion and behavior. Sitting next to a highly focused colleague could boost your conscientiousness, for example, and when more people in a workplace perform positive acts—doing favors for others and going the extra mile—this not only benefits the givers and receivers, but such altruistic ways of behaving are also catching, such that the initial recipients start giving more themselves.[68] In other words, just as a rude company culture can filter through and shape our personalities, an agreeable workplace (and this would likely be true for family or team cultures) can shape your personality in a positive direction.[69] These positive dynamics occur between couples at home too. Another study found that when one partner came home pumped from a good day at the office, this mood affected the other person, boosting that person's own self-esteem levels by the end of the day.[70]

Another factor to consider is that a lot of the situations we find ourselves in and the company we are with are not physical but virtual. If you spend half an hour on Twitter or Facebook arguing with trolls, for instance, this is a strong situation that is going to bear on your mood and your in-the-moment personality, probably leaving you more neurotic and more disagreeable. However, research in this area is mixed, with one study detailing the benefits of social media, such as increasing our feelings of belonging, and another one showing the opposite. But suffice it to say that if you spend time trawling the social feeds of people who upset you or of people you envy, this is likely to have a harmful impact on your short-term moods and emotions. Do this regularly, and it could end up having a chronic effect on your personality.

Whether we're talking about physical situations or virtual ones, the implication is the same: if you want to change yourself, you will find it much easier to become the person you want to be if you are mindful of these social and situational influences on your mood and behavior, especially as any outside pressures can accumulate and mold your personality over the longer term. This sounds like a warning, but there is an upbeat message here. Through being more strategic and thoughtful about where you go, the people you mix with, and what you do, you'll find you can turbocharge your own efforts at personal change.

Ten Actionable Steps to Change Your Personality

To reduce neuroticism	Almost everyone feels anxiety some of the time, but we differ in how we relate to the emotion. Practice seeing anxiety as a motivational friend rather than as an enemy that you need to beat. Channel your anxiety into preparation, and you can get it to work for you. In fact, optimal performance, whether at work or on the sports field, comes from a combination of training and anxiety.	When you're provoked or irritated and feel your blood boiling, picture the situation from a third-person perspective as if you are a fly on the wall. Performing mental distancing in this way has been shown to reduce anger and will help you to avoid losing your temper.
To increase extraversion	The next time you are confronted with a social situation that makes you feel uncomfortable, try reinterpreting it as excitement rather than suppressing these physical sensations. This technique, known as cognitive reappraisal, can help you enjoy yourself more at parties and other social events.	Being extraverted is not just about being chatty and sociable; it's also about being more active. Think about the active things you enjoy, and the next time you are sitting around not doing much, commit to going out and engaging in a pleasurable activity, be that mountain biking, gardening, or volunteering.

Ten Actionable Steps to Change Your Personality *(continued)*

To increase conscientiousness	Make a weekly habit of writing down how your short-term aims and tasks are connected to your longer-term goals and values in life. Your conscientiousness will grow when you can see the link between the effort you put in today and the rewards you will reap in the future.	When you face an arduous task, imagine doing it in the role of a character you admire; it could be a real person or a fictional character like Batman. A recent study found that young children were able to spend more time on task when they adopted the role of Batman, probably because creating distance from the self in this way makes it easier to resist distractions and prioritize longer-term goals.[71] If it works for the kids, why not try it?
To increase agreeability	Each week, think of someone you believe has treated you badly in the past and make an overt declaration to yourself that you forgive the person and he or she owes you nothing. Even putting aside the ethical reasons for practicing regular forgiveness, the habit will have mental and physical well-being benefits for you and increase your proclivity for friendly, altruistic behavior.	Researchers have identified four self-sabotaging habits to resist so as to avoid coming across as a jerk. (1) Don't give backhanded compliments (e.g., "You're strong for a woman"), which will be received as a put-down. (2) Don't humble-brag (e.g., "I've put on so much muscle at the gym, I'll have to get my dress altered"). People just see it as boastful. (3) Don't be a hypocrite (e.g., don't preach about climate change before flying off on vacation). (4) Resist hubris (better to compare your success against your own past performance rather than derogating others).

Ten Actionable Steps to Change Your Personality *(continued)*

| To increase openness | If you have the resources to do so, commit to visiting a variety of unfamiliar places around the world. New sights, sounds, smells, and routines will increase your openness. | Think about the people you spend most of your time with. Research shows that when you feel threatened and disrespected, you are more likely to cling rigidly to your beliefs in a defensive fashion or feign knowing more than you do. By contrast, when you feel trusted and respected, you will naturally be more prepared to be flexible and open-minded. |

115

Chapter 5

CHOOSING TO CHANGE

It was early in my freshman year at college when I began feeling sorry for my fellow student Matt. He hadn't made any friends and was deeply lonely. That his dorm room was on the edge of campus was no doubt partly to blame, but I'll admit, I couldn't help feeling that his personality was also a factor: he was extremely introverted and boring.

I hung out with Matt a couple of times, mainly because he just seemed so sad and lonely. I'll never forget the last time we were together alone, when he told me he'd had a revelation. He said he hadn't come to college to spend time moping around and that he'd made a profound decision: he was going to change himself to become more sociable. I was skeptical. Like lots of other people, I had a sense then that people can't really change, not deep down.

But that was literally the last time I saw Matt on his own. From that point on, he was always surrounded by a coterie of friends or working at one of the campus bars. He always seemed happy and outgoing, usually laughing along with other people. He'd changed, or at least he appeared to. His happiness shouldn't be too surprising: extraverts tend to be happier on average than introverts. In fact, introverts often underestimate how much pleasure they'd get from behaving in extraverted ways more often.[1]

Is Matt's story difficult to believe? It shouldn't be. Remember, a degree of personality change is normal. Your traits are shaped by immediate influences such as mood and present company, and also by dramatic events like marriage and emigration. And all the while, there's that gradual maturing as you mellow into old age.

But of course there's still a world of difference between personality changes arising passively, like a ship buffeted in the wind, and changes arising through deliberate acts of will, as I witnessed in Matt. This raises the tantalizing question: What if you could exploit the plasticity of personality to decide to change yourself in specific ways? What if Matt's story is not an isolated case and by taking up particular activities or making key life choices, you can choose to shape your own personality, to become more extraverted, say, or calmer and more conscientious?

What if a leopard really can swap his spots for stripes?

THE CASE FOR CHANGE

There's more to this topic than personal or scientific curiosity. As discussed in chapter 1, mounting research shows how your personality traits influence the way life unfolds. Extraverts tend to be happier than introverts, but they are also more prone to alcohol and drug problems. Highly neurotic people are at greater risk than average of developing mental health problems and physical illness. In fact, a recent Swiss study that tracked the same group of people through more than three decades found that those who were low in extraversion and high in neuroticism were *six times* as likely to develop depression and anxiety during the course of the research.[2]

Meanwhile, your levels of conscientiousness affect the likelihood that you'll adopt healthy behaviors, like eating well and regularly exercising. You're also more likely to do well in your education and career if you are more conscientious. Having more conscientiousness and openness to experience can even reduce your risk of developing Alzheimer's disease. What's more, research suggests that personality traits can influence the risk of bad things happening—in some cases, creating a vicious cycle, as those unfortunate events are then likely to shape your personality in unhelpful ways. For example, as I discussed in chapter 2, people who score higher in neuroticism and lower in agreeableness are more likely to get divorced. In turn, going through a divorce could reduce your extraversion and lead to you becoming more isolated. Similarly, if you're low in conscientiousness, you're more likely than higher scorers to find yourself out of a job, and, in turn, being unemployed is likely to lower your conscientiousness still further.

How the Main Personality Traits Are Linked with Health and Well-Being

	Prototypical Psychologically Healthy Personality[a]	Aspects of Personality Most Strongly Linked by Psychologists with Various Measures of Well-Being[b]	Aspects of Personality Linked with Physical Health
Neuroticism	Low on neuroticism, especially worry, anger, depressiveness, impulsivity, and vulnerability	Low withdrawal (that is, not easily discouraged or overwhelmed), related to lower neuroticism	High neuroticism linked with having more unhealthy gut bacteria and higher blood pressure
Extraversion	High on extraversion, especially warmth and happiness (and other positive emotions)	High enthusiasm (related to friendliness and warmth), related to the main trait of extraversion	Higher extraversion linked with having more diverse gut bacteria (a marker of better health), but also greater risk of addiction problems
Openness	High on openness to experience, especially being attentive to one's own feelings	High intellectual curiosity (including thinking deeply and being open to new ideas), related to the main trait of openness	Higher openness linked with fewer markers of chronic inflammation in the body
Agreeableness	High on agreeableness, especially in relation to honesty and frankness	High compassion (having empathy and concern for others), related to agreeableness	Lower agreeableness linked with greater risk of cardiovascular disease

How the Main Personality Traits Are Linked with Health and Well-Being *(continued)*

	Prototypical Psychologically Healthy Personality[a]	Aspects of Personality Most Strongly Linked by Psychologists with Various Measures of Well-Being[b]	Aspects of Personality Linked with Physical Health
Conscientiousness	High on conscientiousness, especially having a sense of being capable and in control	High industriousness (gritty, determined, ambitious), related to trait conscientiousness	High conscientiousness linked with lower cortisol levels (a biomarker of stress), less chronic inflammation in the body, and healthier bacteria in the gut

[a]Based on the consensus of 137 personality experts. Wiebke Bleidorn, Christopher J. Hopwood, Robert A. Ackerman, Edward A. Witt, Christian Kandler, Rainer Riemann, Douglas B. Samuel, and M. Brent Donnellan, "The healthy personality from a basic trait perspective," *Journal of Personality and Social Psychology* 118, no. 6 (2020): 1207.

[b]Among the well-being measures were happiness, personal growth, self-acceptance, and having purpose and meaning in life. Jessie Sun, Scott Barry Kaufman, and Luke D. Smillie, "Unique associations between big five personality aspects and multiple dimensions of well-being," *Journal of Personality* 86, no. 2 (2018): 158–172.

What's particularly startling is that in many cases, personality traits exert similar or even greater influence on people's lives than the kinds of factors that you might think of as being important, such as the relative wealth or poverty of the family you were born into, your intelligence, or, when it comes to health outcomes and longevity, your blood pressure.

We hear so much from politicians about their economic plans and public health initiatives. Yet only rarely is there discussion of helping people to develop advantageous personality traits. There are signs this is starting to change—for example, with growing calls to teach "character skills" in schools—but there's still surprisingly little awareness of the immense importance of personality traits to people's lives.

Before looking at whether it really is possible to deliberately change your personality in beneficial ways, including in adulthood, let's take one step back. How natural is it to want to have a different personality? Is this something most of us need to be persuaded about, or do most of us already hanker after change?

Is It Normal to Want to Be Different?

First, what about you? The following short personality test will reveal whether and in what ways you'd like to change your own character, broken down in terms of the Big Five personality traits.[3] Read each description on the left and then give yourself a score based on how much you'd like to be more or less like the kind of person described—or you can decide you are happy now with that characteristic.

How Happy Are You with Your Personality Traits?

		Much More Than I Am (Score +2)	More Than I Am (Score +1)	I'm Happy with How I Am (Score 0)	Less Than I Am Now (Score -1)	Much Less Than I Am Now (Score -2)
1	I want to be more talkative.					
2	I want to have a more vivid imagination.					
3	I want to have a forgiving nature.					
4	I want to be a reliable worker.					
5	I want to be someone who is relaxed and handles stress well.					
6	I want to be someone who is full of energy.					
7	I want to be generally trusting.					
8	I want to be someone who does things efficiently.					

How Happy Are You with Your Personality Traits? *(continued)*

		Much More Than I Am (Score +2)	More Than I Am (Score +1)	I'm Happy with How I Am (Score 0)	Less Than I Am Now (Score -1)	Much Less Than I Am Now (Score -2)
9	I want to be inventive.					
10	I want to be emotionally stable and not easily upset.					
11	I want to have an assertive personality.					
12	I want to like to cooperate with others.					
13	I want to be someone who makes plans and follows through with them.					
14	I want to be curious about many different things.					
15	I want to be someone who remains calm in tense situations.					

To Score Your Test

- Add your responses for items 1, 6, and 11 (remember, you get 2 points for "much more"; 1 point for "more"; 0 for happy as you are; minus 1 point for wanting to be less; and minus 2 points for wanting to be much less). This will give you a total between -6 and 6. The higher your score for these items is, the more *extraverted* you want to be.

- Add your responses for 2, 9, and 14, giving you a total between -6 and 6. The higher your score, the more *open-minded* you want to be.

- Add your responses for 3, 7, and 12, giving you a total between -6 and 6. The higher your score, the more *agreeable* you want to be.

- Add your responses for 4, 8, and 13, giving you a total between -6 and 6. The higher your score, the more *conscientious* you want to be.

- Add your responses for 5, 10, and 15, giving you a total between -6 and 6. The higher your score, the more *emotionally stable* (or *less neurotic*) you want to be.

For each trait, a score of zero suggests you're fairly happy with how you are. Compare your score across traits, and you'll see how satisfied you are with your personality overall and which traits you most and least want to change. Whether your results showed that you harbor desires to change or that you're happy with the way you are, you might be wondering whether your own state of (dis)content is normal.

There are sound reasons for predicting that most people are probably happy with their personalities. Research has long shown that most of us believe we're better than average, from our driving skills to the number of friends we've got. It's a phenomenon that's come to be known as the "Lake Wobegon effect," after Garrison Keillor's fictional town where "the women are strong, the men are good-looking, and all the children are above average." Even prison inmates believe they are more honest and trustworthy (linked with the Big Five trait of agreeableness) than the average member of the public![4] And if you're brilliant already, why mess with perfection, right?

In fact, if your test results showed you're eager to change, you are far from alone. Recent surveys indicate that a large proportion of us *do* harbor the fantasy of personality change. For instance, a survey of students by psychologists at the University of Illinois at Urbana-Champaign found that nearly all of them (over 97 percent) expressed a desire for their personalities to be different in at least some respects.[5]

It's not just US students. Surveys of British, Iranian, and Chinese young people have produced very similar results.[6] And wanting to change isn't purely a young person's desire either. Data from nearly seven thousand people age eighteen to seventy collected through the www .Personality Assessor.com website, where you can take free personality tests, found that even among the oldest participants, 78 percent wanted to be different.[7] It seems that the desire for a personality trait change isn't a purely Western phenomenon or a fixation of youth but a common part of being human.

THE THREE BASIC PRINCIPLES OF SUCCESSFUL PERSONALITY CHANGE

Let's consider three basic principles of an evidence-based approach to deliberate personality change, as laid out recently by personality experts at the University of Zurich:[8]

- A willingness and intention to change your behavior
- A belief in the malleability of personality
- Persistence with your behavioral changes until they become habitual

First, you need to have intentions to change specific trait-relevant behaviors, such as being friendlier to strangers or more talkative at work, either as an end in themselves or as the route toward some higher goal, such as advancing your career or helping poor children in your community. The fundamental, common-sense point here is that intentional personality change isn't going to happen unless you have a clear goal to change your behavior in ways related to your personality.

This is because wanting to change your traits is simply too vague. After all, trait terms like *neurotic* and *extraverted* are simply words to describe your disposition and average behavioral patterns over time. Just as with things like dieting and exercise (where "I'm going to go for a run on Tuesday evenings" is a more effective plan than "I'm going to run more"), the more specific you can make your aims, the more likely you are to succeed. That's why creating a plan to talk to a stranger at least once every day or to start joining your colleagues for after-work drinks at least once a week is more likely to be successful than the abstract ambition of becoming more extraverted (in a pandemic, consider making a plan to go for walks outside with a friend or a colleague, or to join in informal Zoom get-togethers).

The second fundamental principle states that to achieve deliberate personality trait change, you must believe that you are capable of achieving the very behavioral adjustments required to support that change in personality.[9] This sounds a little wishy-washy, resembling the clichéd adage that "believing you can means you're halfway there." But in fact, the importance of your beliefs about the malleability of your traits and abilities has been demonstrated many times, most famously in the influential work of psychologist Carol Dweck. People who see traits and abilities as malleable are said to have a "growth mind-set," and Dweck has shown they tend to respond to obstacles in life by trying harder and finding solutions rather than submitting passively to how things are.[10]

It's a similar story for willpower: research shows that people who believe willpower is limitless tend to recover more quickly from taxing challenges. In fact, a recent study in India, where mental exertion is widely seen as energizing, found that performing a taxing mental task increased people's abilities to persevere on the next task, showing again the importance of our mind-set and beliefs for shaping our psychology.[11] And it's just as true for beliefs about personality. A study Dweck conducted with children showed that teaching them about the malleability of a person's aggressiveness (related to the Big Five traits of agreeableness and conscientiousness) made it easier for them to subsequently learn how to become less aggressive.

If you're interested in changing your personality or helping someone else change theirs, the lesson here is simple: before you get down to the nitty-gritty of enacting deliberate personality change, an important first step is to recognize and learn about how such change is possible and achievable. In fact, regardless of how successful you are at achieving any personality adjustments, simply cultivating the mind-set that personality change is possible is likely to do you good.[12]

To help you think this way, remember that although your personality is partly rooted in the genes you inherited from your parents, it is not entirely determined by those genes (as a crude estimate, it's about 50 percent inherited). What's more, your inherited traits are a little like factory settings: yes, they incline you to act in a certain way in life, but with effort, commitment, and the right strategies, they can certainly be changed. When your current ways of relating to the world and others are not working for you—you're not getting what you want from life or living by your values—then you can choose to mix things up.

The third and final basic principle of willful personality adjustment is that you must repeat the behavioral changes required to achieve the trait change often enough that they become habitual. You have to be persistent and must realize that change takes time and that it might be uncomfortable for a while.

These new ways of behaving might take conscious effort at first, but through repetition, they can become easier and then automatic, just like learning to ride a bike or drive a car. Ultimately it is through acquiring new behavioral habits and ways of responding to the world that you can mold your own personality.

Consider the archetypal quiet, retiring man who wants to be more of an extravert. For him, learning to be more talkative and sociable will likely take a lot of conscious effort at first; it might even feel uncomfortable and forced. But through practice, he'll find that these behaviors can become second nature. Being sociable effectively becomes a reflex, a default setting. Essentially it becomes part of his personality. This works in a similar way for the other traits. Imagine a woman taking up the new habit of attending the theater every week (or watching online productions regularly) as a way to increase trait openness. At first she finds that the situation feels alien, the entertainment strangely unfamiliar. But over time, she comes to recognize certain actors and playwrights and develops her own idiosyncratic tastes and curiosities about the art form. As the psychologists from the University of Zurich put it, "We propose that processes of habit formation help a person to maintain the desired behavior changes across time and, as a consequence, translate them into relatively stable and measurable trait changes."

Looking back to the story of my college friend Matt, it seems clear with hindsight that he was perfectly placed to achieve lasting personality change. He was highly motivated, he believed strongly that change was possible, and he immediately set about changing his behavioral habits, including finding a job in a highly social environment (one of the university bars) where he had little choice but to repeatedly practice socializing with strangers. Matt's story is not a one-off. Psychologists recently compiled a mega-analysis of all the long-term research evidence available on whether people are able to change their personalities, and they concluded that in the majority of cases, they can, especially increasing extraversion and emotional stability.[13]

What's really empowering to note is that all three of the factors associated with the ability for change are themselves eminently changeable. In fact, after reading this book, you will likely find that the first two and maybe even the third now describe you quite accurately, even if they wouldn't have in the past. If you want to change and you've got these three factors sorted, this puts you in a fantastic position to go still further and begin some specific activities and exercises that psychology research says tend to go hand in hand with changes to personality traits.

EVIDENCE-BACKED WAYS TO CHANGE YOUR PERSONALITY

Deliberately setting out to behave in new ways is a crucial part of what's needed to achieve willful personality change, but on its own, this approach is likely to take a huge effort. You're learning to make changes in your outward behaviors—many of which you may find uncomfortable or challenging—in the hope that these efforts eventually will lead to lasting inner changes. Picture the disorganized woman who, in search of more conscientiousness, teaches herself to use a Google calendar, or the self-confessed philistine who forces himself to go to the opera once a month (in the hope of becoming more open-minded).

These deliberate behavioral strategies are an important part of the recipe for change. In fact, a recent study that followed thousands of Dutch people for seven years found that greater cultural activity, such as going to the opera, really does precipitate increases in trait openness.[14] However, a complementary ingredient for successful change is to take up exercises and activities that research has shown have the side effect of being associated with changes to specific personality traits (even though that isn't necessarily most people's usual motive for doing the activity).

While deliberately adopting new habits is important and will change you from the outside in, many of the following activities will change you from the inside out, modifying the basic cognitive and physiological processes that shape your personality. In turn, this will change how you behave, which will alter the situations you find yourself in. For instance, if you regularly complete an activity that has been shown to increase empathy levels (such as reading more literary fiction that features psychologically compelling characters and emotionally sophisticated plots; see page 144 for more details), you will probably begin to

129

act in a more caring way. In turn, this will increase the odds of finding yourself in friendly, trusting company of the kind that will further develop your increasingly agreeable character.

A related point to keep at the back of your mind is that you don't have to make dramatic changes to your traits, such as metamorphosing from wallflower to a stand-up comedian, in order to enjoy meaningful benefits in your life. The reason is that even very modest changes along some or all of the five main personality dimensions can set up an accumulating cascade of real-life consequences in terms of the decisions you make, the activities you spend time on, the people you mix with, and the situations you find yourself in. Whatever your overarching goal, whether to better fulfill your calling in life, be more productive, or have more friends, you will likely find that even subtle modifications to your personality will help you get there, to be who you want to be.

Lower Your Neuroticism

Let's take each trait in turn, beginning with neuroticism—the trait that the evidence suggests more people want to change than any other, with some of the most serious implications for happiness, health, and mental well-being. Recall that neuroticism is the flip side of emotional stability. People who score high on neuroticism are extra sensitive to negative emotion and are hesitant, vigilant, and nervous. So what activities or exercises are associated with alterations to the basic psychological mechanisms that contribute to these characteristics?

You could spend time completing *online memory training* exercises. An increasingly popular theory proposes a good deal of habitual anxiety is caused at a basic level by difficulties in controlling our mental attention, including what we're thinking about at any given time. For instance, when you're trying to give a presentation to your work colleagues, you keep imagining what they might be thinking about you—or when you're on your way to an interview and all you can think about is everything that might go wrong rather than concentrating on rehearsing the excellent answers you've prepared. Online memory training exercises can help by boosting your working-memory capacity, which is your ability to juggle different information simultaneously. In turn, this increases the control you have over your own thoughts.

Consider the findings from a recent study in which thirteen anxious students spent time on a difficult version of what's known in psychology as the *n*-back task.[15] (Google it to find free versions you can try out online.) These tasks involve paying attention to and remembering two streams of information at once. Specifically, the students had to listen to a stream of letters and simultaneously look at a changing grid of squares, and then press a key whenever the current letter or highlighted square was the same as the one that occurred a certain number of items earlier in the stream. The difficulty of the task was intensified by requiring the participants to compare the current square and letter with items further back, and the better the participants performed, the more the difficulty was ratcheted up. (A control group completed a version of the training designed to be too easy to have any benefit.)

The key finding was that after completing thirty minutes of this daily training for fifteen days, the students reported feeling less anxiety than they did before and they were better able to perform under stress. The measures of their brain waves also suggested that they were in a more relaxed state. The training likely had these beneficial effects because it gave the students more control over their own thoughts. People who score high on neuroticism find it difficult not to dwell on future risks and not to ruminate on past mistakes, but after this kind of training, it is easier for them to dial down this anxiety to more manageable levels.

Another activity you could try is performing *regular gratitude exercises*, such as making a short note each day of the things for which you are feeling grateful or writing letters of thanks. Research shows that gratitude can act like a form of emotional armor: people who feel and express more gratitude tend to be less adversely affected by stress in life.[16] There's even neuroimaging evidence suggesting that the more you practice feeling and expressing gratitude, the more your brain adapts to this way of thinking.[17] This suggests that the more effort you make to feel gratitude, the more the feeling will come to you naturally in the future, helping to lower your trait neuroticism.

A further way to alter the basic psychological processes that provide the foundation for neuroticism is to sign up for a course of *therapy*. This might sound like an odd suggestion, but people who take an hour each week to chat with a therapist and reflect on and change their habits of thought are in a sense reshaping their personality.

We don't normally think about therapy in this way; usually the focus is on helping to reduce symptoms or finding inner enlightenment. But recently researchers have started to consider therapy as a form of personality change. For example, in a 2017 paper, Brent Roberts and his team dug up the findings from over 207 psychotherapy trials published between 1959 and 2013, involving more than twenty thousand people, that included before and after measures of the patients' personalities.[18] The team found that just a few weeks of therapy tended to lead to significant and long-lasting changes in patients' personalities, especially reduced neuroticism but also increased extraversion. The reductions in neuroticism were especially impressive, adding up to about half the amount by which the trait normally reduces across an entire lifetime (through the mellowing that is a normal part of getting older).

Cognitive behavioral therapy is one of the most commonly used forms of psychotherapy today. As I mentioned earlier, its focus is on altering a person's negatively biased or unhelpful beliefs and habits of thought. For example, a highly neurotic person might have a tendency to overly focus on criticism or to picture how challenges might go wrong, and CBT will teach him to see the bias in this thinking and correct it.

When researchers examined the effects of just nine weeks of CBT on the personality traits of people with social anxiety, they found it led to reductions in neuroticism and increases in the trust aspect of trait agreeableness.[19] Similarly, after forty sessions of CBT, people with generalized anxiety disorder (a form of chronic anxiety that permeates all aspects of one's life) have been found to show reductions in their neuroticism, as well as increases in their extraversion and agreeableness.[20]

It makes sense that psychotherapy that is targeted at anxious or melancholy ways of thinking should lead to reductions in the trait of neuroticism because personality traits are partly grounded in habits of thought and how we relate to others. You can even think of CBT for mild anxiety and depression as spending time literally learning to make a habit of thinking less like a neurotic person. And when you change your thoughts, it's easier to change your behavioral habits. You start socializing more, make bolder decisions, and live with less fear and angst.

Depending on your socioeconomic or cultural background, starting therapy may seem like an unavailable luxury, or perhaps you see it as a rather drastic intervention suitable only for those who are very unwell. Either way, it's worth bearing in mind the growing evidence for the effectiveness of computerized CBT that you can complete from the comfort of your own home.[21] If you are seeking to lower your own neuroticism scores, it's likely that computerized CBT programs such as Beating the Blues will help by taking you through exercises that offer practice in thinking in ways that foster more emotional stability—for example, by focusing on the aspects of a situation that you can control and considering positive interpretations of past events as much as negative ones.

If seeing a therapist or online therapy aren't your thing, I offer a few tips for thinking in a less neurotic way. (Nevertheless, bear in mind that if you are experiencing significant distress you should seek the help of a suitably qualified mental health professional.) For instance, you could reflect on your relationship with worrying. Research has shown that chronic worriers (which high scorers in neuroticism often are) tend to see worry ultimately as a good thing. This may seem odd given the distress it causes them, but they believe deep down that it can stop bad things from happening. Persistent worriers also tend to be perfectionists in the way they worry, wanting to cover every eventuality. Of course that's impossible, so they end up stuck in an endless worry loop. Psychologists say you can break out of this by simply reminding yourself that it's okay to stop once you've had enough of worrying.

You could also start paying close attention to the way you talk to yourself in your head about upcoming challenges and past mistakes. Especially look out for instances when you hold yourself to impossible standards, making sweeping generalizations, ignoring situational nuances, and using words about yourself like *must* and *should*. Instead try talking to yourself with compassion, more as you would a close relative or friend. People high in neuroticism also tend to have a bias for recalling more negative memories, and to dwell on all the ways that things might go wrong. Recognize this bias and actively address it by deliberately reminiscing about happy memories and past achievements, and set aside time to list the ways that upcoming challenges could go well.

A final activity to lower your trait neuroticism—and a great excuse for traveling—is to try *spending time abroad*. A growing body of research shows that one of the main outcomes of such an experience, especially for young people, is a lowering of neuroticism scores. A few years ago, researchers in Germany assessed more than one thousand university students, some of whom took an extended study trip abroad and others

The Neuroticism Cascade

To stem the cascade, try the following techniques for each stage:

Situation-selection strategy, page 96

Irritability and short temper mean negative experiences are more common through arguments, impatience, and envy

↓

Cognitive reappraisal (this is a chance to learn that the events are not a verdict on you as a person), pages 113, 149

Events are interpreted through "dark glasses" as more catastrophic and personal

↓

Try going for a walk in nature or mindfulness meditation, page 142

The emotional impact is intense and unpleasant

↓

Practice working-memory training to get more control of your thoughts, page 131

The negative effect lingers because of intense rumination and worry

↓

Develop your optimism and practice self-compassion, page 149

Frustration at the repetition of the same bad experiences fuels resentment and low mood

Low mood, low confidence, and pessimism

Psychologists at the University of Iowa believe there is a series of psychological processes—a neuroticism cascade—that traps people high in this trait in a chronic state of negative emotions. Each of the five stages offers opportunities for stemming the cascade using techniques in this book.

who stayed in Germany.[22] They also measured the students' person-alities at the start and end of the year. Unsurprisingly, at the start, the students who planned to travel scored lower on neuroticism on average than those who stayed at home. But even controlling for any differences in initial neuroticism levels, the crucial finding is that by the study's end, students who spent time abroad had experienced greater reduc-tions in their trait neuroticism compared with the students who stayed at home.

By spending time abroad (preferably in a safe, supportive environ-ment), you're giving yourself no option but to deal with uncertainties, new places and people, and new cultures. Although this might be highly challenging, especially if you are fearful by nature, the experience will offer many opportunities for practicing emotional control. On return-ing home, it will be as if your sense of risk and uncertainty has been recalibrated. In personality terms, you will have become less neurotic. Also, many psychologists believe that your personality is relatively stable because it's shaped by the same situations and people you encounter day in and day out. By spending time abroad in an entirely new environ-ment, you give yourself the chance to develop free from the daily forces that usually influence you.

By combining the three foundational principles of willful personal-ity change with these three practical approaches (therapy, travel, and memory training, and the others spread throughout this book), you will give yourself an excellent chance to lower your neuroticism and reap all the benefits associated with being more emotionally stable. And for even more ideas on how to break what some psychologists call the "neu-roticism cascade" see the image on page 135.

Bonus tip: Take a walk! The simple act of putting one foot in front of the other—nothing to do with the effects of fresh air or the purpose of the walk—has been shown to have a beneficial effect on mood even when you don't think it will.[23] Alternatively, take up martial arts. Not only will your new skills give you confidence, research suggests you will develop greater attentional control at a cognitive level, similar to the effect of memory training mentioned on page 131.[24]

Boost Your Conscientiousness

Let's move on to ways to develop more conscientiousness, starting with *finding a job or voluntary role that you find truly meaningful* and to which you are committed. Research shows that feeling personally invested in one's work tends to lead to increases in conscientiousness over time, especially when the demands of the role are transparent.[25] This happens because in a job you love, you're motivated to behave routinely in organized and ambitious ways in pursuit of the aims of the role. This is likely to increase your self-discipline and orderliness if your colleagues and clients reward and reinforce your constructive behavior, setting in motion a virtuous circle that ultimately shifts your trait levels of conscientiousness upward.

Of course, finding a meaningful job is not an easy task. A lot of it may come down to how you think about your job. Studies that have followed workers over many years have found that regardless of the nature of the work, those who see their work as benefiting others are more likely to say that they find it meaningful and important (these people also tend to be happier and more productive in their jobs).[26] So one way to increase your job's meaningfulness, and therefore its chances of boosting your conscientiousness, is to think about how it benefits other people, whether you write Web code that allows people to find the services they want online or you deliver people's mail to their houses. The point is that by seeing the good that you are able to do, you will likely find that your motivation increases and one personal consequence with it is that your conscientiousness is likely to benefit too.

Voluntary roles and constructive hobbies—for example, sitting on the parents' committee at your child's school or on your town's natural resources board—can have a similar influence on your behavior and therefore your conscientiousness. Again there is the challenge of finding a pursuit that means enough to you—a true passion—that it will motivate you to increase your diligence and commitment. Studies of people's passions in life show that you are unlikely to find an activity that fits the bill simply by sitting on your couch and imagining different options. You need to get out in the world and try different endeavors, giving yourself the chance to find a suitable role or activity that may transform your personality for the better. Remember too that it might not be love at first sight. Each time you dabble in a different potential passion, make sure to give it a fair chance to capture your imagination. If you're really stuck for ideas, one catalyst for your imagination could be to take a "career interests" quiz—there are many free examples online.

Another step you can take to boost your conscientiousness is to *practice being savvier about avoiding temptations.* You might think the secret to leading a healthier, more productive (and conscientious) life is iron willpower, but in fact, mounting evidence suggests one secret of people who are adept at resisting temptations is that they avoid them in the first place. Consider the findings of a recent study that asked 159 college students about their four main long-term goals and then surveyed their behavior in detail for a week via random cell phone prompts.[27] Each time their phone went off during the study week, the students had to answer questions such as whether they were currently resisting a temptation and whether they were using their willpower.

When the researchers caught up with the students again at the end of the semester to see which of them had reached their goals (for example, "to learn French"), they found it wasn't the students who had exercised more willpower during the study week; it was those who had faced fewer temptations. The University of Toronto researchers said, "Our results suggest that the path to better self-regulation lies not in increasing self-control, but in removing the temptations available in our environments."

This implies that you can develop your conscientiousness in part by learning strategies to avoid meeting temptation. Diet is a good example. A recent study by Arizona State University found that commuters whose journey featured more food outlets tended to be heavier.[28] Findings like this suggest simply avoiding the route to work that takes you past your favorite bakery or fast-food outlet could help you stay healthier. Similarly, if you find it difficult to resist zoning out on your iPad when you should be sleeping, then make a simple rule: no digital devices in the bedroom. In other words, whether it's technology, fast food, or some other temptation, embrace the idea that you, like most other humans, are weak-willed, and then devise your strategies around that fact. The likely consequence is that you'll become at least a little more conscientious.

Finally, *do your homework!* Okay, so this advice might be coming a little late for many of us, but the same principle applies in adulthood: if you invest greater effort today, be that at work, in your relationships, or in your pastimes, you will come to enjoy the benefits over the longer term, and this will help you develop a more patient, future-oriented mind-set. Researchers showed this recently when they followed thousands of German students over three years. Not only did the students with more conscientiousness put more effort into their homework, but over time, the students who invested more effort into their homework showed subsequent gains in their trait conscientiousness.[29] "Consistent behavioral changes have the potential to lead to persistent changes in students' personality," the researchers said. You could apply the same approach to your hobbies or taking an adult-learning course: apply self-discipline and invest effort today and tomorrow, and soon you will find yourself becoming a more conscientious person. This approach is more likely to be successful if you feel genuinely invested in, and responsible for, what you're doing, and you receive tangible rewards for your hard work over the long term through visible progress or personal feedback (this could come in many forms, from formal exam grades, to creative output, to appreciation from others).

Of course, there's another side to this message from the homework research: if you're a manager, teacher, or parent, there are things you can do to encourage conscientiousness in your staff, pupils, or kids. Be authoritative, but also consistent, warm, and supportive (conscientiousness is more likely to develop when people like and admire their superiors); help individuals understand the link between overcoming today's challenges and obtaining longer-term goals; and provide support during failure. The aim is to convey the message that effort is rewarded; ensure people know what to do to succeed (for example, by having clearly defined roles) and feel ownership and responsibility for their efforts. And above all, try to create an ethos in which success is measured over years, not just days or weeks.

> *Bonus tip:* You can't always avoid temptation, and sometimes you'll have no option but to rely on raw willpower to be more conscientious. In this respect, how you think about willpower could be key, especially whether you see it as a limited resource. I mentioned earlier that in India, challenging tasks are widely seen

as energizing, not tiring. In this context, psychologists have documented what they call "reverse ego-depletion"—the finding that performing one mentally taxing task actually boosted people's performance on a subsequent task, opposite of what's predicted by ego depletion theory, which sees willpower as finite, like the gas in your car. This suggests you should try to think about your willpower as bountiful and unlimited—doing so could help you stay focused for longer.

Changes in Openness

The most obvious approaches to increasing your trait openness are likely to be the most effective. Research that has followed the same people over a number of years has found that spending more time on cultural activities leads to subsequent increases in openness. If you can get yourself into that explorative, experimental mind-set (it could be a willingness to read more books, go to more plays, learn an instrument, take up a new sport, or whatever else), the fact is, this is likely to manifest in your developing a more open-minded personality.

One less obvious way to increase your receptivity to new ideas and to beauty and culture is to *spend time completing puzzles, such as crosswords and sudoku,* which involve what psychologists call inductive reasoning. A recent study involved older participants (age sixty to ninety-four) undertaking a couple of training sessions in strategies for solving crosswords and number puzzles, and then completing home-based puzzles that were continually adjusted to their skill level for an average of eleven hours per week for sixteen weeks. The participants enrolled in this program displayed lasting increases in their trait openness as compared with a control group who didn't complete the training or puzzles.[30] It's likely this benefit arose at least in part by changing how the volunteers felt about themselves intellectually, and you could use mental puzzles and games to your benefit in the same way. Confidence is key to openness because being an open-minded person is about being willing and brave enough to consider different perspectives, new places, and different experiences.

Another surprising activity you can try to boost your openness is *spending time browsing your photo collections or personal movies from years past, or reminiscing with friends about shared memories.* Engaging in nostalgic reverie in this way has been linked to increased creativity (including an ability to write more original and imaginative prose) specifically because it leads to increases in trait openness.[31] The theory is that reminiscing about meaningful past events, especially those featuring encounters with close friends and relatives, can have a range of emotional benefits, including boosting self-esteem. Consequently, this helps us feel more optimistic and engenders a greater willingness to engage with the world and new experiences. Again, this is another example of where confidence can help to foster greater creativity and openness.

Finally, *taking up regular exercise*, such as gym visits or daily walks, is a way to increase, or at least maintain, your openness. When researchers tracked thousands of people over age fifty for several years, they found that those who were more physically active tended to maintain their openness rather than displaying the declines with age some of their peers experienced.[32] The theory is similar to the rationale for completing regular mental puzzles or reminiscing about happy times with friends: being more physically active helps foster confidence and a willingness to try out new things. Developing a more active lifestyle could in fact be one of the simplest steps toward improving your personality.

A related suggestion is to try taking an "awe walk"—that is, walking with the mind-set of a child or first-time visitor, looking for the wonder in all that you see and hear (for example, by paying attention to the staggering variety of patterns in the leaves on the trees; listening to birdsong; or appreciating the local architecture). Awe is known to boost intellectual humility, which in turn will increase your openness.

> *Bonus tip:* If you need some extra motivation, bear in mind that becoming more open-minded could change how you see the world, quite literally. Psychologists recently studied how openness related to people's experience of what's known as binocular rivalry, which is when one visual pattern is presented to one eye and another pattern to the other eye. Usually the subjective experience is to perceive one image, then the other, fluctuating back and forth. Occasionally the two patterns are experienced as mixed together, and research shows that the higher you score in openness, the more time you are likely to see the two patterns merged, suggesting that this personality trait manifests at a very basic level of visual perception.[33]

Increase Your Agreeableness

What about methods for helping yourself become friendlier, warmer, and more trusting—in other words, more agreeable?[34] Preliminary research suggests that an important route to better understanding others is to first *increase how much you understand yourself.*

Researchers in Germany recently outlined a technique for doing this that involved spending time reflecting on the different parts of one's personality, such as "the caring part," "the inner happy child," or "the vulnerable part," and also contemplating one's own thoughts from a detached perspective and allocating them to categories including me/other, past/future, or positive/negative. This was a three-month-long program, and there was also a perspective-taking component for which participants needed a partner (the participants took turns speaking as one part of their personality and their partner had to guess which part), so there's some serious time investment here. However, the researchers found that the more parts of their selves the participants were able to identify (interestingly, especially negative parts), the greater improvement they showed in their empathy skills over the course of the program.[35] This actually fits neuroscience research, showing overlap in the brain areas we use for thinking about ourselves and thinking about others. You may not be able or willing to invest quite so much time as these participants did, but nevertheless there's an important principle to heed: if you want to get better at understanding others, start with better understanding yourself, warts and all.

Another activity to try for boosting empathy is *mindfulness*. Several studies have shown that short courses of mindfulness meditation training—for example, spending thirty minutes a day for a few weeks paying attention in a nonjudgmental manner to the content of one's current thoughts—is associated with gains in empathy.[36] One reason that mindfulness has this benefit is that it teaches you to be observant of your own mental experiences in a nonjudgmental manner, with the side effect that you will become more attentive to other people's concerns in a similarly nonjudgmental fashion (the apps Headspace and Calm are a great way to get started with mindfulness).

You could also make an effort to *read more literary fiction*. Reading complex novels with multilayered characters requires perspective taking and consideration of people's emotions and motives, just the skills you need for getting better at real-life empathy and increasing your agreeableness. Perhaps it's little wonder that several studies have shown that even a short amount of time reading literary fiction seems to have immediate benefits for empathy-related skills, such as identifying others' emotions.[37] This finding of short-term gains hasn't always been successfully replicated, but another study confirmed the principle in a different way: volunteers who were more knowledgeable about novelists (a proxy for having read more literary fiction) also tended to be better at recognizing others' emotions and scored higher on an empathy questionnaire, again suggesting that fiction really does help develop our empathy.[38] There's even neuroscience evidence suggesting the same conclusion: five days spent reading *Pompeii: A Novel* by Robert Harris in the evening was found to alter connectivity patterns in the brain, including in areas involved in taking other's perspectives.[39]

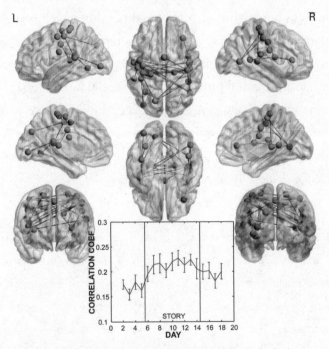

A brain scan study published in 2013 uncovered connections in the brain that were strengthened during and after reading *Pompeii: A Novel,* by Robert Harris on days six through fourteen. These changes might represent the neural basis for the increases in empathy (and greater trait agreeableness) associated with reading literary fiction. Source: *Reproduced from Gregory S. Berns, Kristina Blaine, Michael J. Prietula, and Brandon E. Pye, "Short- and Long-Term Effects of a Novel on Connectivity in the Brain," Brain Connectivity 3, no. 6 (2013): 590–600.*

Finally, try *spending quality time with "outsiders"*—people from a different culture or ethnicity than yourself. For instance, you could join a sports club that you know has ethnic minority members. When psychologists in Italy tested hundreds of high school students twice a year, they found that those who'd spent more high-quality (friendly, cooperative) time with immigrant students through the year also tended to show increases in their agreeableness trait by the end of the study compared with students who didn't have this experience.[40]

It's human nature to be less trusting of people with whom you are unfamiliar, and it's likely that the experience of spending quality time with people from an unfamiliar background teaches us to be more trusting, as well as honing our own social skills, all of which will combine to boost our agreeableness. "Positive intergroup contact experiences may remind an individual that contact is valuable, aiding the development of social skills and broadening one's social horizons," the Italian researchers said. Once again, neuroscience findings have backed up these conclusions. After people have had positive experiences with outsiders, their brains show greater empathy-related activity in response to the sight of outsiders in distress.[41]

> *Bonus tip:* A key characteristic of highly agreeable people is that they tend to be very slow to get angry. This means that getting more control of your own temper is likely to help you become more agreeable. There are many effective anger-management techniques, but perhaps the best evidenced is self-distancing, which means stepping outside the situation. When you feel your temper rising, pause a moment and imagine looking at the situation as if from the perspective of a fly on the wall. Research suggests that doing this has a calming effect and reduces aggression.

Heighten Your Extraversion

Last but not least, what activities and tricks can you use to become more extraverted? One rather radical approach is to *learn to speak a language that has extravert connotations.*[42] When you speak a second language, you acquire some of the personality characteristics that are considered stereotypical of the culture from which that language originates. This has been demonstrated in the case of native Chinese speakers conversing in English, presumably because they see the stereotypical American as more extraverted than is typical in their culture. English speakers could consider learning a language like Portuguese or Italian to adopt the outgoing stereotypes associated with Brazilian or Italian cultures.

Even in your own language, you could try speaking more like an extravert. Extraverts tend to speak in language that is looser and more abstract; for instance, they'll say, "That film was great!" in contrast to introverts, who will make more specific concrete observations, such as, "The plot was very clever." Similarly extraverts are more direct—"Let's grab a drink"—unlike introverts, who might more cautiously say, "Maybe we should try going out for a drink." It's as if extraverts speak with an element of risk and casualness that reflects their approach to life. Adopt the extravert's style, and over time, you may find that doing so rubs off on your personality, even if only a little.

Use if-then implementation plans. Perhaps more than any of the other main personality traits, extraversion and introversion are shaped by habit. If you are used to spending most of your time by yourself, then going to a party will be a shock to the system, potentially making it a nerve-rackingly uncomfortable experience. However, it's a basic fact of human nature that you adapt to what you are used to. Therefore, a simple way to become more extraverted is to habituate yourself to more stimulating environments, in a sense recalibrating your baseline arousal levels. A highly effective way to build new habits is to make explicit if-then implementation plans, such as, "If I am sitting next to a stranger on a train, I will make at least one effort to engage in conversation."

Putting new sociable habits into practice will be easier if you pair up with a gregarious friend or partner. In fact, research with young people finds that following their first romantic relationship, they show gains in extraversion, no doubt related to opportunities to meet new friends and the boost in confidence that comes from being a "we."

Another obvious but easy-to-neglect approach for increasing your extraversion is to do whatever works for you in terms of increasing your confidence. There are some specific psychological tricks you could try, like power posing: this involves you adopting a stance like a superhero with hands on hips and feet spread apart (the idea is to take up as much space as possible). It's a technique that's been ridiculed in some quarters, partly as a reaction to how much the concept has been hyped and also because some studies have failed to replicate some of its supposed effects. But crucially, even the "unsuccessful" studies have all generally found that power posing makes people feel more confident. This could be just the edge you need before heading out to a party or meeting up with a new friend, and that might just nudge you along the extraversion dimension a little.

Of course, if power posing seems ridiculous to you, don't do it. Like an athlete, perhaps try a trusted ritual instead, such as buttoning up your shirt in a particular order.[43] Plenty of research has shown that rituals can boost your confidence even if you know deep down that there's no real logic to what you're doing.[44] The details are not that important. What's crucial is that you increase your optimism that things might go well, a key aspect to extraverts' approach to life. When they go out, they expect to have a good time and they leave themselves open to more opportunities to have fun. Here's a quick fact to help you on your way:

researchers discovered recently that when we act in a more extraverted way (such as being socially confident and talking more energetically), the people we're conversing with are more likely to respond to us in a positive fashion, smiling more and becoming more talkative, thus setting up a welcome feedback loop.[45]

Relatedly, you could *practice trying to be more optimistic*. A recent analysis of twenty-nine studies found that the most effective way to do this is the so-called Best Possible Self intervention, which involves spending half an hour or so "imagining yourself in the future, after everything has gone as well as it possibly could. You have worked hard and succeeded at accomplishing all the goals of your life . . ."[46] Perform this thought experiment regularly, and over time you may find you are more willing to get out and have more fun.

Finally, practice *anxious reappraisal*.[47] Introverts who experience physical sensations that extraverts seek out, like a racing heart and the pulse of adrenaline, find these to be overwhelming and aversive. But introverts will find they can enjoy these sensations more—and so become bolder and less averse to risk—by learning to interpret them as signs of excitement rather than anxiety. Performing this cognitive trick (for example, by telling yourself, "I am excited"[48]) is actually easier than trying to calm yourself down, and in the long run, if you succeed in learning to find challenging situations more enjoyable, you will likely begin to seek them out. You will be becoming more extraverted!

Bonus tip: Especially if you are a strong introvert, you may find your initial attempts to behave in an extraverted fashion exhausting, leading you to grow demoralized. Take heart: research suggests that even extraverts find that extraverted behavior like socializing leaves them feeling tired afterward.[49] Nevertheless, in the moment, acting extraverted has a mood-boosting effect for everyone, introverted and extraverted.[50] Sleepy but happy; that's a good place to be.

BUT WHAT ABOUT AUTHENTICITY OR "BEING TRUE TO YOURSELF"?

The success of books like Susan Cain's *Quiet*, which celebrates the strengths and needs of being an introvert "in a world that can't stop talking," shows how strongly people feel that it is important to stay true to who they are rather than changing themselves to somehow better fit the demands of an unaccepting world. As you contemplate deliberately changing your personality, an understandable concern you might have is whether by doing so, you are somehow being fake or not true to yourself. How do you square these two apparently contradictory ideals—the commonly felt urge to change and the widespread desire to be authentic?

For one thing, setting out to change your personality doesn't have to be an ambition for wholesale metamorphosis. Even quite subtle adjustments to your character could pay dividends. Also, you might wish to accentuate your current traits rather than reverse them. Perhaps you're already more conscientious than average, for example, and wish to build on this strength. You can also take reassurance from research that has followed people for several months and found those who wish for a different personality, and manage to achieve that change, end up happier in the long run.[51]

There is also the question of what it really means to "be authentic." There's evidence that feelings of authenticity are likely to arise when you behave like your ideal self—that is, the kind of person you aspire to be.[52] This suggests that if a shy businessman who wishes to be more extraverted can muster the courage to attend a cocktail party and succeeds in being even modestly sociable, he will enjoy feelings of being true to himself. Similarly, research with couples has found that most important to relationship satisfaction is being with someone who brings out the best in you, helping you to become the person you want to be.[53] Other research has found that feelings of authenticity are brought about not so much through channeling some kind of mythical "true self" but, regardless of our traits, through behaving in ways that make us feel happy and good about ourselves, supporting what the psychologists call the "feeling good=feeling authentic" hypothesis.[54]

Always remember that you are more than your personality traits. You are defined also by your goals and your values and by the people who matter the most to you. It is when you succeed in meeting these goals, living in accord with your values and interacting positively with meaningful others, that you are likely to experience rewarding feelings of being true to yourself—all of which can be aided by the right kind of purposeful personality change.[55]

Recalling the experiences of Matt, the introvert turned extravert I met at college, I think this perspective on authenticity matches his story. In a sense, his true self when I met him fit the description of a strong introvert. But this disposition was making him unhappy, especially because it was thwarting his powerful, authentic desire to forge meaningful relationships. By setting in motion the process of becoming more of an extravert, he found it easier to fulfill the sense of belonging that he craved and that he felt was fundamental to his identity. The new, more garrulous Matt was arguably just as real as the old; it's just that now, his personality was more in sync with his values and goals.

If you want to be different, that aspiration is a valid part of what makes you "you," and satisfying your desire for change is being true to yourself. Moreover, "being authentic" often depends more on what you're doing and who you're with rather than being some kind of permanent achievement. If changing your personality helps you to spend more of your time with the people you want to be with, doing the things you want to do, then changing yourself is going to bring you closer to the real you.

Chapter 6

REDEMPTION

When Bad People Turn Good

As a teenager, Maajid Nawaz's morning routine involved strapping a large knife to his back. That blade was in his hand during a fatal confrontation between Muslim and African students outside the gates of London's Newham College in 1995, which culminated in the murder of a young Nigerian man. Although Nawaz did not hurt anyone himself, he confessed in his 2012 memoir, *Radical*, that he "stood there and watched Ayotunde Obanubi die."[1] Nawaz was a "blindly committed" member of Hizb ut-Tahrir, an organization that aims to create a Muslim caliphate under which everyone must live according to sharia law, meaning, among other things, death to all homosexuals.

Nawaz's support for extreme ideology and his permanently on-the-verge-of-violence lifestyle hadn't come out of nowhere. It was a response to the rampant racism targeted at him and his British Asian friends growing up in Essex, England, in the 1980s and 1990s. Still, if you'd met him at the time of the Newham College murder and listened to his views, you would likely have formed the impression that Nawaz was a dangerous individual with an antisocial personality. This was a young man who as a graffiti artist got a thrill out of evading the authorities. "It was two fingers to the police and law and order," he recalls in *Radical*. This was a man whose own mother at one time thumped her stomach in disgust, wailing, "I curse the womb who gave me such a son."

After the fight outside Newham College, Nawaz compounded the tragedy by traveling with other Muslim gang members to African neighborhoods with the explicit aim of terrorizing other students. In *Radical*, he admitted, "Such a cold-blooded response to the murder of another individual was part and parcel of the person that I'd become."

A sympathizer with the 9/11 terrorists, Nawaz's radical activism set many impressionable youths on the path to violent jihadism. He would travel to Pakistan to foment a military coup there, then later to Egypt, where he was arrested in 2002 by the country's secret police. He spent years in prison. The incarceration would change him profoundly, although not before he made a characteristic vow to unleash deadly revenge on his enemies: "I will kill as many of you as possible before you take me," he fantasized during an initial three-month spell in solitary confinement.

Today Nawaz is a drastically different person. A leading campaigner against radical Islam, he cofounded the anti-extremism group Quilliam and has been feted by, among others, former president George W. Bush and former British prime minister David Cameron. In his many media appearances, articles, and books, Nawaz advocates for compassion over anger and a perspective that recognizes the shared humanity of "the other," whoever they may be.[2]

How did Nawaz achieve this transformation from would-be terrorist to peace activist? It certainly wasn't easy: "Piece by piece I had to reconstruct my entire personality from inside out," he writes in *Radical*. But there are some obvious turning points, themes, and influences, many of which have echoes in other people's stories of redemption.

Education was the first turning point. Nawaz used his jail time to consume enormous amounts of literature—not only Islamic texts but classics of English literature like *Animal Farm* and works by Tolkien. "This combination of rehumanization [rediscovering an empathy for and connection with others], studying Islam from its sources and grappling with moral complexity through literature, affected me in profound ways," he writes. In personality trait terms, Nawaz increased markedly in openness and agreeability.

Aside from education, another major influence on Nawaz's transformation was his experience of being treated with compassion by others. While he was imprisoned in Egypt, Amnesty International categorized him as a prisoner of conscience (someone locked up purely for his beliefs) and campaigned vigorously for his release. Whereas the racism and violence he experienced early in life led Nawaz to feel dehumanized and desensitized him, he says that the compassion that Amnesty showed him had a rehumanizing effect. "I am, in part, the person I am today because of their decision to campaign for me," he says in his memoir.

The final transformative factor for Nawaz was a new purpose in life. He came to see that both Islamophobes and Islamists are the enemies of human rights. He set himself the challenge of forging a new movement to provide a counternarrative, a project that would eventually culminate in 2008 in his cofounding with Ed Husain (also a reformed Islamist radical) of Quilliam, which describes itself as "the world's first counter-extremism organization."[3]

As much as Nawaz's own efforts and motivations, social forces also shaped who he became. Some of his previous allies in Hizb ut-Tahrir unwittingly pushed him away from radicalism. They betrayed him in their own interests, allowing Nawaz to see them for who they really were—not selfless servants of Islam, but selfish, ambitious egotists.

Nawaz's story provides a vivid demonstration of some of the ideas put forward by psychologist Brian Little, who has extensively researched the significance of personal projects to personality development. Essentially, these projects are what you are trying to achieve in life. Little says that if you are driven enough to succeed in the initiatives that mean the most to you, they can change your traits (even if only in key moments) in ways that help you achieve your goals.

In the case of Nawaz, his new purpose may not so much have entirely changed his traits (other than the heightening of his agreeableness and openness) but definitely rechanneled his traits along a more positive path. It's clear that some of the strong extraversion and conscientiousness that once served his radicalism, including his passion and drive and people skills, have since been deployed in his work for Quilliam. "I am nothing if I cannot strive for something," he writes in his memoir. What he calls the "romanticism of struggle," which once propelled him to extremism, remains ever alive in his heart, he says, but is now fueling his peaceful aims.

Your calling in life may not be as grandiose as countering the world's extremism, but if you are interested in changing yourself, it pays to consider how you are shaped by your principal aims and ambitions. They can shape your personality directly and provide the context through which your traits express themselves. If you want to become a better person, you can get closer to achieving this by carefully choosing what goals to prioritize in life. One practical way to do this is by performing a brief reflective exercise that US psychologist Brian Little calls "personal project analysis," as follows:[4]

Exercise: Reflect on Your Main Goals and Callings in Life

- Write down everything you are currently trying to achieve—from getting a new job, to learning to meditate, trying to be a better friend, raising money for charity, promoting a social cause, or losing weight.

- Zoom in on the two or three goals that matter the most to you and are most meaningful. Now make some notes on each one. Are they bringing you joy? Have they come from your own interests and values rather than being imposed on you by others? Do you feel that you're progressing? Are you striving for these goals with others (rather than entirely by yourself)? The more times you answered yes to these questions, the more likely you are to be happy in life.[5]

- If you have identified any goals that don't mean much to you, were imposed on you by others, don't match your values, or are causing you significant stress and frustration, it is worth considering dropping them.

- Alternatively, if you've identified goals that mean a huge amount to you yet you feel you aren't progressing, it's likely these could be causing you unhappiness. You could try reframing these to make them less daunting and less vague (for example, reframe the goal of "Try to write a book" to become "Try to write for half an hour each day"), or you could think about whether you need more support, training, or personal development (using some of the strategies in this book to make changes to your traits could help you on your way).

- If you are interested in personal change, including finding personal redemption, it is important to consider whether your core personal projects are the best way to apply your personality strengths and whether they are likely to be shaping your personality in the ways that you desire. If you strive to be more open-minded, for instance, a core project that involves little experimentation, adventure, challenge, or culture is unlikely to be beneficial. If you wish to be more agreeable, a project that causes you frustration and resentment, that is ultimately selfish, or that upsets others, is bound to be counterproductive.

- If after completing this exercise, you feel you need a new aim in life, don't just introspect about it. Instead, expose yourself to as many possible interests, ideas, social issues, subjects, and activities as possible. Experiment and talk to other people—especially those you feel share your values—about what gets them fired up each day. Passions rarely grab us in one magical eureka moment, so take your time.

OTHER STORIES OF REDEMPTION

The power of passions or callings to shape people's personalities recurs in many stories of redemption. Consider the life of Catra Corbett, who first encountered trouble with the law after shoplifting as a young teenager in California. She went on to become a meth addict and small-time dealer in early adulthood. In her recent autobiography, *Reborn on the Run*, she describes how addiction took over her life, leading her to repeatedly hurt the people she cared about most: "I rarely saw my own family then. I did my mother's hair once a month, and she would suggest that we go to lunch. I would agree to it, and then I would either forget about it, or more often, I just wouldn't show up."[6] Her life as an addict hit its nadir when she was arrested for dealing and she spent a terrifying night in jail. "This is not me," she thought that night. "I really wasn't a bad person. . . . Something had to change."

The problem at first was that Corbett didn't know how to change, and, while she managed to stay off drugs, she didn't have what she calls the "mental tools" to be healthy. From Corbett's own description of her lifestyle, it's highly likely that she was a strong extravert: she had previously had many friends, liked partying, and was lured by the thrill and highs of drugs. To turn her life around, she needed a way to satisfy her extravert nature *and* to combine that with increased conscientiousness to bring greater restraint and order to her life.

As with Nawaz, education played an important part in Corbett's rebuilding of her personality. She went back to her former school and received the diploma she'd failed to obtain as a delinquent teenager. But even more transformative for Corbett was her fortuitous discovery of running. Not too long after her jail experience and getting off drugs, one day—almost at random and perhaps inspired by her much-missed late father who had encouraged her to play sports as a girl—she put on some sneakers and went on an unplanned run with her dog. "I ran around the block, feeling as if I wanted to die. By the time I was done, I felt overheated and exhausted. I plopped down on the front steps and took another deep breath. I felt good. *Wow*, I thought. *I ran the entire way, without walking, or stopping, or any breaks at all. I ran. I ran. I actually ran.* I felt so good, I decided right then that I would become a runner."

For a time, Corbett needed psychological support to overcome an eating disorder (aside from extraversion, part of her vulnerability to addiction and mental health problems likely stems from high trait neuroticism). Eventually her passion for running transformed her personality and her life. Today Corbett is one of the world's foremost ultrarunners; in fact, she is a member of a select club of just four individuals in the world to have run 100 miles in excess of 100 times.[7]

Running came to provide her with an outlet for her extraverted nature ("completing marathons gave me the same kind of elation that the drugs gave me, except running was improving my life, not fucking it up"), and once she fully embraced the sport and set herself progressively tougher challenges, from marathons up to ultra-long-distance trails, it gave her life the structure she needed to boost her trait conscientiousness and calm her emotional instability—a perfect real-life example of the social investment theory that I described in chapter 2. "I was always training for something," she says in her autobiography. "I had a plan for my life. I had what I needed."

A particular advantage of having personal projects like running is that it makes it easy to exploit the *motivating power of milestones*. When you're confronted with an overwhelming challenge, whether it's learning a new language or finding redemption, the struggle to make any apparent progress can be demoralizing. With running and similar activities, it's easy to chart your progress (in terms of distances, like your first 5K or half marathon, and the times you run them in) and to reward yourself for these new achievements, which is powerfully motivating. As the business scholars Chip Heath and Dan Heath explain in *The Power of Moments*, "Milestones define moments that are conquerable and worth conquering," and in doing so they help us "push to the finish line."[8]

With enough imagination and dedication, it may be possible to take this approach regardless of the nature of your goals—for instance, through keeping a diary to note any achievements you've made, no matter how small. In the case of a specific aim like learning a language or a more lofty ambition like finding redemption, for example, it could be making note of the first time that you managed to order a meal in Spanish or the first time that you did someone a favor for purely altruistic reasons. Recording this progress and rewarding yourself can also help to stimulate another power motivator, authentic pride, which, unlike hubristic pride, is based on being pleased with yourself for the fruits of your hard work. Authentic pride feels good, and once you get a taste of it, you will want more, helping to propel you further toward your goals.

As a child and wayward teenager growing up in Pennsylvania, Nick Yarris had what he calls an "impulse control disorder." After trying his first beer at age ten, he never looked back. By the time he was fourteen, he was drinking and using drugs every day. His first arrest came the following year, for stealing, in order to service his growing drug habit. Yarris's life fully derailed in 1981 when, at age twenty, he was pulled over by a traffic officer for running a red light. According to Yarris's account in his memoir *The Fear of 13*, the officer handled him roughly, they had a tussle, and the officer's gun discharged accidentally.[9] This shocked Yarris into surrendering, but the officer was resentful. After the fracas was over, the officer radioed in for backup, bellowing, "Shots fired!" This unleashed a chain of events leading to Yarris being accused of the attempted murder of the officer.

As if matters couldn't get worse, Yarris next concocted a ruse to turn the situation in his favor, claiming that he knew the culprit behind a locally unsolved murder. This scheme backfired, and Yarris himself ended up charged with not only the attempted murder of the officer but also the rape and murder of a local woman. In the ensuing trial, he was found guilty and would go on to endure the most horrific experiences during twenty-two years on death row for a crime he didn't commit.

You might imagine such a life would turn a petty criminal with antisocial tendencies into a vengeful monster. In fact, today Yarris is a role model of decency and humanity. In 2017, he self-published *The Kindness Approach*, in which he shows how to rechannel resentment and anger into forgiveness and compassion.[10]

How did Yarris achieve this transformation? Some of the themes in his story echo those of Nawaz and Corbett: he rebuilt his life in jail, using his addictive personality to educate himself, and to campaign relentlessly, eventually overturning his wrongful conviction. In so doing, Yarris became the first death row prisoner in Pennsylvania to be proven innocent through DNA testing.

The drive to prove his innocence became Yarris's new calling, which helped structure his redemptive personality change. Even after his release, he successfully directed his energy and passion toward living a life of kindness, in part inspired by his mother, who told him his hard-won freedom meant he had a duty to be polite and respectful. This motherly advice struck a chord: "Each day, I have worked so hard to be super-positive and have thrown so much upbeat energy and kindness that I have managed to totally reshape my outlook and approach to life," he writes in *The Fear of 13*.

OBSTACLES TO REDEMPTION

The three stories of redemption—of Nawaz, Corbett, and Yarris—share the same key features: transformative experiences (e.g., going to jail), self-education, a new calling, and the inspiration and encouragement provided by others.

Do these stories mean there is hope for change for people whom society may view as "bad": criminals, cheats, and con artists? Sadly, the reality for many such people is that they do not have the instinct, or the desire, to turn themselves around. Also, prison often does not provide a positive experience that fosters beneficial change; often the opposite is true. It is not realistic for prison authorities to serve up magical transformative moments or influential friends and relatives.

Probably the biggest stumbling block to change, though, is that many offenders do not want to change and see no reason to try. Many criminals have counterproductive habits of thought that allow them to justify their actions and increase their likelihood of offending again in the future.

This idea that criminals have a characteristic way of thinking goes back at least as far as the 1990s and the development by clinical psychologist Glenn Walters of an influential test, the Psychological Inventory of Criminal Thinking Styles—PICTS, for short. It asks people to rate their agreement or disagreement with eighty statements, like those that follow:[11]

Do You Think Like a Criminal?

	Agree	Disagree
I sometimes see or hear things that others can't.		
There is nothing wrong with the way that I behave.		
Society is unfair, and my circumstances leave me no other option than to commit crime.		
I use alcohol to make it easier to break the rules.		
I've been punished enough in the past. I deserve a break.		
Not having control makes me feel uncomfortable; I prefer to have power over others.		
I've avoided getting caught in the past. I'll probably get away with doing what I want in the future.		
I procrastinate a lot.		
I often flake on my social arrangements so I can get high or commit crimes.		

The statements are intended to tap different dimensions of criminal thinking, including (from first to last) confusion, defensiveness, mollification (justifying bad behavior), cutting off guilt and other feelings (using drink and drugs to make it feel easier to commit crimes), entitlement, power orientation, superoptimism, indolence, and discontinuity (an inability to follow through with plans). If you found yourself agreeing with a lot of the statements in the table, the implication is that you have tendencies to think the way a criminal does. But be assured that the full test is much longer and more in-depth, and the results would always be interpreted in the context of a person's background and actual behavior.

Once people with a criminal personality and style of thought end up incarcerated, aspects of the prison environment can unfortunately compound matters by having adverse effects on their personality: the chronic loss of free choice, lack of privacy, daily stigma, frequent fear, the need to wear a constant mask of invulnerability and emotional flat-ness (to avoid exploitation by others), and the requirement, day after day, to follow externally imposed stringent rules and routines. Indeed, long-term imprisonment leads to "fundamental changes in the self," according to interviews with hundreds of prisoners by researchers at the Institute of Criminology at the University of Cambridge.[12] Some experts call this profound personality adaptation to prison life "prisonization."[13]

Even a short stay in prison can have consequences for personality. In 2018, Dutch psychologists tested thirty-seven prisoners twice, three months apart. At the second test, the prisoners showed increased im-pulsivity and poorer attentional control—changes indicative of reduced conscientiousness, which the researchers attributed to the loss of au-tonomy and cognitive challenge in prison.[14]

Adverse personality changes can also linger on after release as a postincarceration syndrome, making it difficult for former prison in-mates to fit back into normal society. In interviews with twenty-five peo-ple in Boston who had served life sentences, psychologists found they had developed various "institutionalized personality traits," especially an inability to trust others (a key feature of low trait agreeability), akin to experiencing a perpetual paranoia.[15]

But there are glimmers of hope that, as in the stories of Corbett, Nawaz, and others, aspects of the prison experience can sometimes also have beneficial effects on personality. For example, a Swedish study from 2017, one of the few to apply the Big Five model to prisoner per-sonality change, compared the personality profiles of maximum secu-rity prisoners with various control groups, including college students and prison guards. While the prisoners scored lower on extraversion, openness, and agreeableness, as you might expect, they actually scored higher on conscientiousness, especially the subtraits of orderliness and self-discipline.[16] The researchers think this could be a form of positive adjustment to an environment with strict rules and regulations, with prisoners gaining in conscientiousness as a way to avoid getting into trouble.

Former prisoners like Nawaz and Yarris who succeeded in using their prison time to rebuild their personalities in beneficial ways seem to have managed to make the most of these positive influences, while containing or minimizing the harmful effects of the prison environment. They also addressed their own criminal thinking styles, in large part through self-education.

Fortunately, there is some evidence that structured rehabilitation programs, such as the Cognitive Self Change intervention, can have a similar effect through encouraging offenders to reflect on and confront the thoughts and beliefs that underlie their criminality, such as believing that life is unfair and so it is justified to harm others, or that it is the fault of others if they leave valuable possessions on display or unprotected.[17] These programs also teach life skills and basic behaviors (such as punctuality and courteousness) to help people deal with issues like relationship problems, stress, and debt in more constructive ways that don't involve resorting to crime (and in so doing, increase offenders' trait conscientiousness and agreeability and lower their scores on the PICTS measure of criminal thinking).[18]

"Time and again I've seen real change happen," Jack Bush, one of the founders of the Cognitive Self Change intervention, told NPR in 2016.[19] Bush gives the example of a lifelong criminal he'd known called Ken, who at one time aimed to be "the baddest criminal anybody had ever seen." However, through the Cognitive Self Change program, he came to recognize how his criminality was rooted in his habits of thought. He later told Bush this led him to develop a new goal: to be an honorable man. "The 20-plus years since his release from prison have been hard, but he's a taxpaying citizen—and an honorable man," Bush said.

A slightly different approach taken by other rehab programs is to target prisoners' distorted moral compass. When people with antisocial personalities are confronted with moral dilemmas, they tend to take a "utilitarian" perspective[20]–that is, they weigh things up in a calculating fashion without feeling, justifying the committing of crimes based on what they consider logical grounds.[21] One of the best-known rehabilitation programs to target morality, moral reconation therapy, uses CBT principles to try to develop offenders' moral sense—for instance, by encouraging greater consideration of consequences, challenging immoral beliefs and thoughts, and teaching more advanced principles of morality.[22]

When it comes to helping prisoners change their personalities for the better, there is plenty of reason for optimism, but it would be a mistake to be complacent. Some well-meaning interventions, including many boot camps based on strict rules and harsh physical activity, have proven harmful. The most infamous example is probably the Cambridge-Somerville Youth Study that was started in 1939 in towns around Boston in which delinquent youths were paired with adult mentors who were meant to take a kind interest in them and encourage their positive personality development. In fact, compared to a control group, those in the intervention showed poorer outcomes, including greater criminality (there are several theories for why this happened, including the delinquent peers in the intervention group leading each other astray).[23] These disappointing outcomes are a reminder that while positive personality change is possible, it is not straightforward or easy. It is not enough to rely on good intentions and plausible-sounding programs; rather it is vital that evidence-based approaches are used.

Perhaps the biggest obstacle to rehabilitation is that many offenders aren't motivated to change and refuse to start programs or soon drop out of them. They don't have any desire to change, and without that, there is little hope. To confront this challenge full on, one pioneering nonprofit program, the Turning Leaf Project in Charleston, South Carolina, has recently taken the unusual approach of paying former offenders $150 a week to participate in daily three-hour CBT classes that target their criminal ways of thinking, until they've notched up at least 150 hours. Despite the payments, only around 35 percent of participants complete the program, but on the plus side, *Vice* magazine reports that so far, no former graduates have been rearrested.[24]

Unaddressed mental health problems are yet another factor that hinders the reform of offenders.[25] Depression, for instance, is around three times more prevalent among prisoners than the general population. Suicide risk is three times higher among male prisoners, and nine times higher among female prisoners, than the general public. Without appropriate therapy or other support, such problems are likely to have an adverse effect on prisoners' personalities and attempts at reform.

Also directly relevant to the chances for successful personality change is the difference between whether offenders have an "antisocial personality disorder"[26]—that is, their criminal habits of thought and behavior are considered a form of mental disorder: extremely serious and enduring but ultimately treatable[27]—or if they instead have a more extreme psychopathic personality, which many believe is not treatable or changeable, although this is controversial.[28]

Although upward of 40 percent of prisoners are considered to have an antisocial personality disorder, far fewer are psychopaths. And whereas all psychopaths have an antisocial personality disorder, the converse is not true.[29] (I cover psychopaths in much more detail in the next chapter.)

On balance, the many personal stories of redemption—from Nawaz, Corbett, Yarris, and others like them—combined with the findings from the research literature on offender rehabilitation, present a hopeful message—one that is consistent with the overarching argument of this book: that personality is malleable. With the right attitude, sufficient motivation, and support from others, some bad people can achieve meaningful, positive change, including individuals with a history of criminality and a reputation for hurting others. Education is often key, as is finding a profound calling or purpose in life that fosters positive personality change and sustains people's journey into the light.

WHEN GOOD PEOPLE TURN BAD

Sadly there are also many tales of heroes transforming into monsters, molesters, robbers, and cheats. Consider the story of Lance Gunderson, who, from his humble roots, raised by a single mother, would go on to survive testicular cancer that had spread to his lungs, stomach, and brain, and become the victor of an unprecedented run of seven Tour de France races and founder of the Live Strong cancer charity that has raised hundreds of millions of dollars for cancer patients. Lance's story of triumph over adversity would inspire a generation, prompting *Forbes* to call him a kind of "secular Jesus."[30] And yet Lance, who later took the surname Armstrong from his mother's second husband, would later admit (following a lengthy investigation by the United States Anti-Doping Agency) to cheating his way to all his cycling titles. Dubbed a "cyclopath" by the *Sunday Times*,[31] Armstrong is accused not only of gross cheating but also of lying and bullying through his many years of denial.[32]

Politics provides similar tales of celebrated individuals, apparent paragons of integrity, turned dirty and corrupt. Think of the onetime US vice presidential nominee, former senator John Edwards, seen as the morally virtuous golden boy of the Democratic Party. He had an extramarital affair while his wife was sick with cancer and lied and

168

schemed to cover up the scandal. Or former congressman Anthony Weiner, the "brash and brilliant" (to quote the *Times of London*) rising political star whose wedding was presided over by President Bill Clinton and was formerly imprisoned for sending lewd images of himself to a fifteen-year-old girl.[33]

What about sporting legend and actor OJ Simpson, infamously accused of murdering his wife and her friend and later imprisoned for armed robbery and kidnapping? Then there's Rolf Harris, the once much-loved Australian children's entertainer, who in 2014 was sentenced to jail for sexually assaulting teenage fans. And perhaps most disturbing of all, the story of Jimmy Saville, the British TV and radio personality, who in life was canonized for his children's entertainment and charity work (he reportedly raised tens of millions of dollars through his philanthropy) but was posthumously accused of assaulting and raping hundreds of victims, including multiple children.

It makes for vivid storytelling to think about these biographies as depicting good people turned evil, like the character Walter White from the TV series *Breaking Bad*, who metamorphoses from hard-working chemistry teacher to ruthless narcotics criminal and murderer. Yet reality is rarely as black-and-white as fiction. While the stories of Armstrong, Saville, Edwards, and others are all depressing tragedies of human weakness and cruelty, it's not clear that they reflect simple or straightforward transformations of personality. In many instances, while the revelations about the dark sides of these celebrity cases were a sudden shock, they had in fact been engaging in wrongdoing for years, often alongside their virtuous and celebrated acts.

Rather than a dramatic personality change, then, it is plausibly the very same traits that propelled these characters' successes—the single-minded determination; you might even call it the arrogance—that in corrupted form facilitated their crimes and transgressions, be that having the gall and guile to lie and cheat or the selfishness and craving to pursue sexual gratification and power. After all, if the fallen celebrities had had nicer, more pliable, easygoing, and selfless personalities in the first place (in trait terms, if they had been higher scorers in agreeability), they would have been unlikely to reach their heights of success and power. So rather than seeing these sorry tales as examples of dramatic personality change, it may be more accurate to see them as examples of people with strong, achievement-oriented traits being diverted by catastrophic lapses of judgment or willpower (facilitated by low, or temporarily diminished, trait conscientiousness), which then spiraled out of control.

In fact, the very idea of purely good people turning entirely bad is an oversimplification because, as humans, we all face a daily battle— between our short-term impulses, our baser desires, on the one hand, and our loftier morals and long-term aspirations on the other. Reflect honestly on your own life, and even if you consider yourself a morally good person most of the time, you will probably be able to recall occasions that you are not so proud of. The last time you received a commendation at work, perhaps you also remembered with a pang of guilt that you got the job by gilding your résumé. As your spouse looked in your eyes and thanked you for your love and support last night, maybe you cringed inside at the way you flirted with your colleague the day before.

For the fallen celebrity and political superstars, the same battles are played out, but in a more dramatic and exaggerated form and in the public eye. Their talents and ambition elevated them onto a pedestal, but these same dizzying heights came with greater temptation— unbridled access to money, drink, drugs, and sex and the chance to bully, seduce, and manipulate suggestible fans and others for short-term gratification or in pursuit of ever-greater success.

Relevant here is evidence that having power over others can lead us to dehumanize them—seeing other people as tools to be manipulated rather than as flesh-and-blood individuals with feelings. Psychologists speculate that in some contexts, such an effect is adaptive—for example, helping political leaders make seemingly impossible decisions that involve weighing the lives of one group against another or giving surgeons the psychological distance they need to slice into another's flesh.

But this still raises the question of why Saville and others committed their abuses over so many years. If they were truly good people, why did they not get themselves back on track? It seems likely that their personalities and morals became corrupted by toxic ways of thinking as they justified their actions to themselves in a similar fashion to how more mundane criminals use warped logic and justifications to explain away and excuse their actions. For instance, having suffered and toiled to achieve their success (and in many cases, having been celebrated for their years of selfless, altruistic efforts), many of these failed celebrities probably told themselves that they had somehow earned the right to satisfy their more carnal desires and increasingly selfish dreams.

You may have practiced this kind of "self-licensing" in a more mundane way—like when you grant yourself a glass of wine after a particularly stressful day at work or you allow yourself to break the muffin ban after a grueling trip to the gym. Imagine this writ large for these once golden individuals who perhaps reasoned with themselves that they had given so many years of their lives for their sport or their art and so they deserved some kind of freedom or payback.

In their book *Out of Character*, psychologists David DeSteno and Piercarlo Valdesolo speculate that self-licensing may have been behind another of the most notorious falls from grace, this one involving the former governor of New York, Eliot Spitzer.[34] A "paragon of moral hypocrisy," Spitzer had campaigned tirelessly against corruption and prostitution, including tightening antiprostitution laws and increasing the severity of charges for using escort services. Scandal hit when he was found to be a regular client of the Emperor's Club, a now-defunct VIP escort agency based in New York City. Self-licensing "may have been partially at play in Spitzer's decisions to indulge himself," write DeSteno and Valdesolo. "After all, didn't all his victories against the scourge of corruption give him license on some level to enjoy himself in an unsavory act now and again?"

The more everyday transformations of people who once seemed so virtuous likely feature the same or similar processes: lapses of self-control and subsequent self-justifications. Think of the dedicated family man who runs off with a younger colleague (and who convinces himself that it is his turn to have some selfish fun), or the honest, hardworking employee who, after getting snubbed for a promotion, begins skimming profits from her company (and then uses her sense of injustice to convince herself it is her due).

When powerful emotions like lust and resentment cause us to act out of character, the repercussions can sometimes lead to more lasting change, especially if there's an effect on your circumstances, priorities, and perspectives. Unforgiven by his spouse, the cheating husband leaves his family and his job and moves away with his mistress, evolving into a less agreeable and less conscientious person, leading to further adverse consequences for his other relationships. The snubbed employee ends up unemployed and grows increasingly bitter, isolated, and demoralized, becoming less extraverted and conscientious in the process, leading to a downward spiral in her career.

Whenever you succumb to temptation and feel your character changing for the worse—cheating at work, say, or pursuing your own pleasures at others' expense—you could heed a lesson from the more infamous tales of disgrace. Often it is the lying to yourself, all the rationalizing and self-serving self-talk, that sustains the fall, followed by the attempts to cover up and justify what you've done. To break that cycle, it is better to admit your mistakes. That honest acknowledgment is the first step toward making amends and planning ahead to try to prevent yourself from lapsing again. In that respect, an important approach is to consider the redemption stories of Nawaz, Corbett, and others and think about how your traits and ambitions could be channeled and satisfied via more constructive outlets.

Many of the stories of fallen celebrities begin with the former hero giving in to temptation in pursuit of sex, power, or greater success. However, there is another form of temptation that can turn good people bad. It's more cerebral and philosophical: people are corrupted by dangerous ideologies, leading them toward extremism. In a way, this is a case of people taking on personal projects that corrupt their morals in a mirror opposite to the uplifting stories of Nawaz and Corbett. Toxic ideologies, beliefs, or ambitions can corrupt people's traits, diminishing their agreeability, openness, and extraversion.

Most of the psychological theories for how people come to be politically or religiously radicalized explain such apparently disturbing shifts in character not as the emergence of some previously hidden psychopathy or as due to an underlying mental illness (there is little evidence that violent radicals are more likely to be mental ill), but as beginning with a change in perspective and loyalty. Usually it is exposure to a seductive new worldview and group identity that speaks to their feelings of grievance and injustice and leads them toward dark and misguided solutions.

So even with once "normal" people who become violent extremists, it's not that a switch is flicked that turns these people from good to bad. Rather, they are tempted down a dark path that they are convinced is morally justified based on some higher aims. A radical preacher may tell them that they must commit violent acts for the greater good of their people, for instance. In such cases, the alteration in mind-set and beliefs comes first. The personality change follows as these individuals become increasingly radicalized, allowing them to justify their increasingly violent and criminal behavior.

Plausibly, the most effective way to steer these individuals away from radicalization is not to start by correcting their unwelcome personality change, but by confronting their distorted beliefs and, some would argue, addressing the social injustices that allowed these beliefs to take root. Recent reinterpretations of some of psychology's most infamous experiments support this idea that when previously good people begin behaving badly, this apparent change in character stems not from the emergence of some kind of latent evil but from their belief that their morally bad behavior is serving a greater purpose.[35]

I've argued that apparently trustworthy, altruistic people can turn bad. Usually it doesn't begin with a transformation in personality, but with one or more initial lapses of judgment or willpower that lead to self-justifications, evasions, and further harmful ripple effects. It can also follow a profound change in outlook, beliefs, and priorities that poison his or her morality and lead to adopting a criminal thinking style and justifying bad acts for some kind of higher cause or out of twisted feelings of entitlement.

Of course, that needn't be the end of the story. If bad people can turn good, there's no reason why some good people who have turned bad can't turn good again. Just look at the reinvention of Tiger Woods.

I outlined in chapter 1 how some psychologists believe that the Big Five traits do not cover the full spectrum of personality and that there is also a dark triad of antisocial traits: narcissism, Machiavellianism, and psychopathy. Perhaps many of our fallen icons harbored these dark traits all along. In fact, they may have contributed to some of their successes before eventually leading them to trouble. The disgraced politician John Edwards, for instance, blamed his transgressions on his narcissism, telling ABC News, "[My experiences] fed a self-focus, an egotism, a narcissism that leads you to believe you can do whatever you want. You're invincible. And there will be no consequences."[36]

Many commentators have similarly labeled the failed sporting icon Lance Armstrong a narcissist, and others have gone further and speculated, on the basis of his years of bullying and lying and his continued self-justifications even after confessing to his cheating, that he may be a psychopath.[37]

In the next chapter, I explore the dark traits in more detail, including looking at whether people with these traits can be rehabilitated and whether we can learn anything useful from their approach to the world without ourselves going over to the dark side.

Ten Actionable Steps to Change Your Personality

To reduce neuroticism	Avoid negative self-talk, which is characterized by black-and-white thinking (e.g., seeing your interview performance as totally awful); exhorting yourself to achieve impossible standards (e.g., to always be honest or witty); and involves overgeneralization (e.g., scolding yourself for being an all-around bad mother because you made a single mistake). Challenge these thinking patterns and aim to speak to yourself with more compassion.	Reflect on the purpose of negative emotions and what they are telling you. For instance, guilt and shame motivate you to be better; sadness can sharpen your attention to detail and provide a blissful contrast for when you come to experience joy. Research suggests that people who enjoy better mental and physical health don't necessarily experience fewer negative emotions, but they are more accepting of them.
To increase extraversion	Meetup.com is an app where people advertise local events they're organizing and invite others to join in. Download the app, and commit to joining one event that appeals to you this coming week. If you're feeling confident, you could progress to organizing your own event and inviting others along. For an alternative, try Eatwith.com—a platform that allows you to enjoy sociable gourmet experiences in hosts' houses.	Habituate yourself to adrenaline and excitement through competitive sports and games or through exciting books, film, and theater. Introverts are more sensitive to such things, but if you get used to a higher level of stimulation through fun activities, you will find social events and other extravert adventures less of a challenge.

Ten Actionable Steps to Change Your Personality *(continued)*

To increase conscientiousness	Social media and nonstop smartphone notifications can put a massive drain on your productivity. Take advantage of available apps, such as Freedom or SelfControl, to create periods of focus. For instance, they allow you to disconnect yourself from the Internet for a set amount of time. Also, create simple rules for yourself, such as that you will check email only once every two hours.	If you want to live a more orderly and self-disciplined life, it often helps to begin with the basics. For instance, start taking more care over your appearance, and you will feel more in control and focused. There is even a phenomenon called "enclothed cognition" that suggests the clothes you wear can affect your mind-set. By dressing smartly, you will begin to feel and act more professional.
To increase agreeability	If you are in a leadership role, concern yourself less with exerting dominance over your subordinates and focus instead on their needs, how you can support them, and the example that you are setting. This is the transformational or prestige-based approach to leadership (as opposed to transactional and dominance-based), and your followers will come to respect you for it.	For the week ahead, be more strategic about the situations you place yourself in, the company you keep, and the media you expose yourself to. Research suggests that one reason highly agreeable people are warm and friendly is that they avoid exposing themselves to conflict and negativity.
To increase openness	Spend time every week completing puzzles like crosswords and sudoku. This will help build your intellectual confidence, which will encourage you to embrace new ideas and seek out new knowledge.	Keep physically active by building regular exercise into your routine—at least two to three times a week if possible. Being confident in your physical abilities will encourage you to try out new activities and visit new places.

Chapter 7

LESSONS FROM
THE DARK SIDE

On September 20, 2017, one of the most powerful Atlantic storms ever recorded made landfall at Puerto Rico. With winds in excess of 100 mph and torrential rain, Hurricane Maria wiped out entire neighborhoods, with a Harvard study published the next year estimating the disaster was responsible for up to eight thousand deaths, including through indirect means, such as loss of medical services.[1]

And yet on October 4, when then US president Donald J. Trump visited Puerto Rico, he told victims they should be "very proud" they hadn't endured "a real catastrophe like Katrina." "What is your death count as of this moment?" he asked. "Seventeen? Sixteen people certified, sixteen people versus in the thousands."[2] At another event in San Juan, he was filmed smiling and throwing paper towels like party gifts into the crowd. Many were shocked by the president's apparent lack of tact and empathy. Whatever his motives, he seemed unaware that his choice of gestures and words might upset the victims. The mayor of

179

San Juan, Carmen Yulín Cruz, described the towel-throwing incident as "terrible and abominable."[3]

Trump's difficulty with empathy became a pattern during his presidency. Shortly after Hurricane Maria, more controversy ensued when he was accused of failing to telephone the families of four US Special Forces soldiers slain in an ambush in Niger. When the former president did make one of those calls, he was again criticized for displaying a lack of empathy, allegedly telling the widow of Sergeant La David Johnson that "he knew what he signed up for" and struggling to remember his name.[4]

We can't read the former president's mind and it's certainly plausible that he did not intend to cause any offense (defending his boss, the White House chief of staff, John Kelly, a four-star marine general, said that he had advised Trump to mention that the fallen had been doing what they loved).[5] However, from a personality perspective, it's not just empathy that Trump struggles with. When he defended himself against the media's criticisms, he also adopted his characteristic style and manner—a toxic mix of self-aggrandizement, extreme sensitivity, and the belligerent derogation of others.

Given how often he behaves this way, many psychologists and psychiatrists believe Trump has a highly "narcissistic personality."[6] The term is borrowed from a figure of Greek mythology, Narcissus, who fell in love with his own reflection. A narcissistic personality is associated with a lack of empathy for others, combined with outward bravura and grandiosity that together conceal a deeply rooted insecurity.

Narcissism is one of the dark triad of personality traits, the others being Machiavellianism and psychopathy. The dark triad traits are related to the Big Five traits and, like them, are made up of more specific characteristics or subtraits—see the table on page 182. Indeed, some experts are skeptical that it is really necessary to invoke another three traits to capture the essence of human personality. Others propose the addition of just one more trait to the Big Five, known as the H-factor, or "Honesty-Humility," low scores on which they say encompass the dark triad.

In this chapter, I address the underlying psychology of narcissists and psychopaths. We will look at what lessons, if any, we can take from people who manage to succeed in life through their darker characters (Trump, after all, succeeded in becoming a US president) and whether it's possible for people with these trait profiles to change.

I'll say a brief word about Machiavellianism, a trait that's named after the sixteenth-century Italian politician Niccolò Machiavelli, who believed that the ends always justify the means, including lying and treachery. To put it bluntly, people who score high on this trait are manipulative, dishonest, selfish jerks; they agree with quiz statements like, "There's a sucker born every minute," and "Make sure your plans benefit you and not others." Both narcissists and psychopaths tend to score very high on Machiavellianism.[7] In fact, some experts question whether it's really a separate trait at all.[8] For that reason, I won't explore Machiavellianism any further and will focus instead on the narcissists and psychopaths in our midst.

ARE YOU A NARCISSIST?

On average, men are more often narcissistic than women. Narcissists take more selfies and are also more likely to follow other narcissists on social media.[9] In terms of the main five personality traits that you took the test for in chapter 1, narcissism tends to go hand in hand with a combination of high extraversion and low agreeableness (see table on following page).

The Dark Triad and Their Relation to the Big Five

	Subtraits	Links with the Big Five Traits
Narcissism	Entitlement, vanity, belief in one's own leadership skills, exhibitionism, grandiosity, manipulativeness	Low agreeableness, high extraversion
Machiavellianism	Cynical worldview, manipulativeness, desire for control, lack of empathy	Low agreeableness, low conscientiousness
Psychopathy	Superficial charm, fearless dominance, lack of empathy, impulsivity, criminality	Low neuroticism, low agreeableness, low conscientiousness, high extraversion

Think back: Did you tend to skip class at college (similarly, do you regularly shirk off work today)? Do you swear a lot and use a lot of sexual language? If so, these could be signs that you are a narcissist. These were the everyday behaviors that correlated with students' narcissism when their behavior was monitored by audio recorder for four days. The psychological explanation is that narcissists are more likely to skip class or work because of their sense of entitlement, and they use more sexual language because they tend to be more promiscuous.[10]

Even the way you present yourself can be revealing. One study found that male narcissists were more likely to wear neat, flashy clothes, and female narcissists were more likely to wear makeup and show their cleavage.[11] Having a huge signature is apparently another give-away.[12] So too is having thick, bushy eyebrows.[13] Admittedly, these are rather crude signs that are likely to miscategorize a lot of people! To be more scientific, a short narcissism questionnaire follows.[14] Rate your agreement as honestly as possible after each statement, from 1, Strongly Disagree, to 5, Strongly Agree. Jot down a 3 if you neither agree nor disagree:

People see me as a natural leader.   _____

I love being the center of attention.   _____

Many group activities tend to be dull without me.   _____

I know that I am special because everyone keeps telling me so.   _____

I like to get acquainted with important people.   _____

I enjoy it if someone compliments me.   _____

I have been compared to famous people.   _____

I am a gifted person.   _____

I insist on getting the respect I deserve.   _____

Total: _____

Add up your scores for each item and divide by 9. How narcissistic are you? For a sense of what's a normal score, you can compare your number against the average number of 2.8 obtained by hundreds of undergraduates when they completed the test. (There's an argument to be had about how normal undergrads are, but let's put that to one side.) If you scored a little bit above or below the students' average, that's unexceptional, but if you scored above 3.7, then you're probably more narcissistic than most others. If you scored above 4.5, well, let's put it this way: I'm impressed you're reading this book rather than gazing in the mirror or posting yet another selfie on Instagram!

What about the people around you? When it comes to that boastful buddy of yours or your grandiose sister, if you suspect they might be narcissistic but wouldn't bet on your chances of getting them to take the test, you could try asking them just one question: "To what extent do you agree with this statement: 'I am a narcissist.'?" (Note that the word *narcissist* means egotistical, self-focused, and vain.) Research with thousands of people has shown that their strength of agreement with this single statement correlates highly with their total score on a comprehensive narcissism questionnaire featuring forty items.[15]

In other words, if you want to know if someone is a narcissist, try asking that person straight-out. Most narcissists are actually pretty unashamed, nay, proud, of the fact they are a narcissist, perhaps because it's yet another way for them to claim that they are somehow special. (Note that the question asks, "Are you a narcissist?" not "Are you narcissistic?" The former makes it more likely that a potential narcissist will answer honestly, based on the opportunity to sign up to a special identity rather than admitting to a description, "narcissistic," which they may recognize as a barely concealed dig.)

THE PROS AND CONS OF NARCISSISM

People will disagree about the advantages or otherwise of having Trump become president. Less controversial is that he provides a highly visible and dramatic case study of a narcissistic personality in action, including its costs and benefits. The indisputable fact that Trump reached the highest office in the world, not to mention his stellar TV career and ability to create an image of huge business success, suggests this personality type must have some upsides. Perhaps the most obvious is that narcissists like him are ready and willing to promote themselves, even at the expense of others.

Consider how at a press conference held on October 16, 2017, shortly after the furor over his telephone calls (or lack thereof) to the families of deceased soldiers, Trump quickly went on the attack, claiming falsely that President Obama and other presidents had failed to call the families of the stricken. A few days later, he told the press, "I am a very intelligent person. . . . Everybody [i.e., the families contacted by reporters] has said unbelievable good things about me." He added, "Nobody has more respect than I do," and, pointing to his head and describing it as "one of the great memories of all time," he further claimed it was inconceivable that he had forgotten the name of La David John-son.[16] The message running through these and many other Trump ut-terances is that he is special, flawless, and better than anyone else at almost everything (research shows that narcissists frequently overesti-mate their abilities and performances).

Before beginning his presidency and describing himself in the third person as is often his style, he told *New York Times* journalist Mark Leibovich that empathy, the very trait that critics say he most lacks, "will be one of the strongest things about Trump."[17] And in an interview broadcast on Trinity Broadcasting shortly after he visited Puerto Rico in the wake of Hurricane Maria, Trump boasted about the reception he received: "There was a crowd and they were screaming and loving everything. . . . I was having fun, they were having fun . . . the cheering was incredible, it was deafening . . . there was love for the fact I went there."[18] The media criticisms, Trump claimed, were "fake news," add-ing that this is "one of the greatest of all terms I've come up with."

Trump watchers will know that this is often the way that the presi-dent responds to criticism: he attacks his critics and then seeks to sell what he sees as his own incredible abilities and prowess. Like a textbook narcissist, almost every Trump utterance betrays an obsession with the self, especially the desire to be special.

His presidency began in this very style with an argument over the size of his inauguration crowd,[19] which Trump claimed, despite evidence to the contrary, was the "biggest in the history of inaugural speeches."[20] When he was challenged by the British interviewer Piers Morgan in 2018 about his retweets of a British far-right group, Trump responded not just that he is not racist but that "I am the least racist person that anybody's ever going to meet."[21]

Other grandiose Trump claims include: "No one respects women more than me" (stated after video footage emerged of him making lewd remarks about women);[22] "Nobody's ever been more successful than me"; "Nobody knows more about taxes than me, maybe in the history of the world"; and "I can be more presidential than anybody."

Trump's narcissistic style arguably reached its peak in January 2018 when excerpts had been published from the forthcoming book *Fire and Fury* by Michael Wolff, which contained unflattering accounts of life inside Trump's White House, subsequently raising concerns about the president's mental state. In response, Trump began by derogating the book, tweeting that "Michael Wolff is a total loser who made up stories in order to sell this really boring and untruthful book." Next, in his usual style, Trump switched to self-aggrandizement, tweeting that his two greatest assets in life had been "mental stability and being, like, really smart." He was, he immediately clarified, "not smart ... but genius and a very stable genius at that." Such overt self-promotion runs counter to many people's ideas of decent behavior, especially for the president, but moral judgments aside, research suggests that narcissists often benefit from their swagger, at least initially.

Consistent with Trump's story, narcissists are more likely than others to emerge as leaders, and at first, they tend to be well liked.[23] British researchers found this when they asked students to fill out personality questionnaires and then to perform group problem-solving tasks together weekly for twelve weeks, rating each other periodically throughout the study. The more narcissistic students were rated by others as especially good group leaders at first. Crucially, though, their appeal waned dramatically over time.[24] The researchers said narcissistic leaders are like chocolate cake: "The first bite of chocolate cake is usually rich in flavor and texture, and extremely gratifying. After a while, however, the richness of this flavor makes one feel increasingly nauseous. Being led by a narcissist could be a similar experience."

The idea that narcissists make a good first impression, at least in some contexts, has also shown up in studies of heterosexual speed dating, in which narcissists are frequently rated as more attractive than nonnarcissists.[25] In the case of narcissistic men, this seems to be because they are seen as sociable and outgoing, which is appealing in a speed-dating context. Narcissistic women are considered more physically attractive, perhaps because they take more care over their appearance and dress more provocatively.

Among friends too, narcissists start off by making a splash. A three-month study into popularity among groups of first-year college students found that the narcissistic students were rated as popular at the beginning, but by the end of the study, their friends had grown sick of them.[26]

Other narcissistic advantages include great persistence, especially if success at a challenge provides the only available opportunity for glory.[27] (Imagine a job in sales where the only metric the boss is interested in is profit, driving the narcissist to hit those targets.) Similarly, narcissists can show great determination to prove others wrong after receiving negative feedback.[28] Their bravado and overt self-belief also seem to help them sell their ideas.[29] No doubt this helped Trump immensely on the campaign trail. In fact, during the Republican primaries for the 2016 election, all the media wanted to talk about was Trump, to the great cost of his rivals.

A clear lesson we can take from narcissists is that there are benefits to acting outgoing and confident when first making your mark, be that in a dating context or starting out as a leader. There are also important moments in life when it's appropriate and beneficial to drop the humility and sell your ideas and achievements with confidence. A problem with narcissists is that they often do this at other people's expense and they don't know when to stop.

To seize the narcissist's advantage without going over to the dark side, you could set a long-term plan to increase your trait extraversion without reducing your trait agreeableness (follow the steps in chapter 5). More specifically, try promoting yourself by making favorable comparisons against your past self rather than against other people (for instance, tell your boss, "I'm much better at this than I used to be"). Or make simple, self-flattering statements that don't involve derogating others (tell an interviewer, "I'm a good teacher," rather than, "I'm better at teaching than my colleagues are"). Another self-promotional strategy is to use a wingman: get a supportive friend or colleague to showcase your achievements.

There's also nothing wrong with patting yourself on the back for your achievements; pride can be incredibly motivating (and a lack of pride can indicate that you're pursuing the wrong goals in life). But a useful and important distinction to recognize is between what psychologists call "hubristic pride" and "authentic pride," also discussed in chapter 6. Narcissists tend to go for the former variety, which is about celebrating what they see as inherently special about themselves. For example, they might claim that their great feedback from customers and clients is due to the fact that they are so charming and charismatic. Former president Trump often makes these kinds of claims, boasting about qualities that are an inherent, innate part of who he is, including his great genes. By contrast, authentic pride is based on recognition of the work and effort we put in. For example, you tell yourself and others that you got great client feedback because you worked exhaustively to provide a good service.

Meanwhile, one strategy to definitely avoid is the humble brag—concealing a boast within a superficial complaint—such as, "Darn it, all my clothes are so baggy since I started this diet and exercise program." Research suggests that these kinds of statements are seen as boasts, and not very effective ones, so you lose on all fronts, seeming neither modest nor impressive.[30]

However, beyond recognizing the importance of making a strong first impression and having the courage to self-promote and take pride when it's appropriate, there's little else to recommend from the narcissists' approach to life. Not only does their appeal wane quickly, but they also have deeply seated problems.

Common sense would suggest that if you have to keep shouting your own greatness from the rooftops, maybe you aren't as confident and sure of yourself as you would like others to think. For example, after President Trump tweeted that he was a "stable genius" early in 2018, journalist Dan Rather tweeted, "Dear Mr. President, A good rule of thumb is that when you've got it, you don't have to say it. People know." Indeed, this idea that a lot of the time narcissism conceals underlying insecurity has been supported by numerous studies. Some experts distinguish "vulnerable narcissism" from so-called grandiose narcissism, which supposedly lacks such inner fragility, but the distinction is disputed.

Consider a cunning experiment that involved volunteers pressing particular computer keys as fast as possible in response to different word categories. The narcissists in the group were extra fast to respond when the same key was allocated for responding to words pertaining to the self (such as *me/myself/I*) and words with a negative connotation (such as *agony* and *death*). This speedy responding indicated that the self and negativity were associated in the narcissists' minds; in other words, they seemed to have a subconscious self-loathing.[31]

Neuroscience supports this interpretation. When researchers scanned the brains of highly narcissistic men while they looked at photographs of themselves, they found that unlike nonnarcissists, they exhibited patterns of neural activity consistent with negative emotion rather than pleasure.[32] In another study, showing how narcissists crave social approval, researchers led teenage boys who scored high on a narcissism questionnaire to believe they'd been rejected by the other players in a video game. The narcissistic teens said they couldn't care less, and yet a scan of their brains taken at the time showed heightened activity in regions known to be associated with emotional pain, more so than seen in the brains of nonnarcissist teens who had been rejected.[33]

All of this suggests that narcissists may talk the talk, but underneath their bravado, they suffer from neediness and self-doubt. This fragile vanity may explain why, following Trump's official medical exam in 2018, he was said to weigh in precisely one pound under the number that would make him formally obese. Film director James Gunn led the skeptics' charge, also known as the #girthers movement, by offering $100,000 to a charity of Trump's choice if he got on a set of scales in public.

Unsurprisingly, there's evidence that this way of relating to the world comes at a cost. One study that tracked volunteers for six months found that the narcissists among them tended to experience more stressful events like relationship problems and poor health.[34] To make matters worse, narcissists also show a heightened physiological reaction to stress, also consistent with the idea that despite their braggadocio, they are thin-skinned and vulnerable.[35]

Looking at how Trump cavorted on the world stage as US president, it may be hard to believe this picture applies to him, but note that according to his biographer, Harry Hurt, Trump spoke of suicide earlier in his life when he used to be more open about his self-doubt. And a former White House deputy chief of staff said of Trump, "He just fundamentally needs to be liked so badly that . . . everything is a struggle for him."[36] Trump's vulnerable side is perhaps best summed up by political columnist Matthew d'Ancona, who refers to him as "snowflake in chief."[37]

The notion that narcissism backfires in the long run applies as much to other political leaders. A study conducted of forty-two US presidents up to George W. Bush found that the higher their narcissism (according to expert ratings), the greater the likelihood was that they had been accused of unethical behavior in office and/or that they had faced impeachment proceedings.[38] Similarly, businesses with a narcissistic CEO are more likely to be subjected to lawsuits, and when this happens, the legal battles tend to be more protracted, partly because of the narcissistic CEO's overconfidence and reluctance to seek help from experts.[39]

DIALING DOWN THE SUPERFICIAL SELF-LOVE

Given the drawbacks to being a narcissist, can you do anything to help yourself or others to become less narcissistic? The good news is that narcissistic traits tend to fade naturally between young adulthood and middle age.[40] To take a more proactive approach in more extreme cases, perhaps the most important target is the narcissist's lack of empathy because this is the reason narcissists lack guilt for their actions and why they show an unwillingness to apologize.[41]

Fortunately, preliminary evidence suggests narcissists are not incapable of empathy. Rather, they lack the motivation or the spontaneous ability to empathize. One relevant study measured students' responses to a video that showed a woman, Susan, describing her traumatic experiences of domestic abuse.[42] As you'd expect, when the researchers didn't intervene, they found that the narcissistic participants showed a lack of empathy toward Susan. They said they didn't care too much about what had happened to her; she had brought things on herself to an extent, and at a physiological level, their heart rates didn't increase in response to her distress.

Crucially, some of the students were given specific instructions before the video, encouraging them to try to empathize with Susan: "Imagine how Susan feels. Try to take her perspective in the video, imagining how she is feeling about what is happening." The narcissists subsequently reported feeling more normal empathy toward Susan, and they showed a normal physiological reaction to her distress (the same as nonnarcissists did). "Although it appears that narcissists' low empathy is relatively automatic and reflected at a physiological level," the researchers concluded that "there is potential for change."

This is promising because when it comes to dealing with the narcissists in your own life (or if you have narcissistic tendencies yourself), it suggests that there is hope. By encouraging narcissists to take other people's perspectives, we can help decrease their selfishness. You could also try encouraging narcissists you know to take up some of the activities that I listed in chapter 5 as ways to increase their trait agreeableness, such as reading more literary fiction or practicing mindfulness, both of which help to boost empathy.

A related approach is to remind narcissists of their social belonging and obligations—how they are not operating in isolation but are part of a larger group, be that their family and friends or a team at work. Psychologists call this a "communal focus," and it's a mind-set that can be triggered by asking leading questions like these: "What makes you similar to your friends and family?" and "What do your friends and family expect you to do in the future?" Adopting a communal mind-set helps to reduce narcissistic tendencies, increasing empathy for others' suffering and making people less interested in fame or personal glory. Encouraging communal thinking in narcissists might similarly help to dial down their self-obsession and boost their empathy.

The second target for helping to reduce narcissism is the narcissist's deeply rooted insecurities and craving for recognition. An effective way to reduce their "look at me" antics is to help heal their inner fragility— no small task. Because narcissists typically act in such a vain, boastful manner, often the last thing we want to do is fuel their apparent self-love.

I've had firsthand experience of this. A narcissist I used to work with is fascinated with himself and takes every opportunity for self-promotion. He begins almost every conversation, every piece of writing, talking about himself, using rehearsed jokes and quips to attract attention and laughs. They seem spontaneous at first, but spend a day with him and you soon see how he operates from a script. The reflex, the temptation, is to bring people like this down a peg or two. But actually I learned that praising this guy and making it clear that I recognized his achievements helped to reduce his narcissistic tendencies and smooth relations.

ARE YOU A PSYCHOPATH?

Narcissists are tiresome and difficult to deal with, but narcissism is just one of the so-called three dark triad traits. Even more troubling than narcissists are high scorers in psychopathy. These folk have ice running through their veins, and in the worst cases, they are the stuff of nightmares. Even so, there may be some lessons we can take from their approach to life.

Rurik Jutting had a privileged upbringing. He grew up in a fairy-tale cottage in a leafy village in Surrey, England. He attended a prestigious private school, Winchester College, where a friend from those days remembers him as "just so normal. He [Jutting] had a sense of humor—he was very sharp, very bright, and perceptive."[43] Then he went to study history at Cambridge University, where he became a rower and secretary of the history society.

After Cambridge, Jutting began a high-flying career in finance, which saw him rise to become a banking whiz for Merrill Lynch in Hong Kong, earning around $700,000 a year. It was at his apartment in Hong Kong that in October 2014, in a cocaine-fueled frenzy, Jutting filmed himself brutally torturing, raping, and murdering two young

Indonesian women. Sentencing Rurik in 2016, the Hong Kong judge described him as "sadistic and psychopathic," and he warned the British authorities (Jutting's defense team were hoping to have him transferred back to the United Kingdom to spend his jail time there) not to fall for his "superficial charm."[44]

Their appearance on the surface as highly competent and charming is one of the hallmarks of psychopaths. As psychologist Kevin Dutton writes in *The Wisdom of Psychopaths*, "If there is one thing that psychopaths have in common, it's the consummate ability to pass themselves off as normal everyday folk, while behind the facade—the brutal brilliant disguise—beats the refrigerated heart of a ruthless, glacial predator."[45] For this reason, one of the pioneers in the field, Hervey Cleckley, titled his 1941 book on psychopaths *The Mask of Sanity*.[46]

This veil of normality, mixed with outward confidence, is a theme in accounts of people who knew Jutting before his ghastly crime. A friend from his university days described him as "incredibly bright . . . rather attractive," with "a sort of controlled poise and a certain understated smugness, a sort of 'superior' air, but lightly worn."[47]

Alongside superficial charm, psychopathy is associated with three features that psychologists call "self-centered impulsivity" (cheating, lying, and generally being selfish and impetuous), "fearless dominance" (extreme confidence and a love of risk and adventure, combined with a lack of anxiety), and "coldheartedness" (a lack of emotion).

Consistent with these key characteristics, studies suggest that psychopaths are particularly drawn to reward (this extreme form of extraversion matches Jutting's playboy lifestyle of drink, drugs, and women). They also have extraordinary calmness and low anxiety, including a lack of related emotions such as shame and guilt; in other words, they are extremely low in neuroticism, which is why they, like Jutting, often excel in high-stress environments like stock trading. And while psychopaths are often perfectly capable of reading people's emotions, they don't seem to feel other people's fear or pain. As Dutton puts it, "They get the words, but not the music, of emotion."

All this manifests at a neural level: the brains of psychopaths literally show less reaction to the sight of other people in pain.[48] They also have shrunken amygdalae, a pair of structures in the brain involved in emotions like fear.[49] In psychological jargon, psychopaths are capable of "cognitive empathy" (they are competent at taking other people's perspectives), but they lack "affective empathy" (which is the precise opposite of autistic people, who *feel* for others but often struggle to see things from their point of view).

Jutting, a charming, fast-living sadistic murderer, fits the Hollywood-based stereotype of what we usually think of when we imagine a psychopath (picture Dexter or Hannibal Lecter). In reality, this pathological, criminal variety of psychopath is relatively rare. What's fascinating, and somewhat disturbing, though, is that psychologists are coming to realize that certain aspects of the psychopathic personality profile manifest in many people but without the violence and criminality. These "successful psychopaths" (other terms are "high-functioning" or "subclinical" psychopaths) have the same charm, cool calmness, and ruthless determination. They also have high levels of self-control and self-discipline and are not usually physically aggressive. In scientific jargon, they typically score extremely high on fearless dominance but low, or at normal levels, on self-centered impulsivity. For a good fictional example, picture the ruthless financier Gordon "greed is good" Gekko from the 1987 movie *Wall Street*.

So what about you? Are you a psychopath reading this book as just another way to get ahead? Perhaps you've come across a supposed test of psychopathy on the Internet that goes something like this: *At her mother's funeral, a woman falls in love with a man there who she'd never met before. After the funeral, she had no way to track him down. A short time later, the woman killed her sister. Why?*

If your answer is that she did this to lure the man to another family funeral, then according to Internet legend you are a psychopath because you've displayed ruthless cunning. Yet experts have actually tried this out on real criminal psychopaths, and this isn't how they tend to answer. Like many ordinary people, most psychopaths said the reason must be due to a love rivalry between the sisters. The test, then, is really no more than a fun riddle.

Other more realistic signs that you or someone you know is psychopathic include having a tendency to enjoy laughing at other people's misfortune and using this as a way to manipulate them. Less obvious is that psychopaths also like being laughed at by others.[50] In fact, it can form part of their superficial charm. Picture the superconfident office boss who tells a few self-deprecating jokes and soon has his staff eating out of the palm of his hand.

According to a personality and occupational survey of nearly four thousand readers of *Scientific American Mind*, people with a more psychopathic personality are also more likely to occupy leadership roles and risky occupations; be politically conservative; be atheists; and reside in Europe rather than the United Sates (it's not clear why this should be).[51] If you went to college (or are at college now), even the major you chose could be revealing: apparently business and economics students tend to score higher on psychopathic traits than psychology students.[52]

To get a more reliable measure of your overall psychopathic tendencies, you're best off taking a short quiz. Here's one that's based on a genuine psychopathy questionnaire. Rate your agreement as honestly as possible after each statement, from 1, Strongly Disagree, to 5, Strongly Agree. Jot down 3 if you neither agree nor disagree:

I like to get revenge on authorities. _____

I'm attracted to dangerous situations. _____

Payback needs to be quick and nasty. _____

People often say I'm out of control. _____

It's true that I can be mean to others. _____

People who mess with me always regret it. _____

I have gotten into trouble with the law. _____

I enjoy having sex with people I hardly know. _____

I'll say anything to get what I want. _____

Total: _____

Add up your scores for each item and divide by 9. How psychopathic are you overall? As with narcissism, you can get a sense of a normal score by comparing your results with the answers given by hundreds of undergraduates. Their average was 2.4. Again, a little over or under this figure is unexceptional, but if you scored above 3.4, you're probably leaning toward being a bit psychopathic. If you scored above 4.4, I wouldn't like to get on your wrong side!

Perhaps more important than your overall score, though, is whether you show a lot of fearless dominance—the trait that successful psychopaths exhibit. To get an idea, here are some statements from another test, specifically tapping fearless dominance: *I take charge; I seek adventure; I remain calm under pressure; I love excitement.*[53] Agree with them all, and it could be a sign that you've got the makings of a successful psychopath! Agreeing with the following statements, however, is an indication of self-centered impulsivity, the aspect of psychopathy that's more associated with criminality and aggression: *I love a good fight; I cheat to get ahead; I break the rules; I act without thinking.* Perhaps if you agreed with all those, you're reading this book in the prison library.

Hopefully it goes without saying that the aggressive, criminal elements of psychopathy are bad news for the individual showing them and for society at large. But what about the psychopathic traits of fearless dominance and coldheartedness? If, like me, you lie much further toward the timid end of the spectrum, is there anything we can learn from the successful psychopaths of this world?

LESSONS IN SUCCESSFUL PSYCHOPATHY

Having the right kind of psychopathic traits certainly seems to help some people in life, depending, of course, on how you measure success. One remarkable study compared thirty-nine British senior managers and CEOs with hundreds of criminally psychopathic inmates incarcerated at the Broadmoor high-security hospital in Berkshire, England (previously home to the Yorkshire Ripper, among others).[54] Incredibly, the CEOs outscored the criminal psychopaths on superficial charm and manipulativeness, matched them on lack of empathy, but, crucially, scored lower on impulsiveness and aggression.

This wasn't a freak result. In the United States, psychologists were able to obtain psychopathy scores from over two hundred corporate professionals enrolled in a management development program. Consistent with the British findings, the managers scored higher on psychopathy than the general public did, and the higher they scored, the better ratings they tended to get for charisma and presentation skills (although they scored worse for being team players and actual performance).[55] Based on his findings, New York psychologist Paul Babiak told the *Guardian* that about one in twenty-five business leaders is likely to be psychopathic.[56]

Some experts even claim that the most successful US presidents have been at least a little on the psychopathic side. One of the leading researchers on successful psychopathy, the late Scott Lilienfeld at

Emory University, asked historical biographers to rate the personality traits of all the presidents up to and including George W. Bush and compared these ratings with historians' estimates of the presidents' performances in office. Again, fearless dominance was key. The presidents who rated high on this trait (the top four scorers were Theodore Roosevelt, John Kennedy, Franklin Roosevelt, and Ronald Reagan; William Taft was the lowest scorer) were also considered more effective in terms of their reputation, electoral outcomes, and the legislation passed during their terms in office.[57]

Aside from senior leadership roles, successful psychopaths are also more likely to be found in competitive, high-risk professions. This includes finance, but also military special forces, emergency services, extreme sports, and even surgery. "Beyond doubt, there's most definitely a place for the psychopath in society," says Dutton.

In fact, a recent paper published by the Royal College of Surgeons was titled "A Stressful Job: Are Surgeons Psychopaths?"[58] The answer was an unequivocal yes. Nearly two hundred doctors took a psychopathy questionnaire, and although they didn't score high on all aspects of psychopathy, they scored higher than the general public on certain traits like stress immunity and fearlessness, and surgeons scored the highest of all. This jibes with the account of a neurosurgeon who told Dutton in *The Wisdom of Psychopaths*, "Yes, when you're scrubbing up before a difficult operation, it's true: a chill does go through the veins."

So why are there so many psychopaths, or at least psychopathically inclined people, in leadership positions and high-paid jobs like surgery? Psychopaths are extreme extraverts, driven by the promise of reward and immune to threats.[59] They even have a heightened response to stimulants; for example, their brains release four times as much dopamine (a brain chemical associated with the anticipation and experience of reward) when they take speed (amphetamine), compared with nonpsychopaths, and they show a similarly heightened brain response in anticipation of getting a cash reward.[60] But the most important reason for the success of high-functioning, noncriminal psychopaths seems to be their ability to switch off their fear and anxiety at appropriate times, be that while performing heart surgery, rescuing victims from a house fire, trading in millions of dollars, or taking part in a daring raid behind enemy lines.

How can you learn from the psychopathic way without going over to the dark side? Long term, and in terms of the Big Five personality traits, the answer is to reduce your trait neuroticism as low as possible and maximize your extraversion.

Reflect honestly on your own life. Assuming you're not a psychopath, there may be times when you shied away from opportunities for fear that you might not meet the challenge or even embarrass yourself. Perhaps you were invited to give a talk to your colleagues at work or offered a work promotion, but you chose to play it safe and avoided the opportunity. In your personal life, maybe you role-played in your head for days or weeks how to go about asking a colleague or friend out on a date, but in the end, you never mustered the courage. These are the kinds of occasions when it might well have helped to channel your inner psychopath.

One way to do this, as I described earlier, is to reframe stressful, anxiety-provoking situations as exciting. Interpret the flood of adrenaline in your system as a buzz rather than as fear, and this will help your performance. This comes naturally to the psychopath, but you can train yourself to have a similar approach when it's called for.

To take this further, a useful strategy is to adopt what psychologists call a challenge mind-set rather than a threat mind-set. When, as a nonpsychopath, you have a threat mind-set, this is because you believe that your abilities don't match the demands of a task. You fear losing control. You're scared you're going to fail and embarrass yourself. The natural response is avoidance.

Having a challenge mind-set, in contrast, comes from believing in your capabilities (to help, remind yourself of the practice and training you've done; if you haven't, then start practicing now, for next time); focusing on those aspects of the task that you can control (rehearsal helps, as does having set procedures and routines that you perform prior to and during a challenge—think of elite athletes and their pregame rituals); and seeing the task less as a test and more as a chance to learn, whatever the outcome. Put simply, focus on what you will gain from trying, not what you might lose, even if the best you can hope for is that it will be a learning experience. Do this, and while you might not quite feel a chill through your veins (like the surgeon Dutton spoke to), you will be better placed to turn your anxiety to your advantage and more likely to seize opportunities when they come, rather than giving way to the office psychopath or some cocky Lothario ready to steal your date.

Importantly, if you adopt a challenge (rather than a threat) mind-set, it also encourages you to practice, or do the research, or whatever else that's needed, to succeed. A study of nearly two hundred employees confirmed this recently. Those who had a challenging day ahead tended to respond by upping their game and taking constructive steps to cope, such as prioritizing their time and seeking support, but only if they had what the researchers called a "positive stress mind-set," similar to a challenge mind-set.[61] Those with a negative stress mind-set, who saw the big day as a threat, stuck their heads in the sand.

A related advantage that successful psychopaths have is their spontaneity and willingness to seize the day. While you're ruminating over whether to apply for that job or make an offer on that house that's for sale, those successful psychopaths have already mailed their CV or called the Realtor, driven by the chance of reward, never mind the risks.

Put simply, psychopaths don't procrastinate. You can even things up by understanding the psychology of procrastination: how we often avoid doing something even though we've decided we should do it, not because of bad time management but because of active avoidance, driven by the uncomfortable fears and negative emotions that the activity provokes (or at least that the thought of it provokes, often irrationally).

A successful approach to avoiding procrastination therefore is to address your fears or take emotion out of the equation altogether. Draw up the pros and cons to an important decision, and consult your friends and family if necessary. Now, having decided that you should go ahead, stop anticipating how things might pan out and simply focus on the next action that you need to take. Then just do it. Go mail your CV. Pick up your phone.

STEERING PSYCHOPATHS TOWARD THE LIGHT

There are moments and situations in life when it might help, depending on your aims in life, to borrow some of the psychopath's strategies, such as when you are competing against pushy, fearless successful psychopaths at work or dealing with difficult, selfish relatives. But as with narcissism, I do not recommend committing yourself wholesale to the dark side!

Remember, psychopathy is associated with a lack of feeling, arguably the very essence of what makes us human. Meaning in life comes from caring about things other than pleasure and self-gratification. Perhaps more than anything else, it comes from your loving relationships. Caring about others might hold you back, but if you succeeded in turning yourself into a coldhearted automaton, what kind of life would that be?

Even if career achievement is the most important thing in life to you, bear in mind that there's evidence that employees suffer under a psychopathic boss[62] and organizations fail over the long term when they are led by psychopaths.[63] This is because effective leadership requires more than gung-ho risk taking. Among other things, understanding and empathy are also important, especially to help talented people grow and to remove hurdles preventing staff achievement.

More generally and totally unsurprisingly, psychopaths are also more likely to die a violent death.[64] And of course they're much more likely than average to find themselves on the wrong side of the law.

So how can you help someone else (or yourself) become less psychopathic? One approach is not to alter their traits per se but to direct them more constructively. The same psychopathic characteristics can fuel selfish ambition or heroism. Jeremy Johnson, a former Utah-based Internet marketing millionaire, lost a fortune gambling, preyed on vulnerable people, and was sentenced to eleven years in jail in 2016 in a bank fraud case. The judge told Johnson, "Your self-importance and the desire to do what you want to do is at the root of this scheme." Yet Johnson didn't just make millions of dollars, he was also a local hero known for his daring rescue missions, including flying his own aircraft to Haiti in 2010 to help earthquake victims. A lifelong friend describes him as "one of the most Christ-like people I have ever come to know."[65]

Johnson is not unusual. One study found a correlation between people's levels of psychopathic traits and their propensity for everyday heroism, such as assisting an unwell stranger or chasing a street crook.[66] An important way to help someone who has a psychopathic kind of personality, then, is to guide that person as far as possible toward careers and roles that maximize the opportunity for heroism and away from the criminal temptations that will ruin him.

Besides trying to steer psychopaths toward the light, can anything else be done to correct or reduce a person's psychopathic traits, or ensure he or she remains of the successful rather than criminal variety? US researchers recently found some success by focusing on the abnormal mental processes that psychopaths display. The premise of this approach is that psychopaths *are* capable of experiencing negative emotions, including regret; it's just that when they are pursuing a goal at any cost, their usual way, they fail to consider the regret they might feel in the future.[67] Cognitive remediation training, which takes place over many weeks and involves repeated prompting to focus on other people's emotions,[68] helps psychopaths pay more attention to the emotional context of what they're doing rather than focusing solely on their main goal. Imagine a psychopath focused on conning someone for personal gain, for example, and ignoring the emotional consequences for their victim.

"They're not cold-blooded; they're simply awful at multitasking," says Arielle Baskin-Sommers at Yale, the scientist leading this research. "So we need to think about how to address the mind of a psychopath in order to help them notice more information in their environment, and harness their emotional experience."[69] This approach is highly experimental, but it jibes with one of this book's key messages: that your personality stems partly from your habits of thought and that by changing these habits, you can change your traits and the kind of person you become.

Ten Actionable Steps to Change Your Personality

To reduce neuroticism	Many chronic worriers develop an unhealthy perfectionistic tendency, believing they can't stop worrying until all problems are solved, which is clearly impossible. When you find your worrying getting out of hand, try this thought-stopping technique: picture a stop signal or simply tell yourself that you've done enough worrying now and have permission to stop.	Practice taking your critical, negative thoughts less seriously. Everyone has them, but they are not gospel and you don't have to let them drag you down. One exercise to help with this is the mind bus technique. Picture your thoughts as unruly children on a school bus and imagine them putting on silly voices. They might be a bit distracting or amusing but they won't stop you as the driver getting to where you want to go.
To increase extraversion	Consider getting a dog or volunteering regularly to help out walking the dogs of your friends or neighbors. Dog owners experience more random social encounters than average because they so frequently bump into other dog owners and engage in small talk.	The next time you go to a party or networking event, rather than sheltering in the corner and fretting over which other guests to speak to, set yourself some modest, fun, and discrete goals in advance, such as finding out the names and occupations of two new people. Treating the event more like a detective challenge than a social gathering will help take the attention off yourself and give you a sense of achievement at the end. The more you do this, the more you will get used to it.

Ten Actionable Steps to Change Your Personality *(continued)*

To increase conscientiousness	Whether it's preparing for exams, training at the gym, or keeping the house tidy, combine any self-disciplined activities that you find a chore with fun elements to make them more immediately rewarding—for example, listen to your favorite music or podcast while you're doing them. Also consider keeping tabs on your progress and planning treats for yourself when you hit key milestones.	Spend some time reflecting on your most important values and goals. Are you currently directing your energies in the right direction? If not, it might be time to change direction. It is far easier to be disciplined and determined if you are in pursuit of overarching aims that resonate with your life values.
To increase agreeability	If you are kind to yourself, you will find it easier to extend warmth and trust to others. There are many self-compassion exercises. One to try is to write a letter to yourself as if from a supportive and sympathetic friend.	Read more literary fiction. This is associated with gains in empathy because reading gives us practice at seeing the perspectives of different characters.
To increase openness	Try learning a new language. Immersing yourself in a different culture (far easier if you are learning their language) will give you a fresh take on the world.	Seek out peak experiences. The obvious is to climb a mountain, but it doesn't have to be that dramatic. It could be planning ahead to take the time to enjoy the next sunset, taking a walk in your local woods, or visiting an art gallery. Your aim is to kindle a sense of oneness with the world and feel your mind open in the process.

Chapter 8

THE 10 PRINCIPLES OF
PERSONAL REINVENTION

Throughout this book I've detailed the various influences constantly molding your personality, including life's many highs and lows. I've shown how it is within your power to take at least some control of this malleability, including describing various exercises and activities that will shift any or all of your main traits in a desired direction, should you wish. I've also touched on some basic principles behind successful deliberate personality change.

In this final chapter, I'll expand on that earlier advice, outlining ten key principles you should hold in mind and return to whenever you are struggling, to help you succeed in your mission to optimize your personality to become the best version of yourself that you can be. Before you read on, now might be a good time to retake the personality test in chapter 1 to see if any of your trait scores have changed at all and, if so, whether they've done so in the direction that you hoped for. You could also consider performing another narrative writing exercise (see chapter

2) to find out whether the overall tone of your reflections has become any more positive. Don't despair if you've yet to make progress. These ten rules will provide you with more ideas for how to succeed:

The Ten Rules for Personal Reinvention

1. Successful change is more likely if it's for a larger purpose.
2. You won't improve unless you appraise yourself honestly.
3. Real change begins with action.
4. Initiating change is easy. Sticking with it is the hard part.
5. Change is an ongoing process, and you need to keep track of it.
6. You need to be realistic about the amount of change that is possible.
7. You're more likely to succeed with the help of others.
8. Life *will* get in the way. The trick is to anticipate and roll with it.
9. Self-kindness is more likely to lead to lasting change than beating yourself up.
10. Believing in the potential for—and continuing nature of—personality change is a philosophy to live by.

RULE 1: SUCCESSFUL CHANGE IS MORE LIKELY IF IT'S FOR A LARGER PURPOSE

Surveys show that most people wish their personality were different in some way. Often it's a vague sense that a change might make you happier in life, more successful at work, or more content in your relationships. Deliberately enhancing your extraversion, conscientiousness, openness, agreeableness, and emotional stability (or just one of these traits) can help you lead a healthier, happier life. However, if you hope for more lasting and radical personal change, it's more likely to come about in the pursuit of some larger purpose or sense of identity.

Research shows that changes in personal values (what most matters to you in life) more often precede personality change rather than the other way around.[1] Becoming a better father, fighting poverty, sharing your love of art, improving your town, volunteering overseas, or learning a new skill: it doesn't matter what we call this motivational pull (psychologists refer variously to "personal projects," "higher callings," or "ultimate concerns"). Seeking deliberate personality change is more likely to be successful and feel authentic if it is in the service of your passion(s) or current purpose and values in life.

Many of the inspiring stories of change I've shared in this book have looked at individuals who have discovered a profound new identity or calling and then worked to improve themselves—through self-education, new relationships, hobbies, and habits—in the service of that higher goal. This then leads to a self-perpetuating effect, where the enactment of that calling and the social roles it entails further shifts your personality in beneficial ways and better channels your existing personality strengths.

If you don't currently have a passion or calling, then before asking yourself, "How do I want or need to change my personality?" it might be more rewarding and effective to ask, "What matters to me?" or even "Who do I want to be?" Of course the answer can change at different times of your life, so it's a question to revisit. For example, you may have been a dedicated parent for many years and seen that as your raison d'être, but once your children grow up and move out, you might feel that you have a hole in your life and are looking for a new purpose.

Whatever time of life you are at, you will not necessarily discover the answer by pondering this question in the comfort of your armchair. You might need to get up and get out and discover through experimentation what ignites that spark inside you. Be patient. It is unlikely to be the first thing you try, and even when you do find your true calling (something that for you provokes enduring fascination and meaning), you might not realize it at first. Passions usually take some time to catch alight.

Once you've found your calling, then is the time to ask, "How might I develop my character to better meet this challenge or live according to these values?" Remember and take to heart that any personality changes you make in pursuit of this calling are more likely to be fully absorbed into your sense of self, to feel authentic, and to last.

Key takeaway: Find your calling in life or reflect on the personal values that matter most to you. This will lay the foundation for meaningful, authentic personality change.

RULE 2: YOU WON'T IMPROVE UNLESS YOU APPRAISE YOURSELF HONESTLY

If you are struggling at work or in your relationships, it can be very tempting to shirk any responsibility and blame it all on circumstances and other people. However, if you are honest, you are often at least partly responsible—possibly with there being a recurring pattern across various situations thanks to a contribution from some of your less helpful traits, perhaps laziness, mood swings, or dogmatism. The first step to improving these less-than-helpful traits is to admit and accept that they need addressing in the first place (without becoming harshly self-critical or disheartened; see rule 9, on page 228).

Taking an honest look at the man or woman in the mirror is easier said than done, however. Massaging our own egos by viewing ourselves in a preferential light is a part of human nature. Most of us—except perhaps the most depressed and highly neurotic—overestimate our abilities and knowledge.[2]

This common self-serving bias can help to sustain your self-esteem and optimism, so it should be handled with care and not shot down in flames. But it can also be a barrier to effective personality change if it prevents you from performing an honest self-appraisal. One way to overcome this is to commit to being as truthful as possible in the way that you answer the personality tests in this book (or any others you take online). Doing so will help you identify the areas of your personality that you could develop to your advantage.

However, even if you are bold enough to take an uncensored view of your personality, it is quite likely that there are things about yourself that you do not know, or at least things that others see in you but that you are unaware of—blind spots, so to speak.

This has been revealed in studies that have asked volunteers to rate their own personality, rate how they think other people see their personality, and then compare those answers with how close friends and family really did rate their personality.[3] The findings showed that while there is a lot of overlap in how you see yourself and how others see you, there are usually also important blind spots—things others agree they can see in you (such as that you are grumpy in the mornings, witty, or too eager to please, or whatever) but you are completely ignorant of yourself.

Tread carefully when exploring these potential blind spots, especially if you are feeling vulnerable or psychologically delicate. What this line of research suggests is that if you are serious about changing your personality for the better, it is a good idea for you not just to rely on your own personality self-ratings, but also to ask some of your close friends, family, and colleagues to score your traits. If you ask enough people, they could even do it anonymously to help avoid any potential risk of offense.

It is worth being careful about who you ask; you don't want to come away from this exercise feeling completely demoralized. Those people whom psychologist Tasha Eurich calls your "loving critics," who have your best interests at heart, are a good choice. Armed with their ratings of your personality, you will then have a better idea of any areas of your personality that may benefit from development.

If you are feeling really brave, you could even take a leaf out of Eurich's excellent book *Insight,* in which she describes an exercise known as the "dinner of truth," in which you go out with a critic who loves you and ask that person to describe the one thing about you that she or he finds most annoying.[4]

If that sounds a bit too risky, another approach to greater self-insight that you can take on your own is to ask yourself the "miracle question" (as described in Chip and Dan Heath's book *Switch*). Imagine that tonight, as you are sleeping, a miraculous change in your personality occurs—one that in the future would ripple out and benefit many areas of your life and relationships. What would this miraculous change be? Reflect on the change in detail and how it would manifest in your life. Would your life be different from the moment you woke, and if so, how? Next, think how you can begin to make this miracle a reality.

> *Key takeaway:* Find out how your close friends and family
> (loving critics) see your personality so that you have a
> fuller picture of the kind of person you are today.

RULE 3: REAL CHANGE BEGINS WITH ACTION

The aspiration to change your personality begins in your mind, but this inner ambition will never be enough on its own. One of the simplest yet most powerful lessons to heed is that unless you *do* something different, nothing will change. Think for a minute about what you have started doing differently since you began reading this book.

If you stick to the same routines, the same hobbies, the same company, the same habits, the same job, the same neighborhood, then it doesn't matter that you privately harbor the desire to be more conscientious, more open-minded, more extraverted, or whatever else because if you're holding everything in your life constant and you are acting as you have always done, then you will be the same person. The moment you break out of those old patterns is when the change process can begin. If you do not know where to start, ask yourself what the very first step is that you need to take to begin the process of change. Then do it. As William James allegedly put it, "Begin to be now what you will be hereafter."

As a writer who spends a lot of time on my own, I'm mindful of how this is probably shaping me to be more introverted. I have for some time been trying to balance that out by finding ways to nurture my extraversion. I'm not saying that introversion is an inherently bad thing, but I have sensed that my circumstances have been molding me to become more introverted than I would like. One step I have taken, like many other solitary workers, is to head out regularly from my home office to do my work at a café. I've done this for years, often lamenting that while I've made the effort to go out into the world, the world in turn has been pretty unimpressed and unrewarding. Sure, my café visits provide a welcome change of scene, but truth be told, after I've ordered my coffee, I rarely speak to anyone. Another thing I do is head to the gym regularly, yet I always cocoon myself within my headphones. Again, I'm out in public yet effectively alone.

Earlier this year, heeding my own advice in this book, it dawned on me that nothing was going to change unless I started *doing* something differently. For years, in my café and gym routines, I had been doing things exactly the same, then complaining that nothing was changing, including my own overly introverted tendencies.

I needed to begin acting differently. At the country club where the café is that I often go to work, I started taking several exercise classes per week, including a boxing-based class that requires partner work—in other words, unavoidable face-to-face socializing. It's early in this experiment and while it felt a little uncomfortable at first not knowing anyone, I can tell you that I am already feeling and acting differently. It may be a subtle change for now, but I feel as though I have come out of my shell at least a little, and it all started by realizing that if I wanted to change, I needed to start by *doing* something differently.

The importance of supporting your intentions to change with actual new behaviors and habits has been backed up by studies. Research volunteers have more successfully achieved their desired personality change when they've been coached to follow specific, relevant behavioral steps to achieve that change, including adopting explicit if-then plans, like, "If I'm in situation X, then I will do Y."

Another recent study showed that wishing to change your personality without actually doing anything about it can even be harmful.[5] Volunteers kept diaries of their intentions for change and whether they'd undertaken any recommended challenges to facilitate that change. Those who completed more of these practical challenges achieved more of their desired change; sadly, those who did not change their behavior, despite pledging to, actually regressed further from their desired personality, perhaps because of their sense of failure. This research backs up my own personal experiences: desiring to change will fail unless you are prepared to act differently.

> *Key takeaway:* Personality change begins with action. What are you going to *do* differently?

RULE 4: INITIATING CHANGE IS EASY. STICKING WITH IT IS THE HARD PART.

Every day, but especially at the start of the year, millions of people around the world make New Year's resolutions to change themselves for the better. Such goals are laudable. Whether it is getting fitter, stopping smoking, reading more, or even changing their personality, the stark truth is that these efforts often peter out as people soon revert to their old habits.

In his book *Change*, psychotherapist and author Jeffrey Kottler cites research suggesting a 90 percent failure rate for people trying to kick habits like gambling and overeating.[6] "Launching changes in your life is relatively easy compared with maintaining them over the long haul," he writes. The reason that it is so difficult to make personal changes stick is that much of how you think and act is habitual (bear in mind that your personality traits are in one sense an overarching description of the many habits that make you the person you are). If something is habitual, it means that it is automatic and effortless. It's how you think, feel, and act without consciously intervening.

When a (low-conscientiousness) smoker reaches for his cigarette during his morning coffee break, it's not something he has to will himself to do; it's just a reflex. When a (highly extraverted) socialite walks into a party full of strangers, she doesn't instruct herself to start chatting to the first person she bumps into; it's just what she does without thinking.

Achieving lasting personality change means shaking things up, unlearning some of your many habits and routines that contribute to the kind of person you are, and overwriting them with new ones. It doesn't mean that you have to suddenly act and think in the same new way every waking second of every single day. Personality change is about shifting your behavioral tendencies. This means you will have to work very hard to develop new habits in how you think and act across various situations until they become second nature—that is, instinctual and automatic.

In order for your new ways of thinking and behaving to become habitual, persistence is key. There is not a great deal of research on how new habits are formed, but to give you an idea of the importance of persistence, a study in 2010 asked students trying to develop a specific new habit to log on to a website every day to record whether they'd performed the habit, as well as how automatic it felt.[7] Examples included going for a run each day before dinner or eating a piece of fruit with lunch (efforts that, if successful, would in personality terms contribute to increased conscientiousness). There was a lot of variation, but the average length of time for a new behavior to become a fully fledged new habit (to reach its peak automaticity) was sixty-six days.

There are various methods you can use to try to increase the chances that your new personality-based habits will stick and to prevent your old ones from relapsing. Many habits unfold in response to specific cues. You tend to do something at a particular time of day (you switch on the TV as soon as you get home from work), or when you are in a certain place (you always order a muffin to go with your morning coffee), or when a particular thing happens (you start thinking of yourself as a failure as soon as something goes wrong at work). Crucial to changing habits is learning to recognize these cues and either avoid them or replace the old reflexive behavior with a new one.

Also important is looking to see what kind of purpose or need your existing, unhelpful habits may serve. You will find it easier to break bad habits if you substitute a healthier behavior for them that satisfies the same need. For instance, that after-work TV habit helps you relax; your midmorning muffin cheers you up; your self-criticism derives from a desire to do better next time. Breaking these habits, which could be part of a wider package of changes aimed at developing your conscientiousness and, in the last case, lowering your neuroticism, will be easier if you find healthier alternatives that bring a similar reward—for instance, chatting with a friend or colleague to cheer yourself up, taking up an after-work sport or hobby as a way to relax, or learning to see failure as a chance to learn and develop.

Of course, you will have lapses when you miss performing a new habit or fall back into an old one. Do not allow this to demoralize you and tempt you to give up. While the great American psychologist William James suggested in his *Principles of Psychology* that a single lapse—a missed run, a conversation avoided, a temptation succumbed to—would be fatal when trying to develop a habit, this has not been supported by research. That study I mentioned before that followed students as they learned new habits found that a single missed day was not too big a deal, although multiple failures did have a cumulative counterproductive effect. It's important to forgive yourself for initial lapses and not let them spiral into something more serious. Try to react by reasserting your determination to stick to the new, healthy habit. This means it's not the initial lapse that's important but what you do next. As the author and habits expert James Clear says, "When successful people fail, they rebound quickly. The breaking of habit doesn't matter if the reclaiming of it is fast."[8]

> *Key takeaway:* To ensure your attempts at personality change last, persist until your new behaviors and tendencies have become habitual.

RULE 5: CHANGE IS AN ONGOING PROCESS, AND YOU NEED TO KEEP TRACK OF IT

You probably don't need to go to the extremes employed by Benjamin Franklin. He started keeping a daily record of his attempts to develop thirteen character virtues (including humility, sincerity, and order) when he was just twenty, noting every instance of failure with a black mark in his notebook. However, in recognizing the importance of tracking his progress, Franklin was shrewd. If you do not keep a record of your attempts at personality change, then it will be difficult for you to know whether you are making any progress, whether to persist with your current efforts, or whether you need to try a different approach.

Unfortunately, it can be tempting to carry on with your change efforts without checking whether they are actually working. Psychologists even have a name for this tendency: the ostrich problem. If you are pleased with yourself for your attempts at change, the last thing you might want is to find out that you haven't been doing as well as you thought or that your efforts have been in vain: they haven't led to the positive benefits that you hoped for or, worse, they've backfired and caused you significant distress. Yet if you are to succeed in the long term, it is vital that you check in regularly to find out whether you're progressing and whether the changes you've made have been beneficial.

Studies conducted in various contexts, from students learning math to patients adopting new, healthy behaviors, have shown that people who track their efforts tend to be more successful at learning and changing. In the context of personality change, this record keeping could take the form of habit tracking: keeping a diary of the new behaviors and other activities that you are undertaking to develop your personality traits to ensure you really are keeping up with your new routines (various apps and smartwatches make this easier today than ever before) and taking periodic personality tests, to see if your traits are responding in the way that you hoped. (This website has free personality tests designed for repeated self-testing: https://yourpersonality.net.)

The most common reason that people avoid tracking their progress is fear of finding out that their efforts are futile or that their apparent achievements are illusory. Overcome this fear by reminding yourself that it's okay to have occasional lapses (see rule 4) and by getting away from an all-or-nothing mind-set as to whether you can do this or you can't. The reality is likely to be more complicated. You might succeed in some ways and not others, or some kinds of progress will come quickly and easily but other targets will be more elusive or unhelpful. Remember that gains are not always linear.

Establishing new routines is an achievement in itself, even if the aim of those new routines takes some time to manifest—whether those ultimate goals are learning a new skill, losing weight, altering your personality traits, or answering your calling in life. In the meantime, rewarding yourself for passing milestones in your attempts at building new routines and habits will be a powerful motivator. Of course, to do this requires that you keep track of your progress. By the way, in a business context, psychologists have found that one of the most important factors driving successful teams is individual team members' sense of making progress toward goals, a phenomenon known as the progress principle that could help you succeed at your personal goals.

Key takeaway: Keep track of your progress so that you know if your efforts are effective, and so that you can reward yourself for passing milestones on the way to lasting personality change.

RULE 6: YOU NEED TO BE REALISTIC ABOUT THE AMOUNT OF CHANGE POSSIBLE

Before explaining the need for realism, let me reiterate: you can and will change. No matter your age, your personality will continue to mature through life. And you can consciously take advantage of this malleability in your character to change yourself in the ways that you want.

This adaptability makes biological sense. Like many of our fellow creatures on this planet, we have evolved the ability to change our behavioral dispositions to suit the environments we find ourselves in. Unlike other animals, we can take conscious control of this inherent flexibility and choose to change ourselves.

The influence on personality that is considered most fixed—placing a limit on how much you can change—comes from the genes that you inherited. Of course, that still leaves plenty of scope for life's slings and arrows to shape you. And what's more, exciting epigenetic research suggests that different experiences can alter how and when your genes are expressed. So even the genetic roots of your personality may not be as fixed as was once thought.

Brent Roberts at the University of Illinois, a leading academic expert on the malleability of personality, describes this as "phenotypic pliability" (that is, how you turn out given the interaction between your genes and the environments you find yourself in). "We use pliability as a metaphor," he writes, "because these modifications to the way DNA is employed result in changes that are permanent in both form and function going forward, much like the way pipe cleaners can be bent and shaped into a form that is enduring."[9]

These facts are exciting and highly motivating for anyone who hopes to change his or her personality. Yet I still believe a fundamental principle of successful personality change is that you are realistic and honest with yourself about how much change is possible. Pause a moment and think about how far you are prepared to go in pursuit of change.

The reason I ask is that while the latest scientific findings suggest that willful personality change is eminently achievable, such change is not easy, and it does not happen by magic (and contrary to the titles of some other books, it will take longer than thirty or fifty-nine seconds).[10] It occurs through dogged persistence and through making changes to your routines—your habits, where you go, what you do, and possibly also whose company you keep. In other words, it involves a lot of disruption. If you are truly honest, how much of your lifestyle do you plan to change? Will you keep the same job, the same friends, the same hobbies, the same daily rituals? Inertia is powerful, and the more in life that is held constant around you, the more that you follow your usual routines, moving in the same circles with the same people, the more constant your personality traits are likely to be.

So while we each have the potential for large-scale personality change, unless you are prepared and able to truly transform your life and your situations and how you interact with them, the level of change that is achievable is likely to be more modest. As Jeffrey Kottler puts it in his book *Change*, "That's not to say that we should give up our dreams but, rather, that there is a compromise we make between what we really, really, want, what is possible, and what we are willing to do to reach that goal."[11]

Another issue to bear in mind is that while you are busy modifying one aspect of your personality, you might find this causes complicating issues with another side of your character. For instance, in my own case, I've found my attempts to increase my conscientiousness have at times given me something else to worry about, thereby nudging up my neuroticism. This shows the importance of taking a holistic perspective even if you have very specific aims for how you'd like to change. In my own case, I've learned to make sure I address my conscientiousness and neuroticism in tandem.

These cautions are not intended to be downbeat. As I've stated before, successful personality change is not an all-or-nothing endeavor. Even quite subtle tweaks to your traits could reap meaningful benefits. These positive effects may snowball, potentially taking your life in different, more advantageous directions.

The point here is to be realistic about the levels of change and transformation we are talking about because unrealistic expectations are a major obstacle to successful change. False hope leads inevitably to disappointment, and, in turn, this can provoke a demotivating spiral and the prospect that you give up any attempts at change at all. Unrealistic fantasies about how you plan to change and how easy it will be may be uplifting at first, but they can lull you into false confidence, tricking your mind into believing that the hard work has been done.

In contrast, a dose of realism about the obstacles in your path will lead you to more success in the long run. Deliberately forcing yourself to consider the setbacks you are likely to encounter in your determination to change can be a helpful exercise that psychologists call "mental contrasting." Try it. Think of one of the main ways that you would like to change, write down three benefits of succeeding (to give your morale a boost), but then pause and consider the three main obstacles in your way and write those down too. Going through this routine will help you take a more realistic perspective and ensure you direct your motivation and energy where they are needed most.

> *Key takeaway:* Be honest with yourself about how far you are prepared to go in pursuit of personality change. It is better to be realistic than to harbor unrealistic expectations.

RULE 7: YOU'RE MORE LIKELY TO SUCCEED WITH THE HELP OF OTHERS

Consider for a moment the role you usually play in your family get-togethers or main friendship groups. In such circles, we often get tagged early on, though not necessarily explicitly, with superficial identities or roles: the nerdy one, the insolent one, and so on (a tendency embraced by the Spice Girls, which gave its members nicknames like "Sporty Spice" and "Posh Spice"). We then live out these social roles almost as if playing a part in a drama or filling our role in a rock band.

Such caricatures or reputations can make for affectionate banter and jokes. In terms of your personality development, if your friends and family see you as the kind of person you aspire to be (your ideal self), that can be liberating and motivating and will help you grow in the ways that you want. But if they see you as nothing like your ideal self and you don't much like the role you've been cast in, this can make your attempts at self-improvement much harder.

Given these dynamics in your innermost social circles, it is not much of a surprise that when researchers have analyzed the kind of stories that people bring to psychotherapy sessions, they have found that they frequently involve anecdotes about wanting close friends and family to be accepting and understanding, but actually finding them "rejecting and opposing" and "controlling."[12] So an important principle of successful personality change is that if you can help your closest family and friends understand, support, and believe in the improvements you are seeking to make, you will find it much easier to change. It is possible to succeed without that backup, but if there is a chance to get meaningful others on your side or even to make new friends who respect and value the kind of person you are trying to be, this will certainly be advantageous. "The single best predictor of a successful change effort is the degree of support you receive from others," writes Jeffrey Kottler in *Change*.[13]

The importance of social backup also applies in the context of your most personal, romantic relationships. Here, psychologists have documented a phenomenon that they call the "Michelangelo effect," named after Michelangelo's description of his sculpting as the process of uncovering the figure that was already present within the stone. If your partner sees you as being like the person you aspire to be and treats you in ways that help you be that person (also if your partner models the kinds of behaviors that you value), then research suggests you will find it easier to become more like your ideal self. As a bonus, you will probably also find a Michelangelo-style relationship more rewarding and feel more authentic.

It is not just the expectations and perceptions of those closest to you that make a difference to your personal development. The wider cultural and behavioral norms (the accepted ways of treating one another and other moral values) that exist in the places where you work or in your friendship circles also shape your personality—either holding back or facilitating the changes you're seeking to make. For instance, if you work in an office with an unfriendly atmosphere and colleagues who frequently snipe at one another, it will be a miracle if this doesn't rub off on you and lower your own trait agreeableness and increase your neuroticism. Indeed, writer and psychologist Alex Fradera calls incivility "the mucus of the workplace" because of the way it can spread through an office culture like a cold.[14] It's not so different within your friendship group. If your friends mostly lack ambition or discipline, for instance, it will be more of a struggle for you to find the motivation to develop these attributes in yourself.

Thankfully, the reverse kind of effect is also true. One study recruited a small number of employees to perform good deeds—favors and minor acts of kindness—for some of their colleagues and then watched for several weeks to see how the recipients felt and behaved. The givers and receivers all benefited in terms of feeling happier and more autonomous, and, most important, the recipients of the contrived acts of kindness ended up being more helpful and kind themselves, thus showing how altruism and agreeableness can spread, just like incivility does.[15]

These various social effects—the roles and expectations others place on you and the influence of your work and friendship cultures—make it vital to consider how the social milieus you move in could be affecting your attempts at personal change. Your options for controlling such things may be limited, but if you can surround yourself with the kind of people who share the characteristics that you value, you will find it easier to develop those traits in yourself.

> *Key takeaway:* Think about the people you spend most of your time with and whether they may be helping or hindering your attempts at personal change.

RULE 8: LIFE *WILL* GET IN THE WAY. THE TRICK IS TO ANTICIPATE AND ROLL WITH IT.

Much of the time it is the multitude of minute and mundane details of daily life that shapes us. Rather than accepting these influences passively, you can exercise your agency and choose to develop new, healthy habits and routines and be more deliberate and strategic about the situations you place yourself in and the company you keep, day in, day out. Doing so will give you an element of control so that you can steer your personality in the directions you want. However, there is no avoiding the fact that aside from your own intentions to change yourself, there will be other forces, often powerful ones, shaping the person you are becoming.

Some of these—positive and negative—will be unavoidable: illness, marriage, accidents, new relationships, bereavements, layoffs at work, promotions, pandemics, relationship breakups, aging, awards and recognition, parenthood, prison, happy holidays, retirement, and more. These side winds may make your attempts at personality change feel as futile as rowing a small boat across the ocean. You paddle in your chosen direction, implementing the strategies and exercises documented in this book, but then the might of the elements stirs the great ocean, sending you the other way. In the worst cases, a single life event might crash over you, leaving you capsized, helpless, and vulnerable.

Of course there is no guaranteed way to inoculate yourself against life's biggest challenges and dangers, but one thing you can do is educate yourself as to how some of the more common experiences are likely to affect you. As I documented in chapter 2, some effects are predictable, such as divorce pushing you toward greater introversion and increased risk of loneliness, and getting fired lowering your conscientiousness, increasing your risk of more prolonged unemployment. Even life's most wonderful highs, such as the arrival of a baby, can bring challenges that may hinder your personality development. For instance, there is the research suggesting that mothers and fathers often struggle with self-esteem and greater neuroticism after childbirth. In being aware of these effects on your personality, you can anticipate them and take ameliorative action to buffer their impact.

That still leaves the risk of a catastrophic event—a crushing wave that casts you adrift. Coping with such turbulent times will nearly always be painful and traumatic. Your best defense is to foster resilience in the good times: develop your emotional stability, openness, agreeableness, and conscientiousness and embed yourself in meaningful, mutually supportive relationships. These traits and your social networks will be the aids that help you survive and heal should a devastating tsunami ever crash over your life.

It may also be a comfort to remember the phenomenon of post-traumatic growth—the fact that many people say that some of the most painful experiences in life changed them for the better, deepening their relationships and bringing them a renewed sense of meaning and perspective. Consider the reflections of David Kushner, whose memoir, *Alligator Candy*, documents the kidnapping and murder of his brother Jon as a child and the aftermath.[16] Of course Kushner's family wished with all their heart that the tragedy had never happened, but somehow they pulled together and survived, and they even grew from the experience. "We've always been haunted by Jon's death, but, perhaps for that reason, we share a drive to get the most out of the lives we have," Kushner writes.

Again, developing your personality could help increase the odds that should catastrophe ever strike, you will be more likely to find some hope and opportunity for positive change. Research suggests that having greater resilience, openness, and, especially, conscientiousness (but perhaps also extraversion and agreeableness) will increase the chance you can capitalize on the potential for personal growth after trauma.[17]

> *Key takeaway:* Develop your resilience in the good times, and when you do hit turbulence, or worse, take heart that these periods can provide the greatest opportunity for personal change.

RULE 9: SELF-KINDNESS IS MORE LIKELY TO LEAD TO LASTING CHANGE THAN BEATING YOURSELF UP

Assuming you are still a ways off from the person you want to be—psychologists would describe this as there being a large gap between your actual self and ideal self—you need to tread carefully. If such personal discontent is extreme and not managed with caution, it can fuel unhappiness and even put you at risk of depression. To cope, you need the right balance of acceptance (including honesty, patience, and realism; see rules 2 and 6) without allowing this to slip into resignation, complacency, and lost motivation. You should aim for honesty, compassion, and understanding toward yourself as you are now while also recognizing your potential for change.

Crucial to your success at striking this balance is how you react when, inevitably, things don't go entirely according to plan. Imagine one of your personality goals is to become more conscientious, yet you find yourself once again staring bleary-eyed into the mirror on another Sunday morning, the previous night's self-indulgence written over you like an act of bodily vandalism. How do you react? With shame and scathing self-criticism? Do you excoriate yourself for the lapse and decide that it is just the latest example of the kind of weak-willed person you are? Do you worry what others will think of you?

Answering yes to these questions would indicate that you are taking the approach of an unhealthy perfectionist, someone prone to pessimism, self-blame, fear of others' harsh judgment, and essentialist thinking—that is, interpreting each setback as providing evidence of the kind of person you are, as if this is something fixed, fundamental, and inherent in you, thus inviting the temptation to give up your efforts at change so as to avoid any risk of failure in the future.

In contrast, you are more likely to maintain your motivation toward successful change if you can think more like a healthy perfectionist by forgiving yourself for your lapse, worrying less about meeting others' expectations, and considering what circumstances and behaviors led to this particular setback (or others like it, such as flaking out on a party invitation, failing an exam, or having a heated argument with your partner—typical, to-be-expected disappointments on the path to greater extraversion, openness, and agreeableness, respectively).

Yes, it is important to be honest with yourself about your current traits (as outlined in rule 2), because deluding yourself about what a great, flawless person you are is not the route to successful personal development, and of course it is right to take responsibility for your mistakes. But try not to think about every failure or lapse as giving a permanent diagnosis about the kind of person you are. Pause to recognize your errors on this occasion, then concentrate more on what you can learn from the experience. What could you do differently next time that might lead to a better outcome? Yes, feel some guilt and responsibility for your lapse and errors. But don't condemn yourself to the shame of concluding that you are, and will always be, a lesser person for this mistake.

Put differently, try not to beat yourself up too much when things don't go according to plan or you fall short of your ambitions. If the process of attempted personality change becomes one painful disappointment after another, you are bound to give up sooner rather than later. The process needs to be bearable at least—even better, highly rewarding. So treat yourself and speak to yourself in your own mind with the same patience and sympathy as you would to a friend you care about. Focus more on the perennial challenge of learning and developing the habits and life skills (so-called mastery goals) that you value. In addition, consider whether you are heading in the right direction to

229

meet your life's calling(s) rather than obsessing too much on whether you managed to hit any particular fixed, arbitrary outcomes or whether you are meeting other people's possibly unfair expectations (so-called performance goals).

> *Key takeaway:* In your pursuit of successful personality change, treat yourself with the same compassion you would a close friend with the same aims.

RULE 10: BELIEVING IN THE POTENTIAL FOR— AND CONTINUING NATURE OF—PERSONALITY CHANGE IS A PHILOSOPHY TO LIVE BY

"People don't change." This is a pessimistic refrain uttered often, usually after a person has erred, and frequently followed by ". . . not deep down." I hope that if nothing else, now that you're reaching the end of this book, you would disagree. Ample anecdotal evidence shows that people can and do change, and so does a stream of objective research studies that has continued to flow during my writing of this book.

Consider a US study released late in 2018 that measured the personality of nearly two thousand people twice, fifty years apart, when they were sixteen years old and then sixty-six. Their scores did not change completely; there was that thread of continuity I've referred to before. But of the ten traits that were measured, 98 percent of the sample showed meaningful change on at least one of them, and nearly 60 percent showed meaningful change on four. Moreover, this change was generally positive, including increased resilience and conscientiousness, for example. "Although individuals maintain some of their core personality across the life span, they also change," the researchers said.[18]

Recognizing this potential for change is immensely empowering. You do not have to accept things the way they are. You can work on changing your habits of thought, behavior, and emotion to improve your life, work, and relationships. Remember that much of the research evidence for people's tendency to change in positive ways is based on what happens naturally, without any purposeful intent, over the course of a lifetime. By making a deliberate commitment to improve your personality and enacting the advice laid out in this book, you are likely to be capable of even greater change than research studies have documented.

The idea that personality is to an extent fluid and continues to change through life echoes Buddhist teachings on the impermanence of the self, as well as the growth mind-set approach put forward by psychologist Carol Dweck. Plenty of research suggests thinking this way about personality is beneficial, making it more likely that you can cope with and adapt to setbacks in life. One study with depressed and anxious teenagers found that a thirty-minute lesson in the malleability of personality helped reduce their symptoms and led them to respond to adversity by thinking about how they could change their behavior to cope (rather than feeling hopeless).[19]

An important part of this approach to life is accepting that change never stops. Securing the personality you would like is not a case of "job done," akin to purchasing the house of your dreams or hanging a medal around your neck. As Anthony Joshua, whose story opened this book, has admitted, "The effort it takes to stay on the straight and narrow is challenging."[20] Striving to be the best version of yourself is a lifelong endeavor as you navigate the different challenges, responsibilities, and pitfalls that cross your path, be they career setbacks, possible ill health, jealous colleagues, or wayward lovers. Time and again you may find yourself developing unhelpful traits, and once more you will need to recommit to enacting positive change. My hope for you is that with enough support and dedication, you will find it is a case of one step back but two steps forward, as you continue to mature and flourish with age.

> *Key takeaway*: Change is constant, and dedicating yourself to being the best version of yourself is a lifelong endeavor.

EPILOGUE

Nedim Yasar could barely have known what hit him. It was early evening in Copenhagen, and there was already a chill in the air. Still buzzing from the cocktail party celebrating the launch of a book about his life, Yasar, a tall, tattooed man, had just folded himself into the seat of his car when he was suddenly shot twice in the head. Emergency services rushed him to a hospital, where he died of his injuries later that night.

The party had been held at the Danish Red Cross youth branch where Yasar, a radio show host, was a mentor to troubled youth. "He was inspiring, but never lecturing. It's a big difference," Anders Folmer Buhelt, the organization's director, told the *New York Times*. "Nedim was very strong on values and very clear on what society he wanted to create. But he was also clear on who he used to be."[1]

Nedim Yasar used to be the leader of the notorious Los Guerreros crime gang. He had left the gang seven years earlier, and with the help of a prison rehabilitation program and inspired in large part by the birth of his son, he had successfully reformed his once ruthless, violent personality. But he could not erase his past, which tragically caught up with him.

Nevertheless, Yasar's inspirational story lives on, another powerful demonstration of the capability people have to change.[2] His radio show editor, Jørgen Ramsov, said after his death that Yasar had come out of the prison rehab program "a totally different man . . . determined to raise his voice against gangs, helping young people understand the criminal life was not good for them."[3] I've filled this book with similar anecdotes and the latest mounting research-based evidence showing that personality change is a reality. In fact, in my previous job as editor of a website covering new psychology findings, barely a week went by that I didn't encounter one or more new studies documenting various aspects of personality change.

And yet pushback against the notion that personality is at all malleable—that people can truly change—remains common. As leading personality researcher Brent Roberts put it recently, "Not only do personality traits exist, you can change them. It kind of screws with everyone's worldview."[4]

I often experience this skepticism firsthand. Recently at a reception held by the British Neuroscience Association after I'd just given a public lecture on brain myths, I had the pleasure of chatting with one of the most eminent and charming psychologists in the United Kingdom, recognized internationally as an elder stateswoman of the discipline. When I told her the topic of this book, her immediate reaction was one of extreme skepticism. Like so many others, including many psychologists who do not specialize in personality research, she believed people do not really change. "But isn't the point that personality traits are stable," she said, "that they don't change?" And with characteristic mental alacrity, she quickly highlighted two individuals well known for their intransigence: Donald Trump and former British prime minister Theresa May.

For a moment, I was caught off guard. Those are perfect examples for anyone arguing against the malleability of personality. Trump and May have remarkably different personalities, but both were criticized frequently while in office for what they had in common: their rigidity. Neither seemed capable of change.

I tried to come up with some counterexamples, but embarrassingly my mind went blank (my excuse is that for the public lecture I'd given, my mind was in brain myths mode). As soon as the conversation moved on to other topics, my head then filled with the names of the many changed individuals documented in this book—people like Maajid Nawaz, the Islamic fundamentalist turned peace campaigner; Anthony Joshua, the petty criminal turned youth role model; Nick Yarris, the criminal delinquent turned bookish champion for compassionate living; Emma Stone, the cripplingly shy teenager turned Hollywood megastar; Catra Corbett, the drug addict turned ultrarunner. In each case, these transformations were reflected in significant changes to their underlying personality traits—especially increases in openness, conscientiousness, and agreeableness and reductions in neuroticism.

I also conjured up in my mind many other retorts I ought to have come up with. First, public figures like Trump and May *are* likely to have changed in some respects, just not in ways that are necessarily visible to the public (usually it's the persistence of their least favorable traits, like Trump's narcissism or May's lack of charisma, that observers are commenting on). But the most important point I wish I had made is that significant personality change may occur only if the person *wants* to change. Both May and Trump, and many others like them, convey strongly that they are happy the way they are and have no desire to change whatsoever—a stubbornness that may be a strength in some respects but also their greatest weakness.

I maintain that if hardened criminals can change their personalities for the better, and psychopaths, and shy students, and even would-be fundamentalist extremists, as shown in the anecdotes and research studies peppered through this book, then I'm confident *you* too can change your personality to *be who you want*.

Acknowledgments

I've never met two of the people I'm especially indebted to for helping make this book a reality: my agent, Nat Jacks, at Inkwell Management and my editor, Amar Deol, at Simon & Schuster. This unusual state of affairs is not a reflection of extreme introversion or avoidance on anyone's part. It's down to the fact that Nat and Amar are in New York and I'm based in the Sussex countryside in England.

I thank Nat for reaching out across the Atlantic and gently encouraging me to write my first "big idea" book. I needed spurring on: it was the year my twins were born, when time and sleep were in short supply. Life has been a roller coaster since then, but Nat has been a constant source of friendly advice and support.

Thanks to Amar for believing in the book and guiding me through the writing process. I'm grateful for his warmth and good humor throughout, and especially the way he gave me the confidence to express myself in the book.

One day I hope to meet Nat and Amar and thank them in person!

Thanks also to Tzipora Baitch at Simon & Schuster, who kindly stepped in to help shepherd *Be Who You Want* through the production process, and to Beverly Miller and Yvette Grant for careful copyediting and production editorial work.

Closer to home in England, I'm grateful to Andrew McAleer at Little, Brown (my British publisher) for all his guidance and enthusiasm for the project. Thanks too to my agent in London, Ben Clark at the Soho Agency.

Over the years that I've been writing about personality psychology for the public, I've drawn on the amazing research and theories of a huge number of psychologists, and I'm indebted to them all, including Brent Roberts, Rodica Damian, Julia Rohrer, Simine Vazire, Scott Barry Kaufman, Brian Little, Dan McAdams, Wiebke Bleidorn, Oliver Robinson, Kevin Dutton, and many others too numerous to mention.

Also, to all the inspiring individuals who feature in this book whose stories show the promise and challenges of personality change: thank you so much.

Not long after I started writing *Be Who You Want*, I also launched my own personality psychology column at BBC Future (where I wrote about some of the ideas covered in this book), and I owe many thanks to my editors there, especially David Robson, Richard Fisher, Zaria Gorvett, and Amanda Ruggeri, for their help honing my writing and showing me ways to relate psychology findings to readers' everyday lives.

As I neared the end of my work on this book in 2019, I also undertook a significant career move, leaving my position at the British Psychological Society, where I'd been an editor for over sixteen years, and joining Aeon to start work on its new sister publication, *Psyche* magazine, which launched in May 2020. Thank you to all my new colleagues at Aeon+Psyche for being so welcoming and inspiring, and especially to Brigid and Paul Hains for believing in me and showing how it's possible to marry intellectual rigor with heart and open-mindedness.

I want to thank John Kemp-Potter. In my years writing this book, our weekly battles for table tennis supremacy have been so much fun and helped keep my neuroticism in check!

It is my close family to whom I owe my deepest gratitude. My kind, loving mum, always there for me, providing comfort and wisdom. My dad, who nurtured my competitive spirit. My beautiful, adorable twins, Rose and Charlie: watching your personalities grow and shine is an unparalleled joy. And thank you to my darling wife and soul mate, Jude: I love you more!

Notes

CHAPTER 1: THE WE WITHIN YOU

1. "Anthony Joshua v Jarrell Miller: British World Champion Keen to Avoid 'Banana Skin,'" *BBC Sport*, February 25, 2019, https://www.bbc.co.uk/sport/boxing/47361869.
2. Michael Eboda, "Boxing Changed Anthony Joshua's Life. But It Won't Work for Every Black Kid," the *Guardian*, May 5, 2017, https://www.theguardian.com/commentisfree/2017/may/05/boxing-changed-anthony-joshua-black-kid-education.
3. Jeff Powell, "Anthony Joshua Vows to Create Legacy in and out of the Ring with His Very Own Museum But Aims to Beat 'Big Puncher' Joseph Parker and Deontay Wilder First," *Daily Mail*, March 30, 2018, https://www.dailymail.co.uk/sport/boxing/article-5563249/Anthony-Joshua-vows-beat-big-puncher-Joseph-Parker.html.
4. David Walsh, "How Tiger Woods Performed Sport's Greatest Comeback," the *Sunday Times*, July 14, 2019, https://www.thetimes.co.uk/magazine/the-sunday-times-magazine/how-tiger-woods-performed-sports-greatest-comeback-png7t7v33.
5. Jonah Weiner, "How Emma Stone Got Her Hollywood Ending," *Rolling Stone*, December 21, 2016, http://www.rollingstone.com/movies/features/rolling-stone-cover-story-on-la-la-land-star-emma-stone-w456742.
6. Alex Spiegel, "The Personality Myth," NPR, podcast audio, June 24, 2016, https://www.npr.org/programs/invisibilia/482836315/the-personality-myth.
7. "Noncommunicable diseases and their risk factors," WHO.Int, accesssed January 25, 2021, at https://www.who.int/ncds/prevention/physical-activity/inactivity-global-health-problem/en/.

8. Gordon W. Allport and Henry S. Odbert, "Trait-Names: A Psycho-Lexical Study," *Psychological Monographs* 47, no. 1 (1949): 171.

9. Other experts believe these dark traits are best captured by a sixth main personality trait that taps humility/honesty.

10. Roberta Riccelli, Nicola Toschi, Salvatore Nigro, Antonio Terracciano, and Luca Passamonti, "Surface-Based Morphometry Reveals the Neuroanatomical Basis of the Five-Factor Model of Personality," *Social Cognitive and Affective Neuroscience* 12, no. 4 (2017): 671–684.

11. Nicola Toschi and Luca Passamonti, "Intra-Cortical Myelin Mediates Personality Differences," *Journal of Personality* 87, no. 4 (2019): 889–902.

12. Han-Na Kim, Yeojun Yun, Seungho Ryu, Yoosoo Chang, Min-Jung Kwon, Juhee Cho, Hocheol Shin, and Hyung-Lae Kim, "Correlation Between Gut Microbiota and Personality in Adults: A Cross-Sectional Study," *Brain, Behavior, and Immunity* 69 (2018): 374–385.

13. Daniel A. Briley and Elliot M. Tucker-Drob, "Comparing the Developmental Genetics of Cognition and Personality over the Life Span," *Journal of Personality* 85, no. 1 (2017): 51–64.

14. Mathew A. Harris, Caroline E. Brett, Wendy Johnson, and Ian J. Deary, "Personality Stability from Age 14 to Age 77 Years," *Psychology and Aging* 31, no. 8 (2016): 862.

15. Rodica Ioana Damian, Marion Spengler, Andreea Sutu, and Brent W. Roberts, "Sixteen Going On Sixty-Six: A Longitudinal Study of Personality Stability and Change Across Fifty Years," *Journal of Personality and Social Psychology* 117, no. 3 (2019): 674.

16. Rafael Nadal and John Carlin, *Rafa* (London: Hachette Books, 2012).

17. "Open Letter to Invisibilia," Facebook, June 15, 2016, https://t.co/jUpXPm cBWq.

18. Angela L. Duckworth and Martin E.P. Seligman, "Self-Discipline Outdoes IQ in Predicting Academic Performance of Adolescents," *Psychological Science* 16, no. 12 (December 2005): 939–944.

19. Avshalom Caspi, Renate M. Houts, Daniel W. Belsky, Honalee Harrington, Sean Hogan, Sandhya Ramrakha, Richie Poulton, and Terrie E. Moffitt, "Childhood Forecasting of a Small Segment of the Population with Large Economic Burden," *Nature Human Behaviour* 1, no. 1 (2017): 0005.

20. Benjamin P. Chapman, Alison Huang, Elizabeth Horner, Kelly Peters, Ellena Sempeles, Brent Roberts, and Susan Lapham, "High School Personality Traits and 48-Year All-Cause Mortality Risk: Results from a National Sample of 26,845 Baby Boomers," *Journal of Epidemiology and Community Health* 73, no. 2 (2019): 106–110.

21. Brent W. Roberts, Nathan R. Kuncel, Rebecca Shiner, Avshalom Caspi, and Lewis R. Goldberg, "The Power of Personality: The Comparative Validity of Personality Traits, Socioeconomic Status, and Cognitive Ability for Predicting Important Life Outcomes," *Perspectives on Psychological Science* 2, no. 4 (2007): 313–345.

22. Christopher J. Boyce, Alex M. Wood, and Nattavudh Powdthavee, "Is Personality Fixed? Personality Changes as Much as 'Variable' Economic Factors and More Strongly Predicts Changes to Life Satisfaction," *Social Indicators Research* 111, no. 1 (2013): 287–305.

23. Sophie Hentschel, Michael Eid, and Tanja Kutscher, "The Influence of Major Life Events and Personality Traits on the Stability of Affective Well-Being," *Journal of Happiness Studies* 18, no. 3 (2017): 719–741.

24. Petri J. Kajonius and Anders Carlander, "Who Gets Ahead in Life? Personality Traits and Childhood Background in Economic Success," *Journal of Economic Psychology* 59 (2017): 164–170.

25. Rodica Ioana Damian, Marion Spengler, and Brent W. Roberts, "Whose Job Will Be Taken Over by a Computer? The Role of Personality in Predicting Job Computerizability over the Lifespan," *European Journal of Personality* 31, no. 3 (2017): 291–310.

26. Benjamin P. Chapman and Lewis R. Goldberg, "Act-Frequency Signatures of the Big Five," *Personality and Individual Differences* 116 (2017): 201–205.

27. David A. Ellis and Rob Jenkins, "Watch-Wearing as a Marker of Conscientiousness," *PeerJ* 3 (2015): e1210.

28. Joshua J. Jackson, Dustin Wood, Tim Bogg, Kate E. Walton, Peter D. Harms, and Brent W. Roberts, "What Do Conscientious People Do? Development and Validation of the Behavioral Indicators of Conscientiousness (BIC)," *Journal of Research in Personality* 44, no. 4 (2010): 501–511.

29. Anastasiya A. Lipnevich, Marcus Credè, Elisabeth Hahn, Frank M. Spinath, Richard D. Roberts, and Franzis Preckel, "How Distinctive Are Morningness and Eveningness from the Big Five Factors of Personality? A Meta-Analytic Investigation," *Journal of Personality and Social Psychology* 112, no. 3 (2017): 491.

30. "The Big Five Inventory-2 Short Form (BFI-2-S)," accessed October 7, 2019, at http://www.colby.edu/psych/wp-content/uploads/sites/50/2013/08/bfi2s-form.pdf.

31. Throughout this book I use the spellings "extravert" and "extraversion" (rather than "extrovert" and "extroversion") because this is how the terms are spelled in the psychological literature, following Carl Jung's seminal writings on personality dimensions.

32. Michael A. Sayette, "The Effects of Alcohol on Emotion in Social Drinkers," *Behaviour Research and Therapy* 88 (2017): 76–89.

33. Dan P. McAdams, *The Art and Science of Personality Development* (New York: Guilford Press, 2015).

34. Michelle N. Servaas, Jorien Van Der Velde, Sergi G. Costafreda, Paul Horton, Johan Ormel, Harriette Riese, and Andre Aleman, "Neuroticism and the Brain: A Quantitative Meta-Analysis of Neuroimaging Studies Investigating Emotion Processing," *Neuroscience and Biobehavioral Reviews* 37, no. 8 (2013): 1518–1529.

35. Evolutionary psychologists also point out that being highly neurotic might have given our ancestors a survival advantage, especially during times of greater threat to life.

36. Achala H. Rodrigo, Stefano I. Di Domenico, Bryanna Graves, Jaeger Lam, Hasan Ayaz, R. Michael Bagby, and Anthony C. Ruocco, "Linking Trait-Based Phenotypes to Prefrontal Cortex Activation During Inhibitory Control," *Social Cognitive and Affective Neuroscience* 11, no. 1 (2015): 55–65.

37. Brian W. Haas, Kazufumi Omura, R. Todd Constable, and Turhan Canli, "Is Automatic Emotion Regulation Associated with Agreeableness? A Perspective Using a Social Neuroscience Approach," *Psychological Science* 18, no. 2 (2007): 130–132.

38. Cameron A. Miller, Dominic J. Parrott, and Peter R. Giancola, "Agreeableness and Alcohol-Related Aggression: The Mediating Effect of Trait Aggressivity," *Experimental and Clinical Psychopharmacology* 17, no. 6 (2009): 445.

39. Scott Barry Kaufman, Lena C. Quilty, Rachael G. Grazioplene, Jacob B. Hirsh, Jeremy R. Gray, Jordan B. Peterson, and Colin G. DeYoung, "Openness to Experience and Intellect Differentially Predict Creative Achievement in the Arts and Sciences," *Journal of Personality* 84, no. 2 (2016): 248–258.

40. Mitchell C. Colver and Amani El-Alayli, "Getting Aesthetic Chills from Music: The Connection Between Openness to Experience and Frisson," *Psychology of Music* 44, no. 3 (2016): 413–427.

41. Douglas P. Terry, Antonio N. Puente, Courtney L. Brown, Carlos C. Faraco, and L. Stephen Miller, "Openness to Experience Is Related to Better Memory Ability in Older Adults with Questionable Dementia," *Journal of Clinical and Experimental Neuropsychology* 35, no. 5 (2013): 509–517; E. I. Franchow, Y. Suchy, S. R. Thorgusen, and P. Williams, "More Than Education: Openness to Experience Contributes to Cognitive Reserve in Older Adulthood," *Journal of Aging Science* 1, no. 109 (2013): 1–8.

42. Timothy A. Judge, Chad A. Higgins, Carl J. Thoresen, and Murray R. Barrick, "The Big Five Personality Traits, General Mental Ability, and Career Success Across the Life Span," *Personnel Psychology* 52, no. 3 (1999): 621–652.

CHAPTER 2: SLINGS AND ARROWS

1. Helena R. Slobodskaya and Elena A. Kozlova, "Early Temperament as a Predictor of Later Personality," *Personality and Individual Differences* 99 (2016): 127–132.

2. Avshalom Caspi, HonaLee Harrington, Barry Milne, James W. Amell, Reremoana F. Theodore, and Terrie E. Moffitt, "Children's Behavioral Styles at Age 3 Are Linked to Their Adult Personality Traits at Age 26," *Journal of Personality* 71, no. 4 (2003): 495–514.

3. M. Spengler, O. Lüdtke, R. Martin, and M. Brunner, "Childhood Personality and Teacher Ratings of Conscientiousness Predict Career Success Four Decades Later," *Personality and Individual Differences* 60 (2014): S28.

4. Philip Larkin, "This Be The Verse," in *Philip Larkin: Collected Poems*, ed. Anthony Thwaite (London: Faber, 1988).

5. Alison Gopnik, *The Gardener and the Carpenter: What the New Science of Child Development Tells Us About the Relationship Between Parents and Children* (New York: Macmillan, 2016).

6. Gordon Parker, Hilary Tupling, and Laurence B. Brown, "A Parental Bonding Instrument," *British Journal of Medical Psychology* 52, no. 1 (1979): 1–10. This is a formal questionnaire that measures authoritarian parenting.

7. Wendy S. Grolnick and Richard M. Ryan, "Parent Styles Associated with Children's Self-Regulation and Competence in School," *Journal of Educational Psychology* 81, no. 2 (1989): 143; Laurence Steinberg, Nancy E. Darling, Anne C. Fletcher, B. Bradford Brown, and Sanford M. Dornbusch, "Authoritative Parenting and Adolescent Adjustment: An Ecological Journey," in *Examining Lives in Context*, eds. P. Moen, G. H. Elder, Jr., and K. Lüscher (Washington, DC: American Psychological Association, 1995).

8. Irving M. Reti, Jack F. Samuels, William W. Eaton, O. Joseph Bienvenu III, Paul T. Costa Jr., and Gerald Nestadt, "Influences of Parenting on Normal Personality Traits," *Psychiatry Research* 111, no. 1 (2002): 55–64.

9. Angela Duckworth, *Grit: The Power of Passion and Perseverance* (New York: Scribner, 2016).

10. W. Thomas Boyce and Bruce J. Ellis, "Biological Sensitivity to Context: I. An Evolutionary-Developmental Theory of the Origins and Functions of Stress Reactivity," *Development and Psychopathology* 17, no. 2 (2005): 271–301.

11. Michael Pluess, Elham Assary, Francesca Lionetti, Kathryn J. Lester, Eva Krapohl, Elaine N. Aron, and Arthur Aron, "Environmental Sensitivity in Children: Development of the Highly Sensitive Child Scale and Identification of Sensitivity Groups," *Developmental Psychology* 54, no. 1 (2018): 51.

12. Jocelyn Voo, "Birth Order Traits: Your Guide to Sibling Personality Differences,"

Parents.com, accessed October 7, 2019, at http://www.parents.com/baby/development/social/birth-order-and-personality/.

13. "How Many US Presidents Were First-Born Sons?" Wisegeek.com, accessed October 7, 2019, at http://www.wisegeek.com/how-many-us-presidents-were-first-born-sons.htm.

14. Julia M. Rohrer, Boris Egloff, and Stefan C. Schmukle, "Examining the Effects of Birth Order on Personality," *Proceedings of the National Academy of Sciences* 112, no. 46 (2015): 14224–14229.

15. Rodica Ioana Damian and Brent W. Roberts, "The Associations of Birth Order with Personality and Intelligence in a Representative Sample of US High School Students," *Journal of Research in Personality* 58 (2015): 96–105.

16. Rodica Ioana Damian and Brent W. Roberts, "Settling the Debate on Birth Order and Personality," *Proceedings of the National Academy of Sciences* 112, no. 46 (2015): 14119–14120.

17. Bart H. H. Golsteyn and Cécile A. J. Magnée, "Does Birth Spacing Affect Personality?" *Journal of Economic Psychology* 60 (2017): 92–108.

18. Lisa Cameron, Nisvan Erkal, Lata Gangadharan, and Xin Meng, "Little Emperors: Behavioral Impacts of China's One-Child Policy," *Science* 339, no. 6122 (2013): 953–957.

19. Jennifer Watling Neal, C. Emily Durbin, Allison E. Gornik, and Sharon L. Lo, "Codevelopment of Preschoolers' Temperament Traits and Social Play Networks Over an Entire School Year," *Journal of Personality and Social Psychology* 113, no. 4 (2017): 627.

20. Thomas J. Dishion, Joan McCord, and François Poulin, "When Interventions Harm: Peer Groups and Problem Behavior," *American Psychologist* 54, no. 9 (1999): 755.

21. Maarten H. W. van Zalk, Steffen Nestler, Katharina Geukes, Roos Hutteman, and Mitja D. Back, "The Codevelopment of Extraversion and Friendships: Bonding and Behavioral Interaction Mechanisms in Friendship Networks," *Journal of Personality and Social Psychology* 118, no. 6 (2020): 1269.

22. Christopher J. Soto, Oliver P. John, Samuel D. Gosling, and Jeff Potter, "Age Differences in Personality Traits from 10 to 65: Big Five Domains and Facets in a Large Cross-Sectional Sample," *Journal of Personality and Social Psychology* 100, no. 2 (2011): 330.

23. Sally Williams, "Monica Bellucci on Life after Divorce and Finding Herself in her 50s," *Telegraph*, July 15, 2017, https://www.telegraph.co.uk/films/2017/07/15/monica-bellucci-life-divorce-finding-50s.

24. Tim Robey, "Vincent Cassel: 'Women Like Security. Men Prefer Adventure,'"

the *Telegraph*, May 28, 2016, http://www.telegraph.co.uk/films/2016/05/28/vincent-cassel-women-like-security-men-prefer-adventure/.

25. Paul T. Costa Jr., Jeffrey H. Herbst, Robert R. McCrae, and Ilene C. Siegler, "Personality at Midlife: Stability, Intrinsic Maturation, and Response to Life Events," *Assessment* 7, no. 4 (2000): 365–378.

26. Emily Retter, "Oldest Ever Bond Girl Monica Bellucci Reveals How a Woman of 51 Can Have Killer Sex Appeal," *Irish Mirror*, October 20, 2015, http://www.irishmirror.ie/showbiz/celebrity-news/oldest-ever-bond-girl-monica-6669965.

27. Jule Specht, Boris Egloff, and Stefan C. Schmukle, "Stability and Change of Personality Across the Life Course: The Impact of Age and Major Life Events on Mean-Level and Rank-Order Stability of the Big Five," *Journal of Personality and Social Psychology* 101, no. 4 (2011): 862.

28. Marcus Mund and Franz J. Neyer, "Loneliness Effects on Personality," *International Journal of Behavioral Development* 43, no. 2 (2019): 136–146.

29. Christian Jarrett, "Lonely People's Brains Work Differently," *New York* magazine, August 2015, https://www.thecut.com/2015/08/lonely-peoples-brains-work-differently.html.

30. Christopher J. Boyce, Alex M. Wood, Michael Daly, and Constantine Sedikides, "Personality Change Following Unemployment," *Journal of Applied Psychology* 100, no. 4 (2015): 991.

31. Gabrielle Donnelly, "'I'd Have Sold My Mother for a Rock of Crack Cocaine': Tom Hardy on his Astonishing Journey from English Private Schoolboy to Drug Addict—and Now Hollywood's No 1 Baddie," *Daily Mail*, January 22, 2016, http://www.dailymail.co.uk/tvshowbiz/article-3411226/I-d-sold-mother-rock-crack-cocaine-Tom-Hardy-astonishing-journey-public-schoolboy-drug-addict-Hollywood-s-No-1-baddie.html.

32. Specht, Egloff, and Schmukle, "Stability and Change of Personality Across the Life Course," 862.

33. Christiane Niesse and Hannes Zacher, "Openness to Experience as a Predictor and Outcome of Upward Job Changes into Managerial and Professional Positions," *PloS One* 10, no. 6 (2015): e0131115.

34. Eva Asselmann and Jule Specht, "Taking the ups and downs at the rollercoaster of love: Associations between major life events in the domain of romantic relationships and the Big Five personality traits," *Developmental Psychology* 56, no. 9 (2020): 1803–1816.

35. Specht, Egloff, and Schmukle, "Stability and Change of Personality Across the Life Course," 862.

36. Tila M. Pronk, Asuma Buyukcan-Tetik, Marina M. A. H. Iliás, and Catrin Finkenauer, "Marriage as a Training Ground: Examining Change in Self-Control and Forgiveness over the First Four Years of Marriage," *Journal of Social and Personal Relationships* 36, no. 1 (2019): 109–130.

37. Jeroen Borghuis, Jaap J. A. Denissen, Klaas Sijtsma, Susan Branje, Wim H. Meeus, and Wiebke Bleidorn, "Positive Daily Experiences Are Associated with Personality Trait Changes in Middle-Aged Mothers," *European Journal of Personality* 32, no. 6 (2018): 672–689.

38. Manon A. van Scheppingen, Jaap Denissen, Joanne M. Chung, Kristian Tambs, and Wiebke Bleidorn, "Self-Esteem and Relationship Satisfaction During the Transition to Motherhood," *Journal of Personality and Social Psychology* 114, no. 6 (2018): 973.

39. Specht, Egloff, and Schmukle, "Stability and Change of Personality Across the Life Course," 862; Sarah Galdiolo and Isabelle Roskam, "Development of Personality Traits in Response to Childbirth: A≠ Longitudinal Dyadic Perspective," *Personality and Individual Differences* 69 (2014): 223–230; Manon A. van Scheppingen, Joshua J. Jackson, Jule Specht, Roos Hutteman, Jaap J. A. Denissen, and Wiebke Bleidorn, "Personality Trait Development During the Transition to Parenthood, *Social Psychological and Personality Science* 7, no. 5 (2016): 452–462.

40. Emma Dawson, "A Moment That Changed Me: The Death of My Sister and the Grief That Followed," the *Guardian*, December 3, 2015, https://www.theguardian.com/commentisfree/2015/dec/03/moment-changed-me-sisters-death.

41. Daniel K. Mroczek and Avron Spiro III, "Modeling Intraindividual Change in Personality Traits: Findings from the Normative Aging Study," *Journals of Gerontology Series B: Psychological Sciences and Social Sciences* 58, no. 3 (2003): P153–P165.

42. Eva Asselmann and Jule Specht, "Till Death Do Us Part: Transactions Between Losing One's Spouse and the Big Five Personality Traits," *Journal of Personality* 88, no. 4 (2020): 659–675.

43. Michael P. Hengartner, Peter Tyrer, Vladeta Ajdacic-Gross, Jules Angst, and Wulf Rössler, "Articulation and Testing of a Personality-Centred Model of Psychopathology: Evidence from a Longitudinal Community Study over 30 Years," *European Archives of Psychiatry and Clinical Neuroscience* 268, no. 5 (2018): 443–454.

44. Konrad Bresin and Michael D. Robinson, "You Are What You See and Choose: Agreeableness and Situation Selection," *Journal of Personality* 83, no. 4 (2015): 452–463.

45. Christopher J. Boyce, Alex M. Wood, and Eamonn Ferguson, "For Better or for Worse: The Moderating Effects of Personality on the Marriage-Life Satisfaction Link," *Personality and Individual Differences* 97 (2016): 61–66.

46. Tasha Eurich, *Insight: The Power of Self-Awareness in a Self-Deluded World* (New York: Macmillan, 2017).

47. Developed by Dan P. McAdams.

48. Dan P. McAdams, *The Art and Science of Personality Development* (New York: Guilford Press, 2015).

49. Jonathan M. Adler, Jennifer Lodi-Smith, Frederick L. Philippe, and Iliane Houle, "The Incremental Validity of Narrative Identity in Predicting Well-Being: A Review of the Field and Recommendations for the Future," *Personality and Social Psychology Review* 20, no. 2 (2016): 142–175.

50. Dan P. McAdams, *The Art and Science of Personality Development* (New York: Guilford Press, 2015).

CHAPTER 3: PATHOLOGICAL CHANGE

1. Chloe Lambert, "A Knock on My Head Changed My Personality: It Made Me a Nicer Person!" *Daily Mail*, January 14, 2013, https://www.dailymail.co.uk/health/article-2262379/Bicycle-accident-A-knock-head-changed-personality-The-good-news-nicer.html.

2. Anne Norup and Erik Lykke Mortensen, "Prevalence and Predictors of Personality Change after Severe Brain Injury," *Archives of Physical Medicine and Rehabilitation* 96, no. 1 (2015): 56–62.

3. John M. Harlow, "Recovery from the Passage of an Iron Bar Through the Head," *Publications of the Massachusetts Medical Society* 2 (1868): 2327–2347.

4. Joseph Barrash, Donald T. Stuss, Nazan Aksan, Steven W. Anderson, Robert D. Jones, Kenneth Manzel, and Daniel Tranel, "'Frontal Lobe Syndrome'? Subtypes of Acquired Personality Disturbances in Patients with Focal Brain Damage," *Cortex* 106 (2018): 65–80.

5. Paul Broks, "How a Brain Tumour Can Look Like a Mid-Life Crisis," *Prospect*, July 20, 2000, https://www.prospectmagazine.co.uk/magazine/voodoochile.

6. Nina Strohminger and Shaun Nichols, "Neurodegeneration and Identity," *Psychological Science* 26, no. 9 (2015): 1469–1479.

7. Lambert, "A Knock on My Head."

8. Even when a brain injury or insult does not affect personality or has a beneficial effect, it is important not to underestimate the impact such an experience can have. Most people suffering a brain injury will live with at least some persistent difficulties for the rest of their lives, even if these are sometimes hidden, such as in the form of memory problems or social difficulties.

9. Damian Whitworth, "I Had a Stroke at 34. I Prefer My Life Now," the *Times*, October 14, 2018, https://www.thetimes.co.uk/article/i-had-a-stroke-at-34-i-prefer-my-life-now-59krk356p.

10. Sally Williams, "I Had a Stroke at 34, I Couldn't Sleep, Read or Even Think," *Daily Telegraph*, August 17, 2017, https://www.telegraph.co.uk/health-fitness/mind/had-stroke-34-couldnt-sleep-read-even-think/.

11. This was the first systematic attempt to identify incidences of positive personality change across a range of different types of brain injury, but there are earlier related reports in the literature. For instance, a 1968 paper in the *British Journal of Psychiatry* featured an evaluation of seventy-nine survivors of ruptured brain aneurysms (weakened blood vessels) and reported that nine experienced a positive personality change. One fifty-three-year-old woman was reported to be friendlier and happier (though also more tactless) and less prone to worry after her neural injury; in fact, she claimed to have received three marriage proposals in the years since it occurred.

12. Marcie L. King, Kenneth Manzel, Joel Bruss, and Daniel Tranel, "Neural Correlates of Improvements in Personality and Behavior Following a Neurological Event," *Neuropsychologia* 145 (2017): 1–10.

13. *Robin Williams* (In the Moment Productions, June 10, 2001).

14. Susan Williams, "Remembering Robin Williams," the *Times* (London), November 28, 2015, https://www.thetimes.co.uk/article/remembering-robin-williams-mj3gpjhcrc2.

15. Susan Schneider Williams, "The Terrorist Inside My Husband's Brain," *Neurology* 87 (2016): 1308–1311.

16. Dave Itzkoff, *Robin* (New York: Holt, 2018).

17. Ibid.

18. Ibid.

19. American Parkinson Disease Association, "Changes in Personality," accessed October 20, 2019, at https://www.apdaparkinson.org/what-is-parkinsons/symptoms/personality-change; Antonio Cerasa, "Re-Examining the Parkinsonian Personality Hypothesis: A Systematic Review," *Personality and Individual Differences* 130 (2018): 41–50.

20. Williams, "The Terrorist Inside My Husband's Brain," 1308–1311.

21. Tarja-Brita Robins Wahlin and Gerard J. Byrne, "Personality Changes in Alzheimer's Disease: A Systematic Review," *International Journal of Geriatric Psychiatry* 26, no. 10 (2011): 1019–1029.

22. Alfonsina D'Iorio, Federica Garramone, Fausta Piscopo, Chiara Baiano, Simona Raimo, and Gabriella Santangelo, "Meta-Analysis of Personality Traits in Alzheimer's Disease: A Comparison with Healthy Subjects," *Journal of Alzheimer's Disease* 62, no. 2 (2018): 773–787.

23. Colin G. DeYoung, Jacob B. Hirsh, Matthew S. Shane, Xenophon Papademetris, Nallakkandi Rajeevan, and Jeremy R. Gray, "Testing Predictions from

Personality Neuroscience: Brain Structure and the Big Five," *Psychological Science* 21, no. 6 (2010): 820–828.

24. Silvio Ramos Bernardes da Silva Filho, Jeam Haroldo Oliveira Barbosa, Carlo Rondinoni, Antonio Carlos dos Santos, Carlos Ernesto Garrido Salmon, Nereida Kilza da Costa Lima, Eduardo Ferriolli, and Júlio César Moriguti, "Neuro-Degeneration Profile of Alzheimer's Patients: A Brain Morphometry Study," *NeuroImage: Clinical* 15 (2017): 15–24.

25. Tomiko Yoneda, Jonathan Rush, Eileen K. Graham, Anne Ingeborg Berg, Hannie Comijs, Mindy Katz, Richard B. Lipton, Boo Johansson, Daniel K. Mroczek, and Andrea M. Piccinin, "Increases in Neuroticism May Be an Early Indicator of Dementia: A Coordinated Analysis," *Journals of Gerontology: Series B* 75 (2018): 251–262.

26. "Draft Checklist on Mild Behavioral Impairment," the *New York Times*, July 25, 2016, https://www.nytimes.com/interactive/2016/07/25/health/26brain-doc.html.

27. Neil Osterweil, "Personality Changes May Help Distinguish between Types of Dementia," *Medpage Today*, May 31, 2007, https://www.medpagetoday.com /neurology/alzheimersdisease/5803; James E. Galvin, Heather Malcom, David Johnson, and John C. Morris, "Personality Traits Distinguishing Dementia with Lewy Bodies from Alzheimer Disease," *Neurology* 68, no. 22 (2007): 1895–1901.

28. "Read Husband's Full Statement on Kate Spade's Suicide," CNN, June 7, 2018, https://edition.cnn.com/2018/06/07/us/andy-kate-spade-statement/index .html.

29. National Institute of Mental Health, "Major Depression," accessed October 20, 2019, at https://www.nimh.nih.gov/health/statistics/major-depression.shtml.

30. American Foundation for Suicide Prevention, "Suicide Rate Is Up 1.2 Percent according to Most Recent CDC Data (Year 2016)," accessed October 20, 2019, at https://afsp.org/suicide-rate-1-8-percent-according-recent-cdc-data-year-2016/.

31. Patrick Marlborough, "Depression Steals Your Soul and Then It Takes Your Friends," *Vice*, January 31, 2017, accessed October 20, 2019, at https://www .vice.com/en_au/article/4x4xjj/depression-steals-your-soul-and-then-it-takes-your-friends.

32. Julie Karsten, Brenda W. J. H. Penninx, Hariëtte Riese, Johan Ormel, Willem A. Nolen, and Catharina A. Hartman, "The State Effect of Depressive and Anxiety Disorders on Big Five Personality Traits," *Journal of Psychiatric Research* 46, no. 5 (2012): 644–650.

33. J. H. Barnett, J. Huang, R. H. Perlis, M. M. Young, J. F. Rosenbaum, A. A. Nierenberg, G. Sachs, V. L. Nimgaonkar, D. J. Miklowitz, and J. W. Smoller, "Personality

and Bipolar Disorder: Dissecting State and Trait Associations between Mood and Personality," *Psychological Medicine* 41, no. 8 (2011): 1593–1604.

34. "Experiences of Bipolar Disorder: 'Every Day It Feels Like I Must Wear a Mask,'" the *Guardian*, March 31, 2017, accessed October 20, 2019, at https://www.theguardian.com/lifeandstyle/2017/mar/31/experiences-of-bipolar-disorder-every-day-it-feels-like-i-must-wear-a-mask.

35. Mark Eckblad and Loren J. Chapman, "Development and Validation of a Scale for Hypomanic Personality," *Journal of Abnormal Psychology* 95, no. 3 (1986): 214.

36. Gordon Parker, Kathryn Fletcher, Stacey McCraw, and Michael Hong, "The Hypomanic Personality Scale: A Measure of Personality and/or Bipolar Symptoms?" *Psychiatry Research* 220, nos. 1–2 (2014): 654–658.

37. Johan Ormel, Albertine J. Oldehinkel, and Wilma Vollebergh, "Vulnerability Before, During, and After a Major Depressive Episode: A 3-Wave Population-Based Study," *Archives of General Psychiatry* 61, no. 10 (2004): 990–996; Pekka Jylhä, Tarja Melartin, Heikki Rytsälä, and Erkki Isometsä, "Neuroticism, Introversion, and Major Depressive Disorder—Traits, States, or Scars?" *Depression and Anxiety* 26, no. 4 (2009): 325–334; M. Tracie Shea, Andrew C. Leon, Timothy I. Mueller, David A. Solomon, Meredith G. Warshaw, and Martin B. Keller, "Does Major Depression Result in Lasting Personality Change?" *American Journal of Psychiatry* 153, no. 11 (1996): 1404–1410; E. H. Bos, M. Ten Have, S. van Dorsselaer, B. F. Jeronimus, R. de Graaf, and P. de Jonge, "Functioning Before and After a Major Depressive Episode: Pre-Existing Vulnerability or Scar? A Prospective Three-Wave Population-Based Study," *Psychological Medicine* 48, no. 13 (2018): 2264–2272.

38. Tom Rosenström, Pekka Jylhä, Laura Pulkki-Råback, Mikael Holma, Olli T. Raitakari, Erkki Isometsä, and Liisa Keltikangas-Järvinen, "Long-Term Personality Changes and Predictive Adaptive Responses after Depressive Episodes," *Evolution and Human Behavior* 36, no. 5 (2015): 337–344.

39. Barnett, "Personality and Bipolar Disorder: Dissecting State and Trait Associations Between Mood and Personality," 1593–1604.

40. Tony Z. Tang, Robert J. DeRubeis, Steven D. Hollon, Jay Amsterdam, Richard Shelton, and Benjamin Schalet, "A Placebo-Controlled Test of the Effects of Paroxetine and Cognitive Therapy on Personality Risk Factors in Depression," *Archives of General Psychiatry* 66, no. 12 (2009): 1322.

41. Sabine Tjon Pian Gi, Jos Egger, Maarten Kaarsemaker, and Reinier Kreutzkamp, "Does Symptom Reduction after Cognitive Behavioural Therapy of Anxiety Disordered Patients Predict Personality Change?" *Personality and Mental Health* 4, no. 4 (2010): 237–245.

42. Oliver Kamm, "My Battle with Clinical Depression," the *Times* (London), June 11, 2016, accessed October 20, 2019, at https://www.thetimes.co.uk/article/id-sit-on-the-stairs-until-i-was-ready-to-open-the-front-door-it-could-take-an-hour-z60g637mt.

43. Shuichi Suetani and Elizabeth Markwick, "Meet Dr Jekyll: A Case of a Psychiatrist with Dissociative Identity Disorder," *Australasian Psychiatry* 22, no. 5 (2014): 489–491.

44. Emma Young, "My Many Selves: How I Learned to Live with Multiple Personalities," *Mosaic*, June 12, 2017, https://mosaicscience.com/story/my-many-selves-multiple-personalities-dissociative-identity-disorder.

45. Bethany L. Brand, Catherine C. Classen, Scot W. McNary, and Parin Zaveri, "A Review of Dissociative Disorders Treatment Studies," *Journal of Nervous and Mental Disease* 197, no. 9 (2009): 646–654.

46. Richard G. Tedeschi and Lawrence G. Calhoun, "The Posttraumatic Growth Inventory: Measuring the Positive Legacy of Trauma," *Journal of Traumatic Stress* 9, no. 3 (1996): 455–471.

47. Michael Hoerger, Benjamin P. Chapman, Holly G. Prigerson, Angela Fagerlin, Supriya G. Mohile, Ronald M. Epstein, Jeffrey M. Lyness, and Paul R. Duberstein, "Personality Change Pre- to Post-Loss in Spousal Caregivers of Patients with Terminal Lung Cancer," *Social Psychological and Personality Science* 5, no. 6 (2014): 722–729.

48. Scott Barry Kaufman, Twitter post, November 23, 2018, 7:35 p.m., https://twitter.com/sbkaufman/status/1066052630202540032.

49. Jasmin K. Turner, Amanda Hutchinson, and Carlene Wilson, "Correlates of Post-Traumatic Growth following Childhood and Adolescent Cancer: A Systematic Review and Meta-Analysis," *Psycho-Oncology* 27, no. 4 (2018): 1100–1109.

50. Daniel Lim and David DeSteno, "Suffering and Compassion: The Links among Adverse Life Experiences, Empathy, Compassion, and Prosocial Behavior," *Emotion* 16, no. 2 (2016): 175.

CHAPTER 4: DIETS, HIGHS, AND HANGOVERS

1. "Obama's Tearful 'Thank You' to Campaign Staff," YouTube video, 5:25, November 8, 2012, https://www.youtube.com/watch?v=1NCzUOWuu_A.

2. Julie Hirschfeld Davis, "Obama Delivers Eulogy for Beau Biden," the *New York Times*, June 6, 2015, https://www.nytimes.com/2015/06/07/us/beau-biden-funeral-held-in-delaware.html.

3. Julie Hirschfeld Davis, "Obama Lowers His Guard in Unusual Displays of Emotion," the *New York Times*, June 22, 2015, https://www.nytimes.com/2015/06/23/us/politics/obama-lowers-his-guard-in-unusual-displays-of-emotion.html.

4. Chris Cillizza, "President Obama Cried in Public Today. That's a Good Thing," *Washington Post*, April 29, 2016, https://www.washingtonpost.com/news/the-fix /wp/2016/01/05/why-men-should-cry-more-in-public/.

5. Kenneth Walsh, "Critics Say Obama Lacks Emotion," *US News and World Report*, December 24, 2009, https://www.usnews.com/news/obama/articles/2009 /12/24/critics-say-obama-lacks-emotion.

6. James Fallows, "Obama Explained," the *Atlantic*, March 2012, https://www.the-atlantic.com/magazine/archive/2012/03/obama-explained/308874/.

7. Walter Mischel, *The Marshmallow Test: Understanding Self-Control and How to Master It* (London: Corgi Books, 2015).

8. It's easy to challenge the extreme situationist arguments. There were methodological holes in Zimbardo's prison study. Recordings have surfaced showing Zimbardo coaching the prison guards to be ruthless and tyrannical, and questions have been raised over whether the kind of people who would volunteer for a "prison study" have typical personalities in the first place. And, contra Mischel, it has become clear that, yes, people do adapt to situations, but if you observe them over an extended period of time and across different situations, they will vary in the average amount of time they act extraverted, aggressive, friendly, and so on, as well as in how intensely they display these behaviors.

9. Kyle S. Sauerberger and David C. Funder, "Behavioral Change and Consistency across Contexts," *Journal of Research in Personality* 69 (2017): 264–272.

10. Jim White, "Ashes 2009: Legend Dennis Lillee Says Mitchell Johnson Could Swing It for Australia," the *Telegraph*, June 26, 2009, https://www.telegraph. co.uk/sport/cricket/international/theashes/5650760/Ashes-2009-legend-Dennis -Lillee-says-Mitchell-Johnson-could-swing-it-for-Australia.html.

11. Nick Pitt, "Deontay Wilder: 'When I Fight There Is a Transformation, I Even Frighten Myself, '" the *Sunday Times* (London), November 11, 2018, https://www.thetimes.co.uk/article/when-i-fight-there-is-a-transformation-i-even -frighten-myself-h2jpq9x9t.

12. Mark Bridge, "Mum Says I'm Starting to Act Like Sherlock, Says Cumberbatch," the *Times* (London), December 27, 2016, https://www.thetimes.co.uk /article/mum-says-i-m-starting-to-act-like-sherlock-57ffpr6dv.

13. Tasha Eurich, *Insight: The Power of Self-Awareness in a Self-Deluded World* (London: Pan Books, 2018).

14. Katharina Geukes, Steffen Nestler, Roos Hutteman, Albrecht C. P. Küfner, and Mitja D. Back, "Trait Personality and State Variability: Predicting Individual Differences in Within- and Cross-Context Fluctuations in Affect, Self-Evaluations, and Behavior in Everyday Life," *Journal of Research in Personality* 69 (2017): 124–138.

15. Oliver C. Robinson, "On the Social Malleability of Traits: Variability and Consistency in Big 5 Trait Expression across Three Interpersonal Contexts," *Journal of Individual Differences* 30, no. 4 (2009): 201–208.

16. Dawn Querstret and Oliver C. Robinson, "Person, Persona, and Personality Modification: An In-Depth Qualitative Exploration of Quantitative Findings," *Qualitative Research in Psychology* 10, no. 2 (2013): 140–159.

17. Melissa Dahl, "Can You Blend in Anywhere? Or Are You Always the Same You?" the *Cut*, March 15, 2017, https://www.thecut.com/2017/03/heres-a-test-to-tell-you-if-you-are-a-high-self-monitor.html.

18. Mark Snyder and Steve Gangestad, "On the Nature of Self-Monitoring: Matters of Assessment, Matters of Validity," *Journal of Personality and Social Psychology* 51, no. 1 (1986): 125.

19. Rebecca Hardy, "Polish Model Let Off for Harrods Theft Gives Her Side," *Daily Mail Online*, August 12, 2017, http://www.dailymail.co.uk/femail/article-4783272/Polish-model-let-Harrod-s-theft-gives-side.html.

20. Robert E. Wilson, Renee J. Thompson, and Simine Vazire, "Are Fluctuations in Personality States More Than Fluctuations in Affect?" *Journal of Research in Personality* 69 (2017): 110–123.

21. Noah Eisenkraft and Hillary Anger Elfenbein, "The Way You Make Me Feel: Evidence for Individual Differences in Affective Presence," *Psychological Science* 21, no. 4 (2010): 505–510.

22. Jan Querengässer and Sebastian Schindler, "Sad But True? How Induced Emotional States Differentially Bias Self-Rated Big Five Personality Traits," *BMC Psychology* 2, no. 1 (2014): 14.

23. Maya Angelou, *Rainbow in the Cloud: The Wit and Wisdom of Maya Angelou* (New York: Little, Brown Book Group, 2016).

24. Thomas L. Webb, Kristen A. Lindquist, Katelyn Jones, Aya Avishai, and Paschal Sheeran, "Situation Selection Is a Particularly Effective Emotion Regulation Strategy for People Who Need Help Regulating Their Emotions," *Cognition and Emotion* 32, no. 2 (2018): 231–248.

25. Zhanjia Zhang and Weiyun Chen, "A Systematic Review of the Relationship Between Physical Activity and Happiness," *Journal of Happiness Studies* 20, no. 4 (2019): 1305–1322.

26. L. Parker Schiffer and Tomi-Ann Roberts, "The Paradox of Happiness: Why Are We Not Doing What We Know Makes Us Happy?" *Journal of Positive Psychology* 13, no. 3 (2018): 252–259.

27. Kelly Sullivan and Collins Ordiah, "Association of Mildly Insufficient Sleep with Symptoms of Anxiety and Depression," *Neurology, Psychiatry and Brain Research* 30 (2018): 1–4.

28. Floor M. Kroese, Catharine Evers, Marieke A. Adriaanse, and Denise T. D. de Ridder, "Bedtime Procrastination: A Self-Regulation Perspective on Sleep Insufficiency in the General Population," *Journal of Health Psychology* 21, no. 5 (2016): 853–862.

29. Ryan T. Howell, Masha Ksendzova, Eric Nestingen, Claudio Yerahian, and Ravi Iyer, "Your Personality on a Good Day: How Trait and State Personality Predict Daily Well-Being," *Journal of Research in Personality* 69 (2017): 250–263.

30. Brad J. Bushman, C. Nathan DeWall, Richard S. Pond, and Michael D. Hanus, "Low Glucose Relates to Greater Aggression in Married Couples," *Proceedings of the National Academy of Sciences* 111, no. 17 (2014): 6254–6257.

31. Rachel P. Winograd, Andrew K. Littlefield, Julia Martinez, and Kenneth J. Sher, "The Drunken Self: The Five-Factor Model as an Organizational Framework for Characterizing Perceptions of One's Own Drunkenness," *Alcoholism: Clinical and Experimental Research* 36, no. 10 (2012): 1787–1793.

32. Rachel P. Winograd, Douglas L. Steinley, and Kenneth J. Sher, "Drunk Personality: Reports from Drinkers and Knowledgeable Informants," *Experimental and Clinical Psychopharmacology* 22, no. 3 (2014): 187.

33. Rachel P. Winograd, Douglas Steinley, Sean P. Lane, and Kenneth J. Sher, "An Experimental Investigation of Drunk Personality Using Self and Observer Reports," *Clinical Psychological Science* 5, no. 3 (2017): 439–456.

34. Rachel Pearl Winograd, Douglas Steinley, and Kenneth Sher, "Searching for Mr. Hyde: A Five-Factor Approach to Characterizing 'Types of Drunks,'" *Addiction Research and Theory* 24, no. 1 (2016): 1–8.

35. Emma L. Davies, Emma-Ben C. Lewis, and Sarah E. Hennelly, "'I Am Quite Mellow But I Wouldn't Say Everyone Else Is': How UK Students Compare Their Drinking Behavior to Their Peers," *Substance Use and Misuse* 53, no. 9 (2018): 1549–1557.

36. Christian Hakuline and Markus Jokela, "Alcohol Use and Personality Trait Change: Pooled Analysis of Six Cohort Studies," *Psychological Medicine* 49, no. 2 (2019): 224–231.

37. Stephan Stevens, Ruth Cooper, Trisha Bantin, Christiane Hermann, and Alexander L. Gerlach, "Feeling Safe But Appearing Anxious: Differential Effects of Alcohol on Anxiety and Social Performance in Individuals with Social Anxiety Disorder," *Behaviour Research and Therapy* 94 (2017): 9–18.

38. Fritz Renner, Inge Kersbergen, Matt Field, and Jessica Werthmann, "Dutch Courage? Effects of Acute Alcohol Consumption on Self-Ratings and Observer Ratings of Foreign Language Skills," *Journal of Psychopharmacology* 32, no. 1 (2018): 116–122.

39. Tom M. McLellan, John A. Caldwell, and Harris R. Lieberman, "A Review

of Caffeine's Effects on Cognitive, Physical and Occupational Performance," *Neuroscience and Biobehavioral Reviews* 71 (2016): 294–312.

40. Kirby Gilliland, "The Interactive Effect of Introversion-Extraversion with Caffeine Induced Arousal on Verbal Performance," *Journal of Research in Personality* 14, no. 4 (1980): 482–492.

41. Manuel Gurpegui, Dolores Jurado, Juan D. Luna, Carmen Fernández-Molina, Obdulia Moreno-Abril, and Ramón Gálvez, "Personality Traits Associated with Caffeine Intake and Smoking," *Progress in Neuro-Psychopharmacology and Biological Psychiatry* 31, no. 5 (2007): 997–1005; Paula J. Mitchell and Jennifer R. Redman, "The Relationship between Morningness-Eveningness, Personality and Habitual Caffeine Consumption," *Personality and Individual Differences* 15, no. 1 (1993): 105–108.

42. Taha Amir, Fatma Alshibani, Thoria Alghara, Maitha Aldhari, Asma Alhassani, and Ghanima Bahry, "Effects of Caffeine on Vigilance Performance in Introvert and Extravert Noncoffee Drinkers," *Social Behavior and Personality* 29, no. 6 (2001): 617–624; Anthony Liguori, Jacob A. Grass, and John R. Hughes, "Subjective Effects of Caffeine among Introverts and Extraverts in the Morning and Evening," *Experimental and Clinical Psychopharmacology* 7, no. 3 (1999): 244.

43. Mitchell Earleywine, *Mind-Altering Drugs: The Science of Subjective Experience* (Oxford: Oxford University Press, 2005).

44. Antonio E. Nardi, Fabiana L. Lopes, Rafael C. Freire, Andre B. Veras, Isabella Nascimento, Alexandre M. Valença, Valfrido L. de-Melo-Neto, Gastão L. Soares-Filho, Anna Lucia King, Daniele M. Araújo, Marco A. Mezzasalma, Arabella Rassi, and Walter A. Zin, "Panic Disorder and Social Anxiety Disorder Subtypes in a Caffeine Challenge Test," *Psychiatry Research* 169, no. 2 (2009): 149–153.

45. "Serious Health Risks Associated with Energy Drinks: To Curb This Growing Public Health Issue, Policy Makers Should Regulate Sales and Marketing towards Children and Adolescents and Set Upper Limits on Caffeine," *ScienceDaily*, November 15, 2017, www.sciencedaily.com/releases/2017/11/171115124519.htm.

46. "MP Calls for Ban on High-Caffeine Energy Drinks," *BBC News*, January 10, 2018, http://www.bbc.co.uk/news/uk-politics-42633277.

47. Waguih William Ishak, Chio Ugochukwu, Kara Bagot, David Khalili, and Christine Zaky, "Energy Drinks: Psychological Effects and Impact on Well-Being and Quality of Life: A Literature Review," *Innovations in Clinical Neuroscience* 9, no. 1 (2012): 25.

48. Laura M. Juliano and Roland R. Griffiths, "A Critical Review of Caffeine Withdrawal: Empirical Validation of Symptoms and Signs, Incidence, Severity, and Associated Features," *Psychopharmacology* 176, no. 1 (2004): 1–29.

49. As of 2020, its recreational use is legal in fifteen US states and Washington, DC.

50. Samantha J. Broyd, Hendrika H. van Hell, Camilla Beale, Murat Yuecel, and Nadia Solowij, "Acute and Chronic Effects of Cannabinoids on Human Cognition: A Systematic Review," *Biological Psychiatry* 79, no. 7 (2016): 557–567.

51. Andrew Lac and Jeremy W. Luk, "Testing the Amotivational Syndrome: Marijuana Use Longitudinally Predicts Lower Self-Efficacy Even After Controlling for Demographics, Personality, and Alcohol and Cigarette Use," *Prevention Science* 19, no. 2 (2018): 117–126.

52. Bernard Weinraub, "Rock's Bad Boys Grow Up But Not Old; Half a Lifetime on the Road, and Half Getting Up for It," the *New York Times*, September 26, 2002, https://www.nytimes.com/2002/09/26/arts/rock-s-bad-boys-grow-up-but-not-old-half-lifetime-road-half-getting-up-for-it.html.

53. John Wenzel, "Brian Wilson on Weed Legalization, What He Thinks of His 'Love & Mercy' Biopic," the *Know*, October 23, 2016, https://theknow.denverpost.com/2015/07/02/brian-wilson-on-weed-legalization-what-he-thinks-of-his-love-mercy-biopic/105363/105363/.

54. Gráinne Schafer, Amanda Feilding, Celia JA Morgan, Maria Agathangelou, Tom P. Freeman, and H. Valerie Curran, "Investigating the Interaction between Schizotypy, Divergent Thinking and Cannabis Use," *Consciousness and Cognition* 21, no. 1 (2012): 292–298.

55. Emily M. LaFrance and Carrie Cuttler, "Inspired by Mary Jane? Mechanisms Underlying Enhanced Creativity in Cannabis Users," *Consciousness and Cognition* 56 (2017): 68–76.

56. Evidence is growing that cannabis use might also increase the vulnerability of some people to experiencing psychosis later in life, though this remains a controversial and open research question.

57. US Dept of Justice Drug Enforcement Administration 2016 National Threat Assessment Summary https://www.dea.gov/sites/default/files/2018-07/DIR-001-17_2016_NDTA_Summary.pdf.

58. Mark Hay, "Everything We Know About Treating Anxiety with Weed," *Vice*, April 18, 2018, https://tonic.vice.com/en_us/article/9kgme8/everything-we-know-about-treating-an.

59. Tony O'Neill, "'My First Time on LSD': 10 Trippy Tales," Alternet.org, June 5, 2014, https://www.alternet.org/2014/05/my-first-time-lsd-10-trippy-tales/.

60. Roland R. Griffiths, Matthew W. Johnson, William A. Richards, Brian D. Richards, Robert Jesse, Katherine A. MacLean, Frederick S. Barrett, Mary P. Cosimano, and Maggie A. Klinedinst, "Psilocybin-Occasioned Mystical-Type Experience in Combination with Meditation and Other Spiritual Practices Produces Enduring Positive Changes in Psychological Functioning and in

Trait Measures of Prosocial Attitudes and Behaviors," *Journal of Psychopharmacology* 32, no. 1 (2018): 49–69.

61. Mark T. Wagner, Michael C. Mithoefer, Ann T. Mithoefer, Rebecca K. MacAulay, Lisa Jerome, Berra Yazar-Klosinski, and Rick Doblin, "Therapeutic Effect of Increased Openness: Investigating Mechanism of Action in MDMA-Assisted Psychotherapy," *Journal of Psychopharmacology* 31, no. 8 (2017): 967–974.

62. Roland R. Griffiths, Ethan S. Hurwitz, Alan K. Davis, Matthew W. Johnson, and Robert Jesse, "Survey of Subjective 'God Encounter Experiences': Comparisons Among Naturally Occurring Experiences and Those Occasioned by the Classic Psychedelics Psilocybin, LSD, Ayahuasca, or DMT," *PloS One* 14, no. 4 (2019): e0214377.

63. Suzannah Weiss, "How Badly Are You Messing Up Your Brain By Using Psychedelics?" *Vice*, March 30, 2018, https://tonic.vice.com/en_us/article/59j97a/how-badly-are-you-messing-up-your-brain-by-using-psychedelics.

64. Frederick S. Barrett, Matthew W. Johnson, and Roland R. Griffiths, "Neuroticism Is Associated with Challenging Experiences with Psilocybin Mushrooms," *Personality and Individual Differences* 117 (2017): 155–160.

65. Lia Naor and Ofra Mayseless, "How Personal Transformation Occurs Following a Single Peak Experience in Nature: A Phenomenological Account," *Journal of Humanistic Psychology* 60, no. 6 (2017): 865–888.

66. James H. Fowler and Nicholas A. Christakis, "Dynamic Spread of Happiness in a Large Social Network: Longitudinal Analysis over 20 Years in the Framingham Heart Study," *BMJ* 337 (2008): a2338.

67. Trevor Foulk, Andrew Woolum, and Amir Erez, "Catching Rudeness Is like Catching a Cold: The Contagion Effects of Low-Intensity Negative Behaviors," *Journal of Applied Psychology* 101, no. 1 (2016): 50.

68. Kobe Desender, Sarah Beurms, and Eva Van den Bussche, "Is Mental Effort Exertion Contagious?" *Psychonomic Bulletin and Review* 23, no. 2 (2016): 624–631.

69. Joseph Chancellor, Seth Margolis, Katherine Jacobs Bao, and Sonja Lyubomirsky, "Everyday Prosociality in the Workplace: The Reinforcing Benefits of Giving, Getting, and Glimpsing," *Emotion* 18, no. 4 (2018): 507.

70. Angela Neff, Sabine Sonnentag, Cornelia Niessen, and Dana Unger, "What's Mine Is Yours: The Crossover of Day-Specific Self-Esteem," *Journal of Vocational Behavior* 81, no. 3 (2012): 385–394.

71. Rachel E. White, Emily O. Prager, Catherine Schaefer, Ethan Kross, Angela L. Duckworth, and Stephanie M. Carlson, "The 'Batman Effect': Improving Perseverance in Young Children," *Child Development* 88, no. 5 (2017): 1563–1571.

CHAPTER 5: CHOOSING TO CHANGE

1. John M. Zelenski, Deanna C. Whelan, Logan J. Nealis, Christina M. Besner, Maya S. Santoro, and Jessica E. Wynn, "Personality and Affective Forecasting: Trait Introverts Underpredict the Hedonic Benefits of Acting Extraverted," *Journal of Personality and Social Psychology* 104, no. 6 (2013): 1092.

2. Michael P. Hengartner, Peter Tyrer, Vladeta Ajdacic-Gross, Jules Angst, and Wulf Rössler, "Articulation and Testing of a Personality-Centred Model of Psychopathology: Evidence from a Longitudinal Community Study over 30 Years," *European Archives of Psychiatry and Clinical Neuroscience* 268, no. 5 (2018): 443–454.

3. "Change Goals Big-Five Inventory," Personality Assessor, accessed November 11, 2019, at http://www.personalityassessor.com/measures/cbfi/.

4. Constantine Sedikides, Rosie Meek, Mark D. Alicke, and Sarah Taylor, "Behind Bars but Above the Bar: Prisoners Consider Themselves More Prosocial Than Non-Prisoners," *British Journal of Social Psychology* 53, no. 2 (2014): 396–403.

5. Nathan W. Hudson and Brent W. Roberts, "Goals to Change Personality Traits: Concurrent Links Between Personality Traits, Daily Behavior, and Goals to Change Oneself," *Journal of Research in Personality* 53 (2014): 68–83.

6. Oliver C. Robinson, Erik E. Noftle, Jen Guo, Samaneh Asadi, and Xiaozhou Zhang, "Goals and Plans for Big Five Personality Trait Change in Young Adults," *Journal of Research in Personality* 59 (2015): 31–43.

7. Nathan W. Hudson and R. Chris Fraley, "Do People's Desires to Change Their Personality Traits Vary with Age? An Examination of Trait Change Goals Across Adulthood," *Social Psychological and Personality Science* 7, no. 8 (2016): 847–856.

8. Marie Hennecke, Wiebke Bleidorn, Jaap J. A. Denissen, and Dustin Wood, "A Three-Part Framework for Self-Regulated Personality Development Across Adulthood," *European Journal of Personality* 28, no. 3 (2014): 289–299.

9. Note that a study published in 2020 found that personality traits change over time regardless of people's beliefs about the malleability of personality, but this research was not focused on *deliberate* personality change. The study was: Nathan W. Hudson, R. Chris Fraley, Daniel A. Briley, and William J. Chopik, "Your Personality Does Not Care Whether You Believe It Can Change: Beliefs About Whether Personality Can Change Do Not Predict Trait Change Among Emerging Adults," *European Journal of Personality*, published online July 21, 2020.

10. Carol Dweck, *Mindset: Changing the Way You Think to Fulfil Your Potential* (UK: Hachette, 2012).

11. Krishna Savani and Veronika Job, "Reverse Ego-Depletion: Acts of Self-Control Can Improve Subsequent Performance in Indian Cultural Contexts," *Journal of Personality and Social Psychology* 113, no. 4 (2017): 589.

12. As an example, a 2017 study led by the University of Texas at Austin showed that teaching teenagers personality is malleable helped them deal with the transition to high school and to experience less stress and better physical health over time as compared to their peers who believed personality is fixed. Other research has shown that people who believe in the malleability of personality cope better with rejection from a romantic relationship because they don't interpret the breakup as saying something fundamental about the kind of person they are.

13. Nathan W. Hudson, R. Chris Fraley, William J. Chopik, and Daniel A. Briley, "Change Goals Robustly Predict Trait Growth: A Mega-Analysis of a Dozen Intensive Longitudinal Studies Examining Volitional Change," *Social Psychological and Personality Science* 11, no. 6 (2020): 723–732.

14. Ted Schwaba, Maike Luhmann, Jaap J. A. Denissen, Joanne M. Chung, and Wiebke Bleidorn, "Openness to Experience and Culture: Openness Transactions across the Lifespan," *Journal of Personality and Social Psychology* 115, no. 1 (2018): 118.

15. Berna A. Sari, Ernst H. W. Koster, Gilles Pourtois, and Nazanin Derakshan, "Training Working Memory to Improve Attentional Control in Anxiety: A Proof-of-Principle Study Using Behavioral and Electrophysiological Measures," *Biological Psychology* 121 (2016): 203–212.

16. Izabela Krejtz, John B. Nezlek, Anna Michnicka, Paweł Holas, and Marzena Rusanowska, "Counting One's Blessings Can Reduce the Impact of Daily Stress," *Journal of Happiness Studies* 17, no. 1 (2016): 25–39.

17. Prathik Kini, Joel Wong, Sydney McInnis, Nicole Gabana, and Joshua W. Brown, "The Effects of Gratitude Expression on Neural Activity," *NeuroImage* 128 (2016): 1–10.

18. Brent W. Roberts, Jing Luo, Daniel A. Briley, Philip I. Chow, Rong Su, and Patrick L. Hill, "A Systematic Review of Personality Trait Change through Intervention," *Psychological Bulletin* 143, no. 2 (2017): 117.

19. Krystyna Glinski and Andrew C. Page, "Modifiability of Neuroticism, Extraversion, and Agreeableness by Group Cognitive Behaviour Therapy for Social Anxiety Disorder," *Behaviour Change* 27, no. 1 (2010): 42–52.

20. Cosmin Octavian Popa, Aural Nireştean, Mihai Ardelean, Gabriela Buicu, and Lucian Ile, "Dimensional Personality Change after Combined Therapeutic Intervention in the Obsessive-Compulsive Personality Disorders," *Acta Med Transilvanica* 2 (2013): 290–292.

21. Rebecca Grist and Kate Cavanagh, "Computerised Cognitive Behavioural Therapy for Common Mental Health Disorders, What Works, for Whom Under What Circumstances? A Systematic Review and Meta-Analysis," *Journal of Contemporary Psychotherapy* 43, no. 4 (2013): 243–251.

22. Julia Zimmermann and Franz J. Neyer, "Do We Become a Different Person When Hitting the Road? Personality Development of Sojourners," *Journal of Personality and Social Psychology* 105, no. 3 (2013): 515.

23. Jeffrey Conrath Miller and Zlatan Krizan, "Walking Facilitates Positive Affect (Even When Expecting the Opposite)," *Emotion* 16, no. 5 (2016): 775.

24. Ashleigh Johnstone and Paloma Marí-Beffa, "The Effects of Martial Arts Training on Attentional Networks in Typical Adults," *Frontiers in Psychology* 9 (2018): 80.

25. Nathan W. Hudson and Brent W. Roberts, "Social Investment in Work Reliably Predicts Change in Conscientiousness and Agreeableness: A Direct Replication and Extension of Hudson, Roberts, and Lodi-Smith (2012)," *Journal of Research in Personality* 60 (2016): 12–23.

26. Blake A. Allan, "Task Significance and Meaningful Work: A Longitudinal Study," *Journal of Vocational Behavior* 102 (2017): 174–182.

27. Marina Milyavskaya and Michael Inzlicht, "What's So Great About Self-Control? Examining the Importance of Effortful Self-Control and Temptation in Predicting Real-Life Depletion and Goal Attainment," *Social Psychological and Personality Science* 8, no. 6 (2017): 603–611.

28. Adriana Dornelles, "Impact of Multiple Food Environments on Body Mass Index," *PloS One* 14, no. 8 (2019).

29. Richard Göllner, Rodica I. Damian, Norman Rose, Marion Spengler, Ulrich Trautwein, Benjamin Nagengast, and Brent W. Roberts, "Is Doing Your Homework Associated with Becoming More Conscientious?" *Journal of Research in Personality* 71 (2017): 1–12.

30. Joshua J. Jackson, Patrick L. Hill, Brennan R. Payne, Brent W. Roberts, and Elizabeth A. L. Stine-Morrow, "Can an Old Dog Learn (and Want to Experience) New Tricks? Cognitive Training Increases Openness to Experience in Older Adults," *Psychology and Aging* 27, no. 2 (2012): 286.

31. Wijnand A. P. van Tilburg, Constantine Sedikides, and Tim Wildschut, "The Mnemonic Muse: Nostalgia Fosters Creativity through Openness to Experience," *Journal of Experimental Social Psychology* 59 (2015): 1–7.

32. Yannick Stephan, Angelina R. Sutin, and Antonio Terracciano, "Physical Activity and Personality Development Across Adulthood and Old Age: Evidence from Two Longitudinal Studies," *Journal of Research in Personality* 49 (2014): 1–7.

33. Anna Antinori, Olivia L. Carter, and Luke D. Smillie, "Seeing It Both Ways:

Openness to Experience and Binocular Rivalry Suppression," *Journal of Research in Personality* 68 (2017): 15–22.

34. If your concern is that you are too agreeable and that this is holding you back in a competitive field, you will find some useful advice in chapter 7.

35. Anne Böckler, Lukas Herrmann, Fynn-Mathis Trautwein, Tom Holmes, and Tania Singer, "Know Thy Selves: Learning to Understand Oneself Increases the Ability to Understand Others," *Journal of Cognitive Enhancement* 1, no. 2 (2017): 197–209.

36. Anthony P. Winning and Simon Boag, "Does Brief Mindfulness Training Increase Empathy? The Role of Personality," *Personality and Individual Differences* 86 (2015): 492–498.

37. David Comer Kidd and Emanuele Castano, "Reading Literary Fiction Improves Theory of Mind," *Science* 342, no. 6156 (2013): 377–380.

38. David Kidd and Emanuele Castano, "Different Stories: How Levels of Familiarity with Literary and Genre Fiction Relate to Mentalizing," *Psychology of Aesthetics, Creativity, and the Arts* 11, no. 4 (2017): 474.

39. Gregory S. Berns, Kristina Blaine, Michael J. Prietula, and Brandon E. Pye, "Short- and Long-Term Effects of a Novel on Connectivity in the Brain," *Brain Connectivity* 3, no. 6 (2013): 590–600.

40. Loris Vezzali, Rhiannon Turner, Dora Capozza, and Elena Trifiletti, "Does Intergroup Contact Affect Personality? A Longitudinal Study on the Bidirectional Relationship Between Intergroup Contact and Personality Traits," *European Journal of Social Psychology* 48, no. 2 (2018): 159–173.

41. Grit Hein, Jan B. Engelmann, Marius C. Vollberg, and Philippe N. Tobler, "How Learning Shapes the Empathic Brain," *Proceedings of the National Academy of Sciences* 113, no. 1 (2016): 80–85.

42. Sylvia Xiaohua Chen and Michael Harris Bond, "Two Languages, Two Personalities? Examining Language Effects on the Expression of Personality in a Bilingual Context," *Personality and Social Psychology Bulletin* 36, no. 11 (2010): 1514–1528.

43. Consider avoiding this approach if you are prone to obsessive or compulsive tendencies.

44. Alison Wood Brooks, Juliana Schroeder, Jane L. Risen, Francesca Gino, Adam D. Galinsky, Michael I. Norton, and Maurice E. Schweitzer, "Don't Stop Believing: Rituals Improve Performance by Decreasing Anxiety," *Organizational Behavior and Human Decision Processes* 137 (2016): 71–85.

45. Mariya Davydenko, John M. Zelenski, Ana Gonzalez, and Deanna Whelan, "Does Acting Extraverted Evoke Positive Social Feedback?" *Personality and Individual Differences* 159 (2020): 109883.

46. John M. Malouff and Nicola S. Schutte, "Can Psychological Interventions Increase Optimism? A Meta-Analysis," *Journal of Positive Psychology* 12, no. 6 (2017): 594–604.

47. Olga Khazan, "One Simple Phrase That Turns Anxiety into Success," the *Atlantic*, March 23, 2016, https://www.theatlantic.com/health/archive/2016/03/can-three-words-turn-anxiety-into-success/474909.

48. Alison Wood Brooks, "Get Excited: Reappraising Pre-Performance Anxiety as Excitement," *Journal of Experimental Psychology: General* 143, no. 3 (2014): 1144.

49. Sointu Leikas and Ville-Juhani Ilmarinen, "Happy Now, Tired Later? Extraverted and Conscientious Behavior Are Related to Immediate Mood Gains, But to Later Fatigue," *Journal of Personality* 85, no. 5 (2017): 603–615.

50. William Fleeson, Adriane B. Malanos, and Noelle M. Achille, "An Intraindividual Process Approach to the Relationship Between Extraversion and Positive Affect: Is Acting Extraverted as 'Good' as Being Extraverted?" *Journal of Personality and Social Psychology* 83, no. 6 (2002): 1409.

51. Nathan W. Hudson and R. Chris Fraley, "Changing for the Better? Longitudinal Associations Between Volitional Personality Change and Psychological Well-Being," *Personality and Social Psychology Bulletin* 42, no. 5 (2016): 603–615.

52. William Fleeson and Joshua Wilt, "The Relevance of Big Five Trait Content in Behavior to Subjective Authenticity: Do High Levels of Within-Person Behavioral Variability Undermine or Enable Authenticity Achievement?" *Journal of Personality* 78, no. 4 (2010): 1353–1382.

53. Muping Gan and Serena Chen, "Being Your Actual or Ideal Self? What It Means to Feel Authentic in a Relationship," *Personality and Social Psychology Bulletin* 43, no. 4 (2017): 465–478.

54. A. Bell Cooper, Ryne A. Sherman, John F. Rauthmann, David G. Serfass, and Nicolas A. Brown, "Feeling Good and Authentic: Experienced Authenticity in Daily Life Is Predicted by Positive Feelings and Situation Characteristics, Not Trait-State Consistency," *Journal of Research in Personality* 77 (2018): 57–69.

55. Alison P. Lenton, Letitia Slabu, and Constantine Sedikides, "State Authenticity in Everyday Life," *European Journal of Personality* 30, no. 1 (2016): 64–82.

CHAPTER 6: REDEMPTION: WHEN BAD PEOPLE TURN GOOD

1. Maajid Nawaz, *Radical: My Journey out of Islamist Extremism* (Maryland: Rowman & Littlefield, 2016).

2. Given that Nawaz now campaigns against Islamist extremism, it won't surprise you that he remains a controversial figure. However, he has a habit of earning apologies and compensation from those who slander and defame his

name. Most recently, in 2018, the Southern Poverty Law Center issued a public apology and promised to pay almost $4 million in compensation after accusing Nawaz of being an anti-Muslim extremist. See Richard Cohen, "SPLC Statement Regarding Maajid Nawaz and the Quilliam Foundation," Southern Poverty Law Center, June 18, 2018, https://www.splcenter.org/news/2018/06/18/splc-statement-regarding-maajid-nawaz-and-quilliam-foundation.

3. https://www.quilliaminternational.com.

4. Inspired by Brian Little's method of "personal project analysis." See Justin Presseau, Falko F. Sniehotta, Jillian Joy Francis, and Brian R. Little, "Personal Project Analysis: Opportunities and Implications for Multiple Goal Assessment, Theoretical Integration, and Behaviour Change," *European Health Psychologist* 5, no. 2 (2008): 32–36.

5. Based on research and writings by Brian Little. See his *Me, Myself, and Us: The Science of Personality and the Art of Well-Being* (New York: Public Affairs Press, 2014).

6. Catra Corbett, *Reborn on the Run: My Journey from Addiction to Ultramarathons* (New York: Skyhorse Publishing, 2018).

7. Emma Reynolds, "How 50-year-old Junkie Replaced Meth Addiction with Ultrarunning," News.com.au, September 28, 2015, https://www.news.com.au/lifestyle/fitness/exercise/how-50yearold-junkie-replaced-meth-addiction-with-ultrarunning/news-story/9b773ee67ffecf27f5c6f3467570fa20.

8. Chip Heath and Dan Heath, *The Power of Moments: Why Certain Experiences Have Extraordinary Impact* (London: Bantam Press, 2017).

9. Nick Yarris, *The Fear of 13: Countdown to Execution: My Fight for Survival on Death Row* (Salt Lake City: Century, 2017).

10. Nick Yarris, *The Kindness Approach* (South Carolina: CreateSpace Independent Publishing Platform, 2017).

11. Based on items published in the Psychological Inventory of Criminal Thinking Styles Part I. See Glenn D. Walters, "The Psychological Inventory of Criminal Thinking Styles: Part I: Reliability and Preliminary Validity," *Criminal Justice and Behavior* 22, no. 3 (1995): 307–325.

12. Susie Hulley, Ben Crewe, and Serena Wright, "Re-examining the problems of long-term imprisonment," *British Journal of Criminology* 56, no. 4 (2016): 769–792.

13. Matthew T. Zingraff, "Prisonization as an inhibitor of effective resocialization," *Criminology* 13, no. 3 (1975): 366–388.

14. Jesse Meijers, Joke M. Harte, Gerben Meynen, Pim Cuijpers, and Erik J. A. Scherder, "Reduced Self-Control after 3 Months of Imprisonment; A Pilot Study," *Frontiers in Psychology* 9 (2018): 69.

15. Marieke Liem and Maarten Kunst, "Is There a Recognizable Post-Incarceration Syndrome Among Released 'Lifers'?" *International Journal of Law and Psychiatry* 36, nos. 3–4 (2013): 333–337.

16. T. Gerhard Eriksson, Johanna G. Masche-No, and Anna M. Dåderman, "Personality Traits of Prisoners as Compared to General Populations: Signs of Adjustment to the Situation?" *Personality and Individual Differences* 107 (2017): 237–245.

17. Jack Bush, Daryl M. Harris, and Richard J. Parker, *Cognitive Self Change: How Offenders Experience the World and What We Can Do About It* (Hoboken, NJ: Wiley, 2016).

18. Glenn D. Walters, Marie Trgovac, Mark Rychlec, Roberto DiFazio, and Julie R. Olson, "Assessing Change with the Psychological Inventory of Criminal Thinking Styles: A Controlled Analysis and Multisite Cross-Validation," *Criminal Justice and Behavior* 29, no. 3 (2002): 308–331.

19. Jack Bush, "To Help a Criminal Go Straight, Help Him Change How He Thinks," NPR, June 26, 2016, https://www.npr.org/sections/health-shots/2016/06/26/483091741/to-help-a-criminal-go-straight-help-him-change-how-he-thinks.

20. To use the hypothetical trolley dilemma as an example, they are usually very happy to push a fat man into the path of a speeding trolley, thus killing him, in order to save the lives of five others, whereas the normal response is to find deliberately harming the fat man unpalatable, even though the greater good would be served.

21. Daniel M. Bartels and David A. Pizarro, "The Mismeasure of Morals: Antisocial Personality Traits Predict Utilitarian Responses to Moral Dilemmas," *Cognition* 121, no. 1 (2011): 154–161.

22. A review of thirty-three studies into the effectiveness of moral reconation therapy found that it leads to a modest, but statistically significant, reduction in rates of recidivism. See L. Myles Ferguson and J. Stephen Wormith, "A Meta-Analysis of Moral Reconation Therapy," *International Journal of Offender Therapy and Comparative Criminology* 57, no. 9 (2013): 1076–1106.

23. Steven N. Zane, Brandon C. Welsh, and Gregory M. Zimmerman, "Examining the Iatrogenic Effects of the Cambridge-Somerville Youth Study: Existing Explanations and New Appraisals," *British Journal of Criminology* 56, no. 1 (2015): 141–160.

24. Eli Hager, "How to Train Your Brain to Keep You Out of Jail," *Vice*, June 27, 2018, https://www.vice.com/en_us/article/nekpy8/how-to-train-your-brain-to-keep-you-out-of-jail.

25. Christian Jarrett, "Research Into The Mental Health of Prisoners, Digested," *BPS*

Research Digest, July 13, 2018, https://digest.bps.org.uk/2018/07/13/research -into-the-mental-health-of-prisoners-digested/.

26. This is a formal, adult psychiatric diagnosis. To meet the criteria, since the age of fifteen, a person must have shown a failure to conform to social norms with respect to lawful behaviors; deceitfulness; impulsivity or failure to plan ahead; irritability and aggressiveness; reckless disregard for safety of self or others; consistent irresponsibility; and lack of remorse.

27. Holly A. Wilson, "Can Antisocial Personality Disorder Be Treated? A Meta-Analysis Examining the Effectiveness of Treatment in Reducing Recidivism for Individuals Diagnosed with ASPD," *International Journal of Forensic Mental Health* 13, no. 1 (2014): 36–46.

28. Nick J. Wilson and Armon Tamatea, "Challenging the 'Urban Myth' of Psychopathy Untreatability: The High-Risk Personality Programme," *Psychology, Crime and Law* 19, nos. 5–6 (2013): 493–510.

29. Adrian Raine, "Antisocial Personality as a Neurodevelopmental Disorder," *Annual Review of Clinical Psychology* 14 (2018): 259–289.

30. Rich Karlgaard, "Lance Armstrong—Hero, Doping Cheater and Tragic Figure," *Forbes*, July 31, 2012, https://www.forbes.com/sites/richkarlgaard/2012/06 /13/lance-armstrong-hero-cheat-and-tragic-figure/#38d88c94795c.

31. "Lance Armstrong: A Ruinous Puncture for the Cyclopath," the *Sunday Times*, June 17, 2012, https://www.thetimes.co.uk/article/lance-armstrong-a-ruinous -puncture-for-the-cyclopath-vh57w9zgjs2.

32. Joseph Burgo, "How Aggressive Narcissism Explains Lance Armstrong," the *Atlantic*, January 28, 2013, https://www.theatlantic.com/health/archive/2013 /01/how-aggressive-narcissism-explains-lance-armstrong/272568/.

33. Will Pavia, "Up close with Hillary's aide, her husband and that sexting scandal," the *Times*, June 21, 2016, https://www.thetimes.co.uk/article/a-ringside-seat-for -the-sexting-scandal-that-brought-down-anthony-weiner-gp9gjpsk9.

34. David DeSteno and Piercarlo Valdesolo, *Out of Character: Surprising Truths About the Liar, Cheat, Sinner (and Saint) Lurking in All of Us* (New York: Harmony, 2013).

35. Take Stanley Milgram's "obedience to authority" experiments in which volunteers followed the order of a scientist and delivered what they thought was a fatal electric shock to another person. Psychologists recently analyzed a post-experimental survey the volunteers answered and found that many had been motivated by the grander cause of helping science—"a cause in whose name they perceive themselves to be acting virtuously and to be doing good." It's a similar story with Philip Zimbardo's notorious Stanford prison experiment,

which had to be aborted prematurely after apparently normal volunteers recruited to play the role of prison guards started abusing the prisoners. Evidence recently emerged that the abusive volunteer guards thought their bad behavior would help make the case for the need for real-life prison reform. Again, bad behavior didn't flow from a sudden change in character so much as a change in perspective — a calculation that certain bad deeds may be for the greater good.

36. Roger Simon, "John Edwards Affair Not to Remember," *Boston Herald*, November 17, 2018, https://www.bostonherald.com/2008/08/18/john-edwards-affair-not-to-remember/.

37. Jeremy Whittle, "I Would Probably Dope Again, Says Lance Armstrong," the *Times*, January 27, 2015, https://www.thetimes.co.uk/article/i-would-probably-dope-again-says-lance-armstrong-j5lxcg5rtb; Matt Dickinson, "Defiant Lance Armstrong on the Attack," the *Times* (London), June 11, 2015, https://www.thetimes.co.uk/article/defiant-lance-armstrong-on-the-attack-9sgfszkzr5t; Daniel Honan, "Lance Armstrong: American Psychopath," *Big Think*, October 6, 2018, https://bigthink.com/think-tank/lance-armstrong-american-psychopath.

CHAPTER 7: LESSONS FROM THE DARK SIDE

1. Arelis Hernández and Laurie McGinley, "Harvard Study Estimates Thousands Died in Puerto Rico Because of Hurricane Maria," June 4, 2018, https://www.washingtonpost.com/national/harvard-study-estimates-thousands-died-in-puerto-rico-due-to-hurricane-maria/2018/05/29/1a82503a-6070-11e8-a4a4-c070ef53f315_story.html.

2. Kaitlan Collins, "Trump Contrasts Puerto Rico Death Toll to 'a Real Catastrophe like Katrina,'" CNN, October 3, 2017, https://edition.cnn.com/2017/10/03/politics/trump-puerto-rico-katrina-deaths/index.html.

3. "Puerto Rico: Trump Paper Towel-Throwing 'Abominable,'" *BBC News*, October 4, 2017, http://www.bbc.co.uk/news/world-us-canada-41504165.

4. Ben Jacob, "Trump Digs In Over Call to Soldier's Widow: 'I Didn't Say What the Congresswoman Said,'" the *Guardian*, October 18, 2017, https://www.theguardian.com/us-news/2017/oct/18/trump-allegedly-tells-soldiers-widow-he-knew-what-he-signed-up-for.

5. Alex Daugherty, Anita Kumar, and Douglas Hanks, "In Attack on Frederica Wilson Over Trump's Call to Widow, John Kelly Gets Facts Wrong," *Miami Herald*, October 19, 2017, http://www.miamiherald.com/news/politics-government/national—politics/article179869321.html.

6. The Goldwater rule, formulated in 1973, forbids psychiatrists and psychologists from making such claims about public officials. The name is a reference to the 1964 Republican presidential nominee, Barry Goldwater, who successfully

sued *Fact* magazine for publishing a poll of two thousand psychiatrists that found half of them considered him "psychologically unfit" for office. During the Trump presidency, however, a growing band of psychiatrists and psychologists believed the danger posed by the former president's personality justified breaking the Goldwater rule.

7. There is a lot of overlap between psychopathy and narcissism, but they are distinct enough for it to be useful to examine them separately.

8. Joshua D. Miller, Courtland S. Hyatt, Jessica L. Maples-Keller, Nathan T. Carter, and Donald R. Lynam, "Psychopathy and Machiavellianism: A Distinction without a Difference?" *Journal of Personality* 85, no. 4 (2017): 439–453.

9. Jessica L. McCain, Zachary G. Borg, Ariel H. Rothenberg, Kristina M. Churillo, Paul Weiler, and W. Keith Campbell, "Personality and Selfies: Narcissism and the Dark Triad," *Computers in Human Behavior* 64 (2016): 126–133.

10. Nicholas S. Holtzman, Simine Vazire, and Matthias R. Mehl, "Sounds Like a Narcissist: Behavioral Manifestations of Narcissism in Everyday Life," *Journal of Research in Personality* 44, no. 4 (2010): 478–484.

11. Simine Vazire, Laura P. Naumann, Peter J. Rentfrow, and Samuel D. Gosling, "Portrait of a Narcissist: Manifestations of Narcissism in Physical Appearance," *Journal of Research in Personality* 42, no. 6 (2008): 1439–1447.

12. Alvaro Mailhos, Abraham P. Buunk, and Álvaro Cabana, "Signature Size Signals Sociable Dominance and Narcissism," *Journal of Research in Personality* 65 (2016): 43–51.

13. Miranda Giacomin and Nicholas O. Rule, "Eyebrows Cue Grandiose Narcissism," *Journal of Personality* 87, no. 2 (2019): 373–385.

14. Adapted from the "short dark triad" personality test available for free use at the website of Delroy Paulhus, accessed November 18, 2019, at http://www2.psych .ubc.ca/~dpaulhus/Paulhus_measures/.

15. Sara Konrath, Brian P. Meier, and Brad J. Bushman, "Development and Validation of the Single Item Narcissism Scale (SINS)," *PLoS One* 9, no. 8 (2014): e103469; Sander van der Linden and Seth A. Rosenthal, "Measuring Narcissism with a Single Question? A Replication and Extension of the Single-Item Narcissism Scale (SINS)," *Personality and Individual Differences* 90 (2016): 238–241.

16. Trump: "I have one of the greatest memories of all time," YouTube, accessed January 25, 2021, at https://www.youtube.com/watch?v=wnVpGoyKfKU.

17. Mark Leibovich, "Donald Trump Is Not Going Anywhere," the *New York Times*, September 29, 2015, https://www.nytimes.com/2015/10/04/magazine/ donald-trump-is-not-going-anywhere.html.

18. Daniel Dale, "Trump Defends Tossing Paper Towels to Puerto Rico Hurricane

Victims: Analysis," *Toronto Star*, October 8, 2017, https://www.thestar.com /news/world/2017/10/08/donald-trump-defends-paper-towels-in-puerto-rico -says-stephen-paddock-was-probably-smart-in-bizarre-tv-interview-analysis.html.

19. Lori Robertson and Robert Farley, "The Facts on Crowd Size," FactCheck.org, January 23, 2017, http://www.factcheck.org/2017/01/the-facts-on-crowd-size/.

20. Harry Cockburn, "Donald Trump Just Said He Had the Biggest Inauguration Crowd in History. Here Are Two Pictures That Show That's Wrong," *Independent*, January 26, 2017, http://www.independent.co.uk/news/world/americas /donald-trump-claims-presidential-inauguration-audience-history-us-president- white-house-barack-a7547141.html.

21. Trump: "I'm the least racist person anybody is going to meet," *BBC News*, January 26, 2018, https://www.bbc.co.uk/news/av/uk-42830165.

22. "Transcript: Donald Trump's Taped Comments about Women," the *New York Times*, October 8, 2016, https://www.nytimes.com/2016/10/08/us/donald-trump -tape-transcript.html.

23. Emily Grijalva, Peter D. Harms, Daniel A. Newman, Blaine H. Gaddis, and R. Chris Fraley, "Narcissism and Leadership: A Meta-Analytic Review of Linear and Nonlinear Relationships," *Personnel Psychology* 68, no. 1 (2015): 1–47.

24. Chin Wei Ong, Ross Roberts, Calum A. Arthur, Tim Woodman, and Sally Ake-hurst, "The Leader Ship Is Sinking: A Temporal Investigation of Narcissistic Leadership," *Journal of Personality* 84, no. 2 (2016): 237–247.

25. Emanuel Jauk, Aljoscha C. Neubauer, Thomas Mairunteregger, Stephanie Pemp, Katharina P. Sieber, and John F. Rauthmann, "How Alluring Are Dark Personalities? The Dark Triad and Attractiveness in Speed Dating," *European Journal of Personality* 30, no. 2 (2016): 125–138.

26. Anna Z. Czarna, Philip Leifeld, Magdalena Śmieja, Michael Dufner, and Peter Salovey, "Do Narcissism and Emotional Intelligence Win Us Friends? Modeling Dynamics of Peer Popularity Using Inferential Network Analysis," *Personality and Social Psychology Bulletin* 42, no. 11 (2016): 1588–1599.

27. Harry M. Wallace, C. Beth Ready, and Erin Weitenhagen, "Narcissism and Task Persistence," *Self and Identity* 8, no. 1 (2009): 78–93.

28. Barbora Nevicka, Matthijs Baas, and Femke S. Ten Velden, "The Bright Side of Threatened Narcissism: Improved Performance following Ego Threat," *Journal of Personality* 84, no. 6 (2016): 809–823.

29. Jack A. Goncalo, Francis J. Flynn, and Sharon H. Kim, "Are Two Narcissists Better Than One? The Link Between Narcissism, Perceived Creativity, and Creative Performance," *Personality and Social Psychology Bulletin* 36, no. 11 (2010): 1484–1495; Yi Zhou, "Narcissism and the Art Market Performance," *European Journal of Finance* 23, no. 13 (2017): 1197–1218.

30. Ovul Sezer, Francesco Gino, and Michael I. Norton, "Humblebragging: A Distinct—and Ineffective—Self-Presentation Strategy," Harvard Business School working paper series 15-080, April 24, 2015, http://dash.harvard.edu/handle /1/14725901.

31. Virgil Zeigler-Hill, "Discrepancies Between Implicit and Explicit Self-Esteem: Implications for Narcissism and Self-Esteem Instability," *Journal of Personality* 74, no. 1 (2006): 119–144.

32. Emanuel Jauk, Mathias Benedek, Karl Koschutnig, Gayannée Kedia, and Aljoscha C. Neubauer, "Self-Viewing Is Associated with Negative Affect Rather Than Reward in Highly Narcissistic Men: An fMRI study," *Scientific Reports* 7, no. 1 (2017): 5804.

33. Christopher N. Cascio, Sara H. Konrath, and Emily B. Falk, "Narcissists' Social Pain Seen Only in the Brain," *Social Cognitive and Affective Neuroscience* 10, no. 3 (2014): 335–341.

34. Ulrich Orth and Eva C. Luciano, "Self-Esteem, Narcissism, and Stressful Life Events: Testing for Selection and Socialization," *Journal of Personality and Social Psychology* 109, no. 4 (2015): 707.

35. Joey T. Cheng, Jessica L. Tracy, and Gregory E. Miller, "Are Narcissists Hardy or Vulnerable? The Role of Narcissism in the Production of Stress-Related Biomarkers in Response to Emotional Distress," *Emotion* 13, no. 6 (2013): 1004.

36. Michael Wolff, *Fire and Fury: Inside the Trump White House* (London: Abacus, 2019).

37. Matthew D'Ancona, "Desperate for a Trade Deal, the Tories Are Enabling Donald Trump," the *Guardian*, January 14, 2018, https://www.theguardian.com /commentisfree/2018/jan/14/trade-deal-tories-donald-trump.

38. Ashley L. Watts, Scott O. Lilienfeld, Sarah Francis Smith, Joshua D. Miller, W. Keith Campbell, Irwin D. Waldman, Steven J. Rubenzer, and Thomas J. Faschingbauer, "The Double-Edged Sword of Grandiose Narcissism: Implications for Successful and Unsuccessful Leadership among US Presidents," *Psychological Science* 24, no. 12 (2013): 2379–2389.

39. Charles A. O'Reilly III, Bernadette Doerr, and Jennifer A. Chatman, "'See You in Court': How CEO Narcissism Increases Firms' Vulnerability to Lawsuits," *Leadership Quarterly* 29, no. 3 (2018): 365–378.

40. Eunike Wetzel, Emily Grijalva, Richard Robins, and Brent Roberts, "You're Still So Vain; Changes in Narcissism from Young Adulthood to Middle Age," *Journal of Personality and Social Psychology* 119, no. 2 (2019): 479–496.

41. Joost M. Leunissen, Constantine Sedikides, and Tim Wildschut, "Why Narcissists Are Unwilling to Apologize: The Role of Empathy and Guilt," *European Journal of Personality* 31, no. 4 (2017): 385–403.

42. Erica G. Hepper, Claire M. Hart, and Constantine Sedikides, "Moving Narcissus: Can Narcissists Be Empathic?" *Personality and Social Psychology Bulletin* 40, no. 9 (2014): 1079–1091.

43. Joshi Herrmann, "'I Wouldn't Want to Spend More Than an Hour with Him but He Was . . .'," *Evening Standard*, November 4, 2014, https://www.standard.co.uk/lifestyle/london-life/i-wouldn-t-want-to-spend-more-than-an-hour-with-him-but-he-was-incredibly-bright-rurik-juttings-old-9837963.html.

44. Paul Thompson, "'The evil that I've inflicted cannot be remedied . . .'" *Daily Mail*, November 8, 2016, https://www.dailymail.co.uk/news/article-3906170/British-banker-Rurik-Jutting-GUILTY-murder-350-000-year-trader-faces-life-jail-torturing-two-sex-workers-death-luxury-Hong-Kong-apartment.html.

45. Kevin Dutton, *The Wisdom of Psychopaths* (New York: Random House, 2012).

46. Hervey Milton Cleckley, *The Mask of Sanity: An Attempt to Clarify Some Issues about the So-Called Psychopathic Personality* (Ravenio Books, 1964).

47. Herrmann, "'I Wouldn't Want to Spend More Than an Hour with Him but He Was . . .'"

48. Ana Seara-Cardoso, Essi Viding, Rachael A. Lickley, and Catherine L. Sebastian, "Neural Responses to Others' Pain Vary with Psychopathic Traits in Healthy Adult Males," *Cognitive, Affective, and Behavioral Neuroscience* 15, no. 3 (2015): 578–588.

49. Joana B. Vieira, Fernando Ferreira-Santos, Pedro R. Almeida, Fernando Barbosa, João Marques-Teixeira, and Abigail A. Marsh, "Psychopathic Traits Are Associated with Cortical and Subcortical Volume Alterations in Healthy Individuals," *Social Cognitive and Affective Neuroscience* 10, no. 12 (2015): 1693–1704.

50. René T. Proyer, Rahel Flisch, Stefanie Tschupp, Tracey Platt, and Willibald Ruch, "How Does Psychopathy Relate to Humor and Laughter? Dispositions Toward Ridicule and Being Laughed At, the Sense of Humor, and Psychopathic Personality Traits," *International Journal of Law and Psychiatry* 35, no. 4 (2012): 263–268.

51. Scott O. Lilienfeld, Robert D. Latzman, Ashley L. Watts, Sarah F. Smith, and Kevin Dutton, "Correlates of Psychopathic Personality Traits in Everyday Life: Results from a Large Community Survey," *Frontiers in Psychology* 5 (2014): 740.

52. Verity Litten, Lynne D. Roberts, Richard K. Ladyshewsky, Emily Castell, and Robert Kane, "The Influence of Academic Discipline on Empathy and Psychopathic Personality Traits in Undergraduate Students," *Personality and Individual Differences* 123 (2018): 145–150; Anna Vedel and Dorthe K. Thomsen, "The Dark Triad Across Academic Majors," *Personality and Individual Differences* 116 (2017): 86–91.

53. Edward A. Witt, M. Brent Donnellan, and Daniel M. Blonigen, "Using Existing

Self-Report Inventories to Measure the Psychopathic Personality Traits of Fearless Dominance and Impulsive Antisociality," *Journal of Research in Personality* 43, no. 6 (2009): 1006–1016.

54. Belinda Jane Board and Katarina Fritzon, "Disordered Personalities at Work," *Psychology, Crime and Law* 11, no. 1 (2005): 17–32.

55. Paul Babiak, Craig S. Neumann, and Robert D. Hare, "Corporate Psychopathy: Talking the Walk," *Behavioral Sciences and the Law* 28, no. 2 (2010): 174–193.

56. Steven Morris, "One in 25 Business Leaders May Be a Psychopath, Study Finds," *Guardian*, September 1, 2011, https://www.theguardian.com/science/2011/sep/01/psychopath-workplace-jobs-study.

57. Scott O. Lilienfeld, Irwin D. Waldman, Kristin Landfield, Ashley L. Watts, Steven Rubenzer, and Thomas R. Faschingbauer, "Fearless Dominance and the US Presidency: Implications of Psychopathic Personality Traits for Successful and Unsuccessful Political Leadership," *Journal of Personality and Social Psychology* 103, no. 3 (2012): 489.

58. J. Pegrum and O. Pearce, "A Stressful Job: Are Surgeons Psychopaths?" *Bulletin of the Royal College of Surgeons of England* 97, no. 8 (2015): 331–334.

59. Anna Katinka Louise von Borries, Inge Volman, Ellen Rosalia Aloïs de Bruijn, Berend Hendrik Bulten, Robbert Jan Verkes, and Karin Roelofs, "Psychopaths Lack the Automatic Avoidance of Social Threat: Relation to Instrumental Aggression," *Psychiatry Research* 200, nos. 2–3 (2012): 761–766.

60. Joshua W. Buckholtz, Michael T. Treadway, Ronald L. Cowan, Neil D. Woodward, Stephen D. Benning, Rui Li, M. Sib Ansari, Ronald M. Baldwin, Ashley N. Schwartzman, Evan S. Shelby, et al., "Mesolimbic Dopamine Reward System Hypersensitivity in Individuals with Psychopathic Traits," *Nature Neuroscience* 13, no. 4 (2010): 419.

61. Anne Casper, Sabine Sonnentag, and Stephanie Tremmel, "Mindset Matters: The Role of Employees' Stress Mindset for Day-Specific Reactions to Workload Anticipation," *European Journal of Work and Organizational Psychology* 26, no. 6 (2017): 798–810.

62. Clive R. Boddy, "Corporate Psychopaths, Conflict, Employee Affective Well-Being and Counterproductive Work Behaviour," *Journal of Business Ethics* 121, no. 1 (2014): 107–121.

63. Tomasz Piotr Wisniewski, Liafisu Yekini, and Ayman Omar, "Psychopathic Traits of Corporate Leadership as Predictors of Future Stock Returns," SSRN 2984999 (2017).

64. Olli Vaurio, Eila Repo-Tiihonen, Hannu Kautiainen, and Jari Tiihonen, "Psychopathy and Mortality," *Journal of Forensic Sciences* 63, no. 2 (2018): 474–477.

65. Natasha Singer, "In Utah, a Local Hero Accused," the *New York Times*, June 15, 2013, http://www.nytimes.com/2013/06/16/business/in-utah-a-local-hero -accused.html.

66. Sarah Francis Smith, Scott O. Lilienfeld, Karly Coffey, and James M. Dabbs, "Are Psychopaths and Heroes Twigs off the Same Branch? Evidence from College, Community, and Presidential Samples," *Journal of Research in Personality* 47, no. 5 (2013): 634–646.

67. Arielle Baskin-Sommers, Allison M. Stuppy-Sullivan, and Joshua W. Buckholtz, "Psychopathic Individuals Exhibit but Do Not Avoid Regret during Counterfactual Decision Making," *Proceedings of the National Academy of Sciences* 113, no. 50 (2016): 14438–14443.

68. Arielle R. Baskin-Sommers, John J. Curtin, and Joseph P. Newman, "Altering the Cognitive-Affective Dysfunctions of Psychopathic and Externalizing Offender Subtypes with Cognitive Remediation," *Clinical Psychological Science* 3, no. 1 (2015): 45–57.

69. Arielle Baskin-Sommers, "Psychopaths Have Feelings: Can They Learn How to Use Them?" *Aeon*, November 18, 2019, https://aeon.co/ideas/psychopaths-have-feelings-can-they-learn-how-to-use-them.

CHAPTER 8: THE 10 PRINCIPLES OF PERSONAL REINVENTION

1. Amber Gayle Thalmayer, Gerard Saucier, John C. Flournoy, and Sanjay Srivastava, "Ethics-Relevant Values as Antecedents of Personality Change: Longitudinal Findings from the Life and Time Study," *Collabra: Psychology* 5, no. 1 (2019).

2. This is the phenomenon I mentioned in chapter 5 that psychologists call the "better-than-average" effect, or the Lake Wobegon effect, after the fictional town where "all the women are strong, all the men are good-looking, and all the children are above average."

3. Alice Mosch and Peter Borkenau, "Psychologically Adjusted Persons Are Less Aware of How They Are Perceived by Others," *Personality and Social Psychology Bulletin* 42, no. 7 (2016): 910–922.

4. Tasha Eurich, *Insight: The Power of Self-Awareness in a Self-Deluded World* (New York: Macmillan, 2017).

5. Nathan W. Hudson, Daniel A. Briley, William J. Chopik, and Jaime Derringer, "You Have to Follow Through: Attaining Behavioral Change Goals Predicts Volitional Personality Change," *Journal of Personality and Social Psychology* 117, no. 4 (2019): 839.

6. Jeffrey A. Kottler, *Change: What Really Leads to Lasting Personal Transformation* (Oxford: Oxford University Press, 2018).

7. Phillippa Lally, Cornelia H. M. Van Jaarsveld, Henry W. W. Potts, and Jane Wardle, "How Are Habits Formed? Modelling Habit Formation in the Real World," *European Journal of Social Psychology* 40, no. 6 (2010): 998–1009.

8. James Clear, *Atomic Habits: An Easy & Proven Way to Build Good Habits & Break Bad Ones* (New York: Penguin, 2018).

9. Brent W. Roberts, "A Revised Sociogenomic Model of Personality Traits," *Journal of Personality* 86, no. 1 (2018): 23–35.

10. Richard Wiseman, *59 Seconds* (London: Pan Books, 2015); Gary Small and Gigi Vorgan, *Snap! Change Your Personality in 30 Days* (West Palm Beach, FL: Humanix Books, 2018).

11. Jeffrey A. Kottler, *Change: What Really Leads to Lasting Personal Transformation* (Oxford: Oxford University Press, 2018), 63.

12. Lester Luborsky, Jacques Barber, and Louis Diguer, "The Meanings of Narratives Told during Psychotherapy: The Fruits of a New Observational Unit," *Psychotherapy Research* 2, no. 4 (1992): 277–290.

13. Kottler, *Change*, 92.

14. Alex Fradera, "When and Why Does Rudeness Sometimes Spread Round the Office?" *BPS Research Digest*, May 4, 2018, https://digest.bps.org.uk/2016/10/11/when-and-why-does-rudeness-sometimes-spread-round-the-office/.

15. Joseph Chancellor, Seth Margolis, Katherine Jacobs Bao, and Sonja Lyubomirsky, "Everyday Prosociality in the Workplace: The Reinforcing Benefits of Giving, Getting, and Glimpsing," *Emotion* 18, no. 4 (2018): 507.

16. David Kushner, "Can Trauma Help You Grow?" the *New Yorker*, June 19, 2017, https://www.newyorker.com/tech/annals-of-technology/can-trauma-help-you-grow.

17. Yuanyuan An, Xu Ding, and Fang Fu, "Personality and Post-Traumatic Growth of Adolescents 42 Months after the Wenchuan Earthquake: A Mediated Model," *Frontiers in Psychology* 8 (2017): 2152; Kanako Taku and Matthew J. W. McLarnon, "Posttraumatic Growth Profiles and Their Relationships with HEXACO Personality Traits," *Personality and Individual Differences* 134 (2018): 33–42.

18. Rodica Ioana Damian, Marion Spengler, Andreea Sutu, and Brent W. Roberts, "Sixteen Going on Sixty-Six: A Longitudinal Study of Personality Stability and Change across 50 Years," *Journal of Personality and Social Psychology* 117, no. 3 (2019): 674.

19. Jessica Schleider and John Weisz, "A Single-Session Growth Mindset Intervention for Adolescent Anxiety and Depression: 9-Month Outcomes of a Randomized Trial," *Journal of Child Psychology and Psychiatry* 59, no. 2 (2018): 160–170.

20. "Anthony Joshua v Andy Ruiz: British Fighter Made 'Drastic Changes' after June Loss," *BBC Sport*, https://www.bbc.co.uk/sport/boxing/49599343.

EPILOGUE

1. Martin Selsoe Sorensen, "Reformed Gang Leader in Denmark Is Shot Dead Leaving Book Party," the *New York Times*, November 21, 2018, https://www.ny times.com/2018/11/21/world/europe/denmark-gang-leader-book-nedim-yasar .html.

2. Marie Louise Toksvig, *Rødder: En Gangsters Udvej: Nedim Yasars Historie* (Copenhagen: People'sPress, 2018).

3. "Newsday—Former Gangster Shot Dead—as He Left His Own Book Launch— BBC Sounds," *BBC News*, November 22, 2018, https://www.bbc.co.uk/sounds /play/p06shwwm.

4. Jill Suttie, "Can You Change Your Personality?" *Greater Good*, February 20, 2017, https://greatergood.berkeley.edu/article/item/can_you_change_your_personality.

Index

277

Index